Human Management
in the **Public Sector**
Policies and Practices

Human Resource Management
in the **Public Sector**
Policies and Practices

John L. Daly

M.E.Sharpe
Armonk, New York
London, England

Library of Congress Cataloging-in-Publication Data

Daly, John L., 1952–
  Human resource management in the public sector : policies and practices /
by John L. Daly.
    p. cm.
  Includes bibliographical references and index.
  ISBN 978-0-7656-1702-6 (pbk. : alk. paper)
  1. Local government—United States—Personnel management. 2. Civil service—
United States—Personnel management. I. Title.

  JS358.D35 2011
  352.6′2140973—dc22   2011005569

Printed in the United States of America

The paper used in this publication meets the minimum requirements of
American National Standard for Information Sciences
Permanence of Paper for Printed Library Materials,
ANSI Z 39.48-1984.

SP (p)   10   9   8   7   6   5   4   3   2   1

Contents

Preface

Human Resource Management in the Public Sector: Policies and Practices introduces human resource management and personnel foundations, policies, and practices pertinent in public organizational settings. This book employs pragmatic applications of human resources suitable to any governmental or nonprofit system, but which best fit within a municipal government context.

This book distinguishes itself from other books in two unique ways. Initially, during its development, I envisioned the target audience as upper-division undergraduate students and master-level public administration and public policy graduate students (many of whom are also practitioners) interested in acquiring human resource management insights. I assumed that while most readers required a basic knowledge about human resource management, most would never serve directly in a human resource management capacity. The irony here lies in the reality that all organizational leaders, including unit supervisors, must demonstrate human resource talents and insights. Without such strengths, their managerial effectiveness will suffer, as will their employees' performance.

A second significant difference between *Human Resource Management in the Public Sector* and other human resource efforts occurs through its substantial integration of "work-life balance" concepts as critical to public organization human resource management success. In local government today, public servants and their human resource systems confront enormous obstacles, including resource shortfalls, growth in unfunded service mandates, calls for staffing reductions, wage stagnancy, and employee security benefits givebacks. In this climate, it is easy to understand why employees' commitments are declining with regard to sustaining long-term employment within their public service agencies.

Active learning questions at the end of each chapter allow course participants to test their skills in addressing some of the human resource problems associated with the concepts and issues discussed in the chapter readings. Questions encourage students to reflect on the issues at hand in a short period of time, either in small groups or individually. Ideally, students and teams will share with each other their findings, recommendations, and resolutions on these end-of-chapter questions. Sharing results allows participants to compare their abilities and skills at addressing challenging and often intractable human resource problems against responses offered by others.

ACKNOWLEDGMENTS

Development of a comprehensive, yet compact manuscript can be a lonely endeavor. Fortunately, I have had the good fortune of ample support from my colleagues in the University of South Florida's Department of Government and International Affairs and its Public Administration Program, where I serve as director. I have also benefited immensely from discussions with my graduate students in our human resource management courses. Furthermore, I want to offer my gratitude with special thanks to Beverly D. Douglas, SPHR, for sharing her insights about human resource management in the trenches. Harry Briggs served as the executive editor during the publication of my initial book with M.E. Sharpe, *Training in Developing Nations: A Handbook for Expatriates*. Then, as now, Harry's insight, advice, and patience have proved invaluable.

Finally, I am profoundly grateful to my wife, Debra Liebenow Daly, who deserves sainthood for her editing expertise, her steadfast support for me, and her belief in my work. This book is dedicated to Debby, whose love and courage inspire me to appreciate life each and every day and live it as though each day could be my last one.

Human Resource Management
in the **Public Sector**
Policies and Practices

1 | Twenty-first Century Human Resource Management

The public sector is about service. It is about community and making a difference. I would rather work for state or local government and make a real contribution to my community than make gobs of money working for a corporation that has no understanding of the various elements of its own community. I made the right decision.

—Anonymous Harvard Business School MBA graduate

After reading this chapter, you will

- understand the influences of environmental changes on human resource management strategies, policies, and practices;
- grasp the significance of values-based human resource systems;
- appreciate historical events that have stimulated the growth, development, and application of professional human resource management;
- recognize human resource system's role in reshaping local governments to become innovative, learning-based organizations;
- comprehend emerging public workforce trends and their influence on the practice of human resource management in the twenty-first century.

The arrival of the third millennium now is a reality and so is the need for twenty-first century human resource management. Yet many human resource practitioners, especially in the public sector, appear unprepared for the challenges they will experience over the next quarter century. Our society faces immense transformation, much of it caused by global, technological, demographic, political, and economic forces of change. Lavigna and Hays (2004, 238) confirm this concern: "At a time when governments need to be most adept at luring talent to the public service, their ability to do so has rarely been so constrained and complicated by economic, social, and organizational pressures." Our transition from an industrial to a knowledge-based society is still in its infancy. For example, Ray Kurzweil indicates in *The Age of Intelligent Machines* that America is less than 1 percent into the job loss it will experience due to the emergence of electronic intelligence. Samson notes also that within the next 50 to 100 years we will experience a transformation of jobs based on electronic intelligence beyond things we can even imagine (Marshall 2003, 23). Change is upon us as never before. Local governments must address these challenges and identify innovative ways to sustain high-quality services; otherwise, they will lose legitimacy in the eyes of the public they serve.

Public organizations and their human resource staffs must develop and adapt innovative human capital. All sectors, whether public, not-for-profit, or private, face the need for creating "organizational learning cultures." According to John Luthy (2000, 20), organizations exhibiting learning characteristics seek improvements at all levels and have more initiative, creativity, spirit, ability to collaborate, productivity, and quality than those that remain static (i.e., those that maintain traditional management practices). Unfortunately, Peter Senge's (1994) research indicates that the public sector's utilization of learning cultures has not been effectively promoted nor actively practiced. Learning cultures facilitate the necessary adaptive capacity that organizations need in order to succeed in increasingly complex and competitive environments. For many organizations (including those in the public sector), a culture of learning, growth, and adaptation to change will constitute, over the next quarter century, the difference between success and failure. Sustaining acceptable productivity is no longer sufficient for today's public organization. Citizens demand more from government, and if more cannot be delivered they will call for change in either the leadership of the organization or the ownership of service production; that is, the public will demand the privatization of public services. As Stephen Covey (2004) states, service levels and quality today must exceed the expectation of customers if organizations hope to remain a viable force in the marketplace. Local governments must strive to achieve similar outcomes so their legitimacy will not be questioned nor their survival threatened.

American citizens are impatient consumers of government services. They expect government, at all levels, to provide high-quality services in a timely manner and within existing resource bases. The lethargic response in early September 2005 by the U.S. Federal Emergency Management Agency (FEMA), following the devastation of Hurricane Katrina in New Orleans and other southern gulf coast communities, demonstrated the level of public wrath that results when expectations of timely service delivery are not met. Clearly, meeting these expectation levels challenges public workforces. Such pressures mandate increased program innovation, higher public employee commitment, better program planning, and enhanced coordination across interagencies of government. Unfortunately, what worked well in the past becomes the road map for doom for tomorrow's public sector unit and its human resource system. Citizens demand quality services, even though their trust and expectation that government can deliver has dwindled over the past half-century and remains low today (Thompson and Radin 1997).

Public sector human resource systems today also face internal questions of legitimacy. A disturbing paradox exists for many public sector human resource units. At a time when human resource expertise is most needed, operational staffs least desire it. In many local governments, department supervisors and their employees detest their human resource management units. Some view human resources as "those people who do things to us" rather than "those professionals who do things for us." As Lavigna and Hays (2004) note, job applicants often equate applying for a public position with visiting a dentist, except that the pain of the application process persists longer. Movement beyond this obstructionist perception (and in some instances reality) requires both a shift in the mind-set of the workforce and, more importantly, an alteration of the human resource unit itself. This entails more than a complete and thorough reexamination of human resource processes, practices, and policies. It warrants a cultural transformation of human resource management with an eye to service, rather than compliance, within the organization.

WHAT IS HUMAN RESOURCE MANAGEMENT?

Human resource (HR) management[1] consists of dedicated professionals working cooperatively with other talented organizational (and community) members to achieve the organization's vision, mission, goals, and values. As such, HR management operates as a service unit for other operational units. HR strives to develop policies, plans, programs, and initiatives that advance other working units' human capacity and their ability to provide high-quality products and services to customers, clients, or citizens (in the case of government).

HR began as personnel administration. Many of the same tasks that personnel administration units coordinated in the past continue to be part of HR management today. Chapter 2 will discuss more comprehensively the three levels of HR management. Operational-level HR (i.e., the work of coordinating personnel functions on a day-to-day basis) incorporates many of the traditional personnel administration functions. Today, however, HR systems cannot simply focus on coordination of the organization's human capital needs in a present sense. HR units increasingly are moving toward serving in a strategic capacity, assisting other organizational units to identify and reward talent, as well as identifying methods and strategies for improving organizational outcomes.

HUMAN RESOURCES' SIX CORE VALUES

Strongly held and effectively practiced values significantly influence the quality of HR services offered to individuals seeking professional assistance. These values must be living standards that guide HR practitioners' policies, attitudes, actions, and behaviors. Progressive personnel units' principles drive the team's responsiveness to internal customers (i.e., those departments and people that HR assist in their organizations) and external customers (e.g., the media, individuals seeking employment information, and other units of government). The six core values fundamental to high effectiveness and to quality public sector HR units are:

1. Responsiveness to the public's will
2. Social equity
3. Mission-driven focus
4. Skills-based competency in employment practices
5. Professional human resource competency
6. Ethically based organizational culture

RESPONSIVENESS TO THE PUBLIC'S WILL

The principal responsiveness to the public's will demands that public employees act in the citizens' best interest. The public's will is determined through the electoral process and expressed through public policy decisions offered by their elected representatives. In this instance, the public servant's actions ultimately follow the policy directives of elected leaders unless some compelling reason dictates otherwise. Compelling exceptions might include officials' attempts to circumvent existing laws, actions patently serving private interest or benefit at the expense of the public's good, and situations violating the ethical or professional standards of one's profession. In these circumstances, public employees face difficult professional (and personal) decisions. Voicing opposition (e.g., whistle-blowing) to anticipated or actual practices may be one path of action. A second recourse is to remain quiet while resigning one's position with the organization. A final approach may be to bring questionable practices to the attention of leaders (and, if necessary, legal authorities) while remaining a force for meaningful change. Each whistle-blowing scenario requires personal fortitude and a strong character, as individuals experiencing these circumstances often suffer greatly for maintaining high public standards.

SOCIAL EQUITY

The second value, social equity, stresses the fair treatment to all members of society, including employees (and protected group members seeking entry) in public organizations. Social equity, in a HR context, focuses on the employment-related decisions affecting protected class groups (e.g., women, aging employees, the disabled, veterans, and people of color and other ethnic affiliations). Employment-related actions include recruitment and selection practices and outcomes, promotion and demotion decisions, training and development policies and programs, employee discipline processes, and downsizing, outplacement, and termination strategies.

HR systems serve as gatekeepers of fair treatment across competing interests. Arbitration of conflict here can be a most formidable task, as social equity issues often come in direct conflict with the skills-based principle (discussed below). In addition, employee-related decisions often result in zero-sum outcomes (i.e., one party wins while others lose), raising the likelihood for conflict (Thurow 1980). Intraorganizational harmony may become the casualty of organizational decisions. Frequently, nonwinners in these zero-sum decisions place the blame on HR units and maintain high resentment for officials centrally placed in such decision-making authority.

MISSION-DRIVEN FOCUS

Over the past quarter century, public organizations have incorporated mission statements as an integral component of their management planning process and organizational philosophy. Mission statements give organizations purpose, vision, and meaningful directions for seeking collective agency accomplishments. These benchmarks also serve as the barometer of mission-driven success. Traditionally, organizations have viewed efficiency and effectiveness as measures of success. Paradoxically, organizational activities can be both efficiently administered with desired outcomes yet fail to achieve an organization's purpose and longer-range mission. Paraphrasing a quote that the author read years ago, "A speeding train moving in the wrong direction gets nowhere fast." Thus, HR units play a significant role in the identification and attainment of the organization's mission by assisting in the identification of human capital trends and aiding departments through necessary organizational restructuring. Furthermore, HR helps employees gain new skills and leadership development. Finally, through effective human capital planning, HR assists employees to acquire the requisite talent needed to succeed in executing policies, plans, and programs that sustain the organization's mission.

SKILLS-BASED COMPETENCY IN EMPLOYMENT PRACTICES

The principle of skills-based competency relates to the identification and selection of individuals with the demonstrated talents and capacity to function effectively in the position they hold or seek. Typically, a person's qualifications for employment are determined through a combination of educational attainment, position examinations predicting high job content knowledge, and an on-the-job demonstration of job abilities. Job content-based testing and appropriate skill-based selection techniques seek to offset the heavy use of politically based hiring in public sector. Past patronage selection systems were criticized for selecting job applicants based on whom the applicants knew rather than what they knew; a plum job, for example, might go to an unqualified long-time political contributor to the recently elected mayor's campaign or a lifelong associate of a powerful local politico. In contrast, the principle of skills-based competency ensures that hiring a professional and talented public employee, such as the city's next human resource director, will be determined according to the applicant's relevant job knowledge, past indications of performance, and demonstrated successes.

PROFESSIONAL HUMAN RESOURCE COMPETENCY

HR practitioners also aspire to attain professional skill competency. In this profession, one's actions impact the lives of others on a daily basis. HR decisions affect who is hired, the content of training and development afforded to employees, and the nature of measuring performance levels in the agency. In addition, these decisions influence the distribution of organizational resources, including employee compensation and benefits along with a myriad of other critical factors that affect employees' lives both on and off the job.

Personnelists have a professional and ethical obligation to maintain professional competency in their positions. Recent Society for Human Resource Management (SHRM) data indicate substantial growth in the number of professionals attaining human resource management certification. SHRM's HR Certification Institute (HRCI) offers three certification programs: the Global Professional in Human Resources (GPHR), the Senior Professional in Human Resources (SPHR), and the Professional in Human Resources (PHR). The GPHR and SPHR include experienced HR professionals with typically six to eight years of HR management practice. Both require time in service experience and successful passing of a written exam. The GPHR is designed for international HR specialists, while the SPHR applies primarily to the U.S. market. The PHR serves as an entry-level certification program and requires two years of HR professional work experience and successful passing of an in-depth exam. As of October 2010, approximately 108,000 HR professionals in more than 70 countries worldwide had attained one or more of these certifications (HRCI 2010). Growing attainment of these certifications demonstrates that HR staffs take their own professional development seriously.

ETHICALLY BASED ORGANIZATIONAL CULTURE

The final HR value, creating standards for improved ethical behavior in public organizations, ranks among the most significant concerns in today's public sector environment. The National Association of Schools of Public Affairs and Administration (NASPAA), for example, has adopted curriculum standards for ethics training as part of its recommended coursework provided at schools possessing NASPAA accreditation. HR officers frequently face difficult ethical issues in their work. They must contemplate their own personal ethical values in relation to those exhibited by their organization and its executive leaders.

Value-driven HR management principles strengthen the attainment of an organization's goals and mission. Moreover, these six core values influence the development of the type of positive and enduring cultures that HR management systems need in order to develop sustainable policies that improve twenty-first century workforces as they tackle dynamic forces for change.

HISTORICAL EMERGENCE OF HUMAN RESOURCE MANAGEMENT

Today's American organizations face immense change. Employees often claim that "the only constant we face is the certainty of change." In reality, public organizational change has always occurred, but in recent decades its magnitude has rocketed exponentially. Historically, pressures forcing change and organizational adaptability have been common in the American economic fabric. America's Industrial Revolution, commencing in the mid-nineteenth century, created technological advances, especially in machinery and harvesting equipment. Such technological advances reduced the need for manual labor on America's farms. Many displaced workers (including freed slaves) fled to American cities, hoping to create new lives and to locate new employment. As a nation in transformation from an agricultural to an industrial society, America was challenged to design new techniques for managing growing pools of workers. American government also sought improved organizational structures and practices to deal effectively with its growing urban centers (like New York, Boston, Philadelphia, Chicago, and Saint Louis). America needed better government to sustain its growing national economy.

At the start of the twentieth century, professional management principles, like those espoused by Frederick Taylor in his "scientific management" theory, began to be applied in American industry and government. The call for increased professionalism in management applications significantly influenced changes in management philosophies and practices. Woodrow Wilson's seminal article in 1887, "The Study of Administration," for example, heightened awareness of the need to run government in a "business-like" fashion with improved precision and increased organizational efficiency. Other events also created opportunities to transform governmental practices. The assassination of President James Garfield in 1881 by a disgruntled civil servant applicant served as a major catalyst for reform, resulting in the passage of the Pendleton Act. This act, also known as the Civil Service Act of 1883, created the U.S. Civil Service Commission. One of its primary goals was to create a system to instill merit principles into the process of hiring in place of political patronage. Patronage hiring had gained growing acceptance in government since Andrew Jackson's election as president in 1828. American society, however, was changing rapidly by the end of the nineteenth century. As its urban centers developed and formal organizations grew, so did the need for professional staffs to bring about greater organizational efficiency and accountability, to reform government at all levels, and to create systems for facilitating growing HR needs in these organizations.

Ironically, HR management's significance grew at the beginning of the twentieth century as a result of this industrial expansion. Initial adoption of personnel departments occurred between 1900 and 1910. Early application of personnel practices was most common in rapidly growing economic sectors—especially in the railroad and steel industries.

Personnel staffs, policies, and functions expanded as business and government developed in America. Personnel, as a professional discipline, widened as social science research began recognizing the significance of human behavior, social and group interactions, and the roles they played in achieving desired organizational outcomes. Elton Mayo and Fritz Roethlisberger's research at Western Electric's plant in Hawthorne, Illinois, during the 1930s led to the "discovery" of the Hawthorne effect. Their research originally sought to determine the effects of plant lighting variations on worker productivity. Ultimately, they discovered that lighting did not significantly affect performance outcomes as much as did behavioral changes in the work productivity of employees, who were under study. These findings suggested that the social needs of workers influenced outcomes as much, if not more than, the workplace design or standard operating procedures. In this instance, performance improved as a result of the employees feeling a part of a special group under examination. Thus, the Hawthorne Effect suggests that social factors and the treatment of people significantly influence performance outcomes and must be considered when assessing work structure and design. Their work spawned the human relations movement following World War II. American personnel departments' scope of responsibilities also increased with the expansion of America's labor movement in the 1930s and 1940s. The enactment of the National Labor Relations Act of 1935 (also known as the Wagner Act) strengthened workers' rights and legitimized collective bargaining in many private sector settings. Furthermore, the introduction of the Fair Labor Standards Act of 1938 required regulation of minimum wages, overtime pay, and child labor. Enactment of these federal laws created further demand for personnel specialists capable of ensuring workforce compliance with federal and state regulations.

Personnel systems experienced smooth growth and relative stability from the end of World War II in 1945 through the early 1960s. Unprecedented growth occurred in the American economy during this period with substantial increases overall in state and local government employment. HR–related legislation intensified during President John F. Kennedy's administration (1961–1963). It erupted with President Lyndon B. Johnson's Great Society initiatives. The 1960s could be characterized as the high point for the development of landmark civil rights legislation. In particular, the Equal Pay Act of 1963, Title VII of the 1964 Civil Rights Act, and the Age Discrimination in Employment Act of 1967, all antidiscrimination policies designed to enhance minority- and gender-based social equity, influenced further the demand for personnel specialists. Judicial activism also created a need for additional expertise. This became especially true for labor-law attorneys, who could be called on to counsel management regarding changes in personnel regulations and strategies for remaining in compliance with increasingly complex and taxing regulatory policies.

Societal confidence in government began to erode during the middle 1960s and continued in the 1970s. Simultaneously, the conservatism movement grew while antigovernmental attitudes developed. Growing state tax revolts in California, Texas, and Ohio exemplified distrust of government. California's Proposition 13 referendum, approved by voters in June 1978, cut California property tax rates by as much as 30 percent. It also placed limits on future tax rate increases. Within five years of Proposition 13's passage, nearly half the states had placed similar restraints on lawmakers' taxing authority (Moore 1998). These actions forced local Californian communities to rethink (i.e., reinvent) service delivery strategies and community priorities due to the dramatic revenue shortfalls they created (Osborne and Gaebler 1992). Declining local revenues forced greater focus on entrepreneurial methods for delivering local government services. Local government personnel systems were tested during this period. Less progressive systems that could not adapt quickly enough were perceived as superfluous.

In the 1980 presidential campaign, Ronald Reagan gained significant political support when he claimed, "Government is not the solution to the problem. Government IS the problem" (Quotes for All 2005). Criticism of affirmative action (i.e., programs to facilitate increased workforce participation and upward mobility of minority members) also increased. *Regents v. Bakke* (1978) is one example. Alan Bakke, a Caucasian applicant to the University of California-Davis medical school, was twice denied admission. At the same time, the university admitted minority candidates with lower qualifying standards (as determined by undergraduate grades and medical school entry examination test scores), utilizing affirmative action policies. In response, Bakke filed a "reverse discrimination" lawsuit. Ultimately, Bakke was admitted to the medical school (independent of judicial intervention), while the U.S. Supreme Court upheld America's affirmative action policy. Nevertheless, this case served as a focal point and catalyst for criticism of affirmative action programs and called into question the legitimacy of affirmative action applications. Norma Riccucci (1997, 57) notes that, "almost since its inception, affirmative action has been pummeled by attacks from the citizenry, scholars, and even individual lawmakers and jurists. Efforts to curb discrimination (i.e., in the form of equal employment opportunity—EEO—programs) have been subject to the whims of hiring authorities and policymakers." Riccucci also notes that the 1990s witnessed growing grassroots efforts to dismantle all types of affirmative action programs. The 1996 California Civil Rights Initiative (CCRI, also referred to as California Proposition 209) asked state voters to determine whether "the state shall not discriminate against, or grant preferential treatment to, any individual or group on the basis of race, sex, color, ethnicity or national origin in the operation of public employment, public education, or public contracting" (American Civil Rights Institute n.d.). Although opposed by the Clinton administration, Proposition 209 received the voters' approval with 54 percent of the vote. This law limits preferential treatment in virtually all of California's public sector, including state and local governments, public schools (including California's public universities and community colleges), special districts, and other political subdivisions. It is noteworthy that this law does not apply to the private sector, which found increased diversity in its organizations beneficial in opening new markets and better understanding new customers' consumption desires and service needs.

The last two decades have witnessed further transformations of HR management practices. This period can best be characterized by (1) the devolution of state and local government civil service systems and (2) the growth of decentralized applications of HR at the operational level. The State of Georgia's civil service reform in 1996 serves as the best recent example of civil service system reforms. In effect, the state dismantled its civil service system and the protections afforded new employees. All new hires beginning work after July 1, 1996, would serve on an "at will" basis (Gossett 2002). "At will" means that they serve at the pleasure of their superiors. They can leave "at will," without notice, but their employment also can be terminated at the will of their employer. This change lessened protections for new employees while increasing employment flexibility. Ultimately, this reform gives Georgia state government greater latitude to decrease the size (and cost) of its workforce.

The use of the "new public management" (also known as "New Public Administration") principles—which focuses on improved public service efficiency through greater market competition—also has had considerable effects on HR practices. Some personnel activities, such as the selection and hiring of new employees, have been devolved to operating units. This change grants these units greater control over the hiring of individuals, as well as often reducing the time necessary to bring new selections on board. Lavigna and Hays (2004, 240) note that "widespread initiatives have been undertaken to 'de-bureaucratize' HRM by eliminating unnecessary rules and regulations." In May 2010, the U.S. Office of Personnel Management (OPM) launched a new initiative designed to streamline the federal government's recruitment and selection system. Two primary goals of the new hiring process are to reduce the burdens placed on job applicants seeking employment and to reduce the time it takes for agencies to make hiring decisions (Crum 2010). Ultimately, reforms like these being initiated in OPM, while painful for traditional HR operations, will both advance the image of HR management and facilitate the needs of operating units in an increasingly competitive labor market. Thus, HR management, by relinquishing some bureaucratic power and control, gains immense strength providing assistance in other areas, like strategic workforce forecasting, that are more appreciated and relevant to the organizations it serves.

TWENTY-FIRST CENTURY WORKFORCE DEMOGRAPHICS AND DIVERSITY

To succeed in the twenty-first century, America's workplace must embrace the challenges of a new economy—this includes knowledge of how people work, where they work, and how they balance professional and family needs (Chao 2001). Traditional paternal protections, such as stable employment for workers in return for their loyalty and commitment to the organization, no longer exist in many workplaces. Even the concept of tenure (i.e., employment for life) that public organizations used in the past to attract and retain public servants is fading. Today, the average thirty-four-year-old American employee already has worked for nine different companies during his or her brief career (Chao 2001).

Employee organizational trust is disintegrating. Diminishing job satisfaction, motivation, and long-term organizational commitment in many workplace settings reflect this change. It should come as no surprise that the traditional psychological contract between employer and employee, whereby the employee relinquishes decision-making authority to the boss in exchange for job stability and progressive promotions based on seniority, is dying, if not dead. Workers' attitudes, especially among younger cohorts, differ significantly from those of earlier generations (Kaye, Scheff, and Thielfoldt 2003). Younger workers, especially millennial[2] employees (born between 1977 and 1997) currently entering the workforce, demand greater decision-making involvement and control over their work assignment and work environment. Paul Light's research suggests that today's youth are intolerant of "thick hierarchies, rule-bound processes, and limited opportunities for meaningful work [that] keep government from offering the kind of challenging work necessary to draw and retain top people" (quoted in Frisby 2003, 10). Clearly, many will "walk" (i.e., voluntarily resign their positions) if shared work autonomy is not granted. Moreover, their primary commitment is to their own professional skills development, not to their employers. Many younger generation workers believe that those who maintain high loyalty to their organizations are fools. They witnessed their parents' loyalty being disregarded during frequent American corporation downsizing during the 1980s and 1990s. They refuse to fall for the same "loyalty ruse." Thus, retaining high-quality human capital today is no longer simply a matter of providing better compensation. This remains a necessary condition but an insufficient strategy. HR planners must think more creatively, addressing work assignments and the developmental needs of their employees. They also must consider their employees' broader familial needs. In particular, an organization must balance employees' work with their family obligations. Achieving such balance is critical, requiring due diligence of HR systems. Without family friendly working initiatives in place, sustaining worker satisfaction, organizational commitment, performance outcomes, and the organization's human capital will be difficult, if not impossible, to achieve.

DEMOGRAPHIC CHANGE AND JOB SHORTAGES

Demographers researching American population trends of the past two decades have predicted skills shortages in critical occupational fields in the near future. Levine and Kleeman (1986) refer to this situation, as it relates to the public sector, as the "quiet crisis." This term epitomizes their concern for the federal government's increasing inability to recruit, motivate, and retain high-quality civil servants. Recent economic slowdowns have moderated in some occupational fields. An American Association of Retired People's (AARP) 2008 survey found that approximately 25 percent of respondents age forty-five years and older indicated that they might delay early retirement if economic conditions did not improve (Fox 2010). Nevertheless, Department of Labor economists still project workforce shortages caused by skills gaps in some occupational areas in information technology (Fox 2010). Progressive municipal HR systems, like the City of Phoenix, recognized this fact early, especially relating to the hiring and retention of its information technology (IT) staff. Wisely, it adjusted city HR policies to compete more aggressively to attract the best talent in the marketplace (Lan, Riley, and Cayer 2005). Applicant availability is not the issue for Phoenix as many job seekers continue to apply for open positions. Rather, Phoenix's concern is locating and acquiring individuals with the best talent and skill sets needed to excel in a twenty-first century organization.

Local government executive leadership also might be in short supply in the near future. Green (2000) notes that in the near future local governments will be adversely affected by retirements. Sam Ehrenhalt (now deceased) served as a Senior Fellow at the Rockefeller Institute of Government. His findings, as reported by Green (2000, 439), indicate that "the proportion of older government workers aged forty-five to sixty-four has risen from 36.8 percent in 1994 to 41.7 percent in 1998." Furthermore, the International City/County Management Association (ICMA) expresses concern about the aggregate aging of local government city managers. The association expects an increasing percentage of these leaders to retire over the next decade. The ICMA recently noted: "The local government management profession is approaching a crossroads as baby boomers that comprise the majority of local government managers approach retirement at a quickening pace, and statistics indicate that the greatest numbers of retirees will come from the managerial ranks" (ICMA n.d., n.p.). Furthermore, it expresses concern for a declining number of youth entering the city manager profession, suggesting a potential void in talent once current executives vacate their positions. The ICMA has repeatedly heard from its members "that today's young people have a limited knowledge of how their communities operate and lack an interest in pursuing careers in local government management" (Frisby 2003, 8).

WOMEN IN THE WORKFORCE

Gender redistribution in America's workplace has significantly evolved in recent years. Between 1970 and 2004, women increased their labor force participation from 43 to 59 percent (Bureau of Labor Statistics ([BLS] 2005). The days of white-male-dominated staffs have disappeared. Today, the workforce is more gender-blended. BLS gender-related employment statistics bear out the radical transformation that occurred over the past quarter-century. Today, women account for about one-half of America's labor market. Historically, education has been strongly linked to both employability and upward employment mobility. Among 2004 U.S. high school graduates, more females enrolled in college than their male counterparts. Of this graduating class, 72 percent of females entered college compared to 61 percent of male graduates (BLS 2005). Assuming this trend continues, women are likely to ascend to positions of higher authority and responsibility in the coming years. Some evidence exists supporting this observation, as women's earnings—as a percentage of men's earnings between 1979 and 2004—increased from 62 to 80 percent (BLS 2005). Recent findings of the Institute for Women's Policy Research (2010), however, indicate that progress has slowed considerably in recent years: median weekly earnings of full-time working women have been essentially flat since 2005.

Balancing family and work obligations has become an increasingly formidable burden for American workers. Family friendly organizations, which allow the flexibility and assistance for individuals to balance these competing work-family obligations, position themselves at a competitive advantage compared with more traditional organizations. Working women, in particular, value flexible policies and initiatives that allow them to function dually as a contributing parent and productive employee. Position attractiveness increases considerably when the organization provides family friendly policies such as flexible working hours, flexible leave programs, on-site childcare programs or childcare referral assistance, and other desired benefits and perks.

ETHNIC DIVERSITY

America's population continues to become increasingly diverse in terms of both race and ethnicity. As of August 2008, minorities accounted for one-third of the U.S. population. If growth trends continue, this group will reach majority population status by 2042 (U.S. Census Bureau 2010). In terms of the federal government's work composition, as of June 30, 2010, non-Hispanic whites constitute 66.5 percent of the permanent U.S. federal government's civilian workforce, with the remaining 33.5 percent being minority status members (U.S. Office of Personnel Management 2010).

By 2100 the Caucasian population will have shrunk to only 40 percent of the population (Centers for Disease Control and Prevention n.d.). Today, African-American and Hispanic populations are approximately equal, each group constituting 13 to 14 percent of the population. The African-American population is likely to remain about the same at 14 percent of the overall population. By 2050 the Hispanic population will account for 25 percent of the population. Much of the growth in the Hispanic population will result from higher family birthrates (relative to other groups) and the continuation of significant Hispanic immigration from other countries (Klingner and Nalbandian 2003).

Changes in the nation's population certainly will influence the racial and ethnic diversity in the American workplace. Increased interest in diversity training, for example, is one outcome of greater demographic diversity in the country's communities as well as in its workforce. Understanding cultural differences across social groups will be an important factor in interacting with the public. The outcome of the beating of Rodney King in Los Angeles on March 3, 1991, for example, demonstrates the need for better understanding of cultural and diversity differences across social groups. Mr. King, an African-American driving under the influence, led police on a high-speed chase. Ultimately, Los Angeles Police Department (LAPD) apprehended King. Four of its officers beat King brutally during his arrest. A bystander videotaped this incident and, subsequently, the video was broadcast repeatedly over national newscasts. In 1992 the State of California tried the LAPD officers, with the jury verdict calling for their acquittal. Los Angeles community race riots followed the decision. Eventually, federal trials for civil rights violations ensued with jury decisions finding two of the four officers guilty of federal civil rights violations for which they served time in prison. The two remaining LAPD officer gained acquittals of the charges.

Clearly, social equity legislation and judicial intervention since the 1960s have opened doors of opportunity for ethnic minorities (and women) that were previously locked. The U.S. labor market reflects greater minority participation today than ever before.

America's Aging Workforce

America's population, like that of many developed nations, is growing older. As society ages, HR systems logically are concerned about future staff availability. In addition, personnel policies and planning must be crafted to deal with staffing transition. Common questions asked in today's large organization abound: How can we retain our senior talent? Where will we find qualified applicants to replace this talent? How can we develop personnel policies that can attract and retain our human capital? How do we legally protect the organization against litigation associated with the aging process?

As society ages, the costs for health care and pension benefits will increase. HR strategies must anticipate that over the next ten to twenty years, as the baby boom generation (i.e., those born between 1945 and 1964) ages, its members will seek favorable public policy initiatives to protect their self-interests, both in the workplace and in general. Policies dealing with aging must be factored into organizational strategies and planning to protect the organization's human capital investment, maintain desired productivity outcomes, and sustain a smooth staffing transition. BLS data displayed in Figure 1.1 demonstrate the aging of America over the past quarter-century.

HR systems can create procedures and plans to smooth the workforce lumpiness that will be experienced between now and 2025. Progressive HR units already have begun addressing these concerns, realizing the benefits of their actions.

Chapter Summary

This chapter addressed the definition of HR management and the importance of its six core values. The chapter also examined the historical factors and demographic

Figure 1.1   **Aging of American Society**

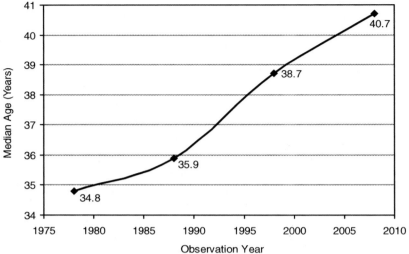

Source: Bureau of Labor Statistics (n.d.).

influences that have shaped HR practices in the past as well as in the twenty-first century.

The next chapter turns its attention toward specific activities and responsibilities found in HR systems. A review of these major activities serves as a bridge for an in-depth focus on each of these activities in subsequent chapters.

KEY CONCEPTS AND TERMS

aging of America's workforce

Civil Service Act of 1883

gender and ethnic transformations in the American workforce

HR Certification Institute and certification programs (GPHR, SPHR, and PHR)

National Association of Schools of Public Affairs and Administration (NASPAA)

six core values of HR management

U.S. Office of Personnel Management

PRACTICAL LEARNING ACTIVITIES

1. Break into small groups of three to five students. Identify one group member to serve as spokesperson for the group's findings. Discuss how diversity in the workplace has changed the nature of managing people and reshaped the culture of most organizations today. Reflect upon how a predominantly

white and male organization would differ from a robust organization that is diverse in terms of gender and ethnicity. Also, consider the pressures that ethnicity and gender changes exert on reshaping the practices and policies of HR systems today.

2. The instructor will identify and place each student into one of six teams. Each team will review one of the six core values of HR management (see numbered list on page 5). Each team will discuss how HR management systems benefit by possessing significant levels of the value that it has been asked to review. For example, if the group has been selected to assess an "ethically based organizational culture," discuss how highly ethical work units might differ from units lacking such ethical standards.

3. America's workforce is aging, as is evident from a review of Figure 1.1. What is likely to be the impact of aging in the workplace on future personnel policies, performance outcomes, medical and health care planning, and succession planning? What can HR systems do to facilitate organizational planning as they prepare to deal with the effects of aging in the workplace?

NOTES

1. For the purposes of general discussion, the terms "human resources" and "personnel" will be used interchangeably, even though distinctions between the two terms do exist.

2. Some of the other names attributed to this generation of workers are "digital generation," "the D [digital] generation," "nesters," "generation Y," and "net generation."

REFERENCES

American Civil Rights Institute. n.d. California's Proposition 209. www.acri.org/209/209text.html.

Bureau of Labor Statistics (BLS). 2005. News: Women in the labor force: A data book. www.bls.gov/bls/databooknews2005.pdf.

Bureau of Labor Statistics (BLS). n.d. The labor force is getting older. www.bls.gov/opub/working/data/chart2.txt.

Centers for Disease Control and Prevention. n.d. Racial & ethnic populations. www.cdc.gov/omhd/Populations/definitions.htm.

Chao, E. 2001. Message from the Secretary of Labor. Washington, DC: Bureau of Labor Statistics. www.bls.gov/opub/rtaw/pdf/message.pdf.

Covey, S. 2004. *The Seven Habits of Highly Effective People*. New York: Free Press.

Crum, J. 2010. Hiring reform next steps: Issues of merit. Washington, DC: U.S. Merit System Protection Board.

Fox A. 2010. At work in 2020. *HR Magazine*. www.shrm.org/Publications/hrmagazine/EditorialContent/2010/0110/Pages/0110fox.aspx.

Frisby, M. 2003. What can be done? Attracting young adults to careers in local government. *Public Management* (January–February), 8–14.

Gossett, C. 2002. Civil service reform: The case of Georgia. *Review of Public Personnel Administration* 22, 2 (Summer), 94–113.

Green, M. 2000. Beware and prepare: The government workforce of the future. *Public Personnel Management* 29, 4 (Winter), 435–444.

HR Certification Institute (HRCI). 2010. About the HR Certification Institute. www.hrci.org/about.

Institute for Women's Policy Research. 2010. The gender wage gap: 2009 (Fact Sheet—IWPR #C350). www.iwpr.org/pdf/C350.pdf.

International City/County Management Association (ICMA). n.d. What are ICMA's next generation initiatives? http://icma.org/en/icma/priorities/next_generation.

Kaye, B., D. Scheff, and D. Thielfoldt. 2003. Engaging the generations. In *Human Resources in the 21st Century*, ed. M. Effron, R. Gandossy, and M. Goldsmith. Hoboken, NJ: John Wiley.

Klingner, D., and J. Nalbandian. 2003. *Public Personnel Management: Context and Strategies* (5th ed.). Upper Saddle River, NJ: Prentice Hall.

Lan, G., L. Riley, and N. Cayer. 2005. How can local government become an employer of choice for technical professionals? Lessons and experiences from the City of Phoenix. *Review of Public Personnel Administration* 25, 3 (September), 225–242.

Lavigna, R., and S. Hays. 2004. Recruitment and selection of public workers: An international compendium of modern trends and practices. *Public Personnel Management* 33, 3 (Fall), 237–253.

Levine, C., and R. Kleeman. 1986. *The Quiet Crisis of the Civil Service: The Federal Personnel System at the Crossroads*. Washington, DC: National Academy of Public Administration.

Luthy, J. 2000. Leaving a leadership legacy. *Public Management* 82, 9, 18–22.

Marshall, J. 2003. Assessing the future of work. *Financial Executive* (December), 22–25.

Moore, S. 1998. Proposition 13 then, now and forever. Cato Institute. www.cato.org/dailys/7–30–98.html.

Osborne, D., and T. Gaebler. 1992. *Reinventing Government: How the Entrepreneurial Spirit Is Transforming the Public Sector*. New York: Penguin.

Quotes for All. 2005. Quotes of Ronald Reagan. www.quotesforall.com/r/reaganronald.htm.

Regents v. Bakke. 1978. 438 U.S. 265.

Riccucci, N. 1997. Will affirmative action survive into the twenty-first century? In *Public Personnel Management: Current Concerns, Future Challenges* (2nd ed.), ed. C. Ban and N. Riccucci. New York: Longman.

Senge, P. 1994. *The Fifth Discipline*. New York: Doubleday.

Thompson, F., and B. Radin. 1997. Reinventing public personnel management: The Winter and Gore initiatives. In *Public Personnel Management: Current Concerns, Future Challenges* (2nd ed.), ed. C. Ban and N. Riccucci. New York: Longman.

Thurow, L. 1980. *The Zero-Sum Society: Distribution and the Possibilities for Economic Change*. New York: Basic Books.

U.S. Census Bureau. 2010. Minority Census Population. http://2010.census.gov/mediacenter/awareness/minority-census.php.

U.S. Office of Personnel Management. 2010. Ninth Annual Report to the President on Hispanic Employment in the Federal Government. www.opm.gov/Diversity/Hispanic/annual/reports/April2010/HispanicEmployment-2010.pdf

Wilson, W. 1887. The study of administration. *Political Science Quarterly* (June 2), 197–222.

2 Human Resources in the Emerging Organization

Success is not the key to happiness. Happiness is the key to success. If you love what you are doing, you will be successful.

—Albert Schweitzer

After reading this chapter, you will

- recognize the importance of the human factor in achieving successful organizational outcomes;
- gain an initial understanding of the major activities that human resource systems perform for their organizations;
- realize the human resource system's roles and responsibilities at the strategic, tactical, and operational levels of an organization;
- appreciate the paradigmatic distinctions between traditional and progressive approaches to human resource management;
- understand better the opportunities available for individuals interested in pursuing careers in the field of human resource management.

Public organizational achievement is best fostered when policies, programs, and outcomes affirm the organization's mission. Achievement of such results does not come easily for any organization, including public organizations like municipal governments. Here are the six key factors that positively influence organizational success:

- good organizational leaders at all levels;
- strong community support and engagement;
- sufficient financial resources to achieve what the community asks of its public servants;
- positive organizational culture, which includes strong organizational communication, coordination, cooperation, and commitment;

- effective organizational design, structured in a manner that facilitates the efficient utilization of financial, technological, and human capital; and
- human resources consisting of people with the experience, skills and talent, and commitment to achieve the organization's goals.

All six factors drive local government. Of these elements, however, the sixth—the people—is the most important.

We know from experience that people find significant meaning and value in their work, almost as much as they do in their personal lives. This is particularly true for career professionals. Police officers and firefighters, for example, invest so much psychic capital in their work that they often find it difficult to cope in retirement. Human resource (HR) professionals need to refer to these six characteristics frequently when contemplating the quality and contribution of their work. For just as human capital (i.e., the people) is critical to organizational success, HR management (i.e., those professionals in the HR division) provides critical linkages to the people. HR actions alone do not dictate success or failure in these six factors, but their efforts do matter significantly. HR activities, when properly crafted and effectively implemented, improve the potential for achieving goal-driven outcomes. Furthermore, by being cognizant of employees' needs, HR can offer the types of initiatives that benefit employees personally (e.g., competitive pay plans, desired medical benefits, day-care assistance) by allowing them to remain focused on their jobs and achieve desired goals.

PRINCIPAL ACTIVITIES OF HUMAN RESOURCE MANAGEMENT

Often, employees take for granted HR programs. This should not surprise anyone. Workers tend to place greater value on their positions relative to aspects of work performed in other organizational units. Many of my graduate students, with in-service work experiences, have mentioned their surprise at the scope of HR–related activities. Comments like, "I never realized just how diverse and complex human resource activities are" or "Now I have much greater respect for what my HR department does" are common among students nearing the completion of their HR course.

HR's breadth of activities and work responsibilities is immense. Often, HR systems appear ineffective or incapable of managing and tracking employee and performance-related information. The level of data collected and retained within HR units is voluminous and growing. Progressive HR systems adopt information technology, like HR managements systems (HRMS), to ease this "paper burden." Likewise, increasing emphasis on strategic planning, performance outcomes, and quality of service improvements helps explain why cutting-edge HR systems are devolving. HR data collection increasingly occurs within operating departments or is outsourced to private HR services.

Figure 2.1 provides a brief synopsis of the major management oversight activities performed by HRMS. One important observation should be noted here. Not all municipal governments have formal HR management units, but all have individuals responsible for these HR functions. Municipalities with less than 150 employees often

Figure 2.1 **Human Resource Activities**

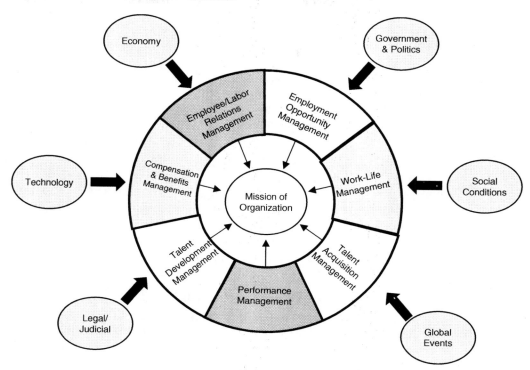

do not have a recognized HR unit. In situations like these, either the chief administrator (e.g., city manager, city clerk, town manager) or a selected representative (e.g., assistant to the city manager, assistant city manager, administrative assistant) manages these activities. Municipalities larger than 150 employees increasingly will find the need for specialized professionals trained in HR management to handle the HR service delivery of the local government. Thus, as the organization's workforce increases in size, so will the likelihood that it will create a distinct HR management unit.

HR leadership also becomes more significant as organizational size increases. This is especially true for cities with more than 250 employees, as it becomes increasingly difficult for the city administrative leader to know each employee personally.

This book focuses on the seven most significant HR interrelated functions: Employment Opportunity Management, Work-Life Management, Talent Acquisition Management, Performance Management, Talent Development Management, Compensation and Benefits Management, and Employee and Labor Relations Management (see Figure 2.1). HR systems coordinate these activities in order to facilitate the attainment of the local government's primary mission and most desired accomplishments. As noted previously, HR systems should not act alone when considering appropriate policies and strategies to enhance organizational outcomes. HR systems must share information and work in conjunction with the wants and needs of each operating department. Among the poorest decisions that HR leaders can make is choosing to remain isolated from the organization's leadership and operating staff. Unfortunately, this often remains the case in traditional bureaucratic and risk-adverse HR units.

Achieving the organization's mission and its near-term and longer-term goals requires the benefit of unified commitment and coordination across all local government departments. The implementation of a community event—for example, an Independence Day celebration—requires significant coordination among a number of local government units. Crowd and traffic control require police involvement. The Fire Department must be available for fire control associated with fireworks displays and the provision of medical care in case citizens in the crowd are injured or need other immediate medical assistance. Parks and Recreation units will have to set up for the event venues, often moving city equipment for event seating, sound systems, and so on. Other city departments will also be involved in parade and firework permits, parking, transportation coordination, and a myriad of issues associated with such an event. Notably, this example illustrates only one event among the many services cities provide every day for their community. Intragovernmental and intergovernmental coordination is essential in achieving desired organizational ends and outcomes.

ENVIRONMENTAL INFLUENCES

In addition, environmental factors affect and influence HR activities identified in Figure 2.1. The oval shapes in this figure depict some of the common environmental factors influencing the practice of organizational management activities today. Environmental factors include those events, issues, pressures, and influences occurring outside of the organization that affect the organization's practices and policies as well as the attainment of desired performance outcomes. Systems theory, for example, advises organizational leaders that they cannot close themselves off from outside influences and stakeholders without potential threats to their legitimacy, sustainability, and long-term survival. As David Easton (1957) suggests, organizations that do so will experience negative entropy; that is, they will become less significant to those they serve, threatening their own organizational survival.

The most common categories of external pressures that municipal governments face are identified below.

Economic Conditions

Economic conditions affect governments' abilities to provide community services. For example, declines in the local economy reduce revenues, stalling capital projects, forcing employee downsizing, and curtailing training and development initiatives for existing employees.

Technological Advances

Advances in technology, such as computer-aided design technology, create employment opportunities for some while displacing others. The American Federation of Labor and Congress of Industrial Organizations (AFL-CIO 1998), for example, reports that occupations in technician and related support fields—such as jobs for drafters, surveyors, licensed practical nurses, dental hygienists, and emergency medical technicians—are expected to grow rapidly in the near future, especially various computer-based occupations. Organizations and HR systems must anticipate technological change and facilitate its application and implementation. In addition, HR systems must identify methods for transitioning employees as a result of changing technology.

Governmental and Political Change

Activities and public policy at other levels of government may affect programs offered at the local level. For example, America's war in Iraq adversely affected staffs in local government as a result of military call-ups. In 2004 California had more than 10,300 National Guard members and reservists called for active duty. A large number of these soldiers were public employees, many of whom worked in law enforcement or the state prison. California's controller calculated that these call-ups cost the state an average of $1,500 a month in salary adjustment and benefits for each activated state employee reservist (Tempest 2004).

Legal and Judicial Decisions

Legislative and judicial decisions from federal, state, and local jurisdictions influence the practice of HR management. In some instances, lower-level courts and/or local government councils address issues based on local needs, even when higher-level governments (federal or state governments' judiciary or legislatures) remain mute on the issue. One classic example is protection provided for sexual orientation. Some state and local governments have enacted progressive legislation to protect individuals against discrimination based on their sexual orientation or gender identity. As of March 2011, however, no federal legislation had been passed to protect against discrimination based on sexual orientation or gender identity. Congress continues to consider legislation known as the Employment Non-discrimination Act, which if approved, would provide sexual orientation protection in private non-religious organizations employing fifteen or more full-time equivalent workers. By comparison, thirty-one states legislate protection for individuals against discrimination based on their sexual orientation (Human Rights Campaign 2010).

Socioeconomic Conditions

Unstable socioeconomic conditions in a community (i.e., poor housing, racism and civil unrest, high crime, declining educational levels) may cause social unrest from isolated and disaffected local stakeholder groups. In recent years, HRMS have provided diversity training for their workforces as a means of understanding and interacting more effectively with individuals from diverse social and cultural backgrounds.

Global Events

Natural disasters, wars, incidences of terrorism, and health pandemics all are recent global events that affect government and their HR practices. Acts of terrorism clearly have reshaped local governments' policies especially in the area of security, for protection of both their communities and their municipal workplaces. HR policies, accepted practices in government, and resource allocations have all changed because of global events like 9/11.

Environmental scanning monitors external forces, seeking to understand changing conditions and how those changes affect the organization's internal processes, operations, and policies. Vigilant monitoring of change aids the organization to prepare for and institute changing policies and practices when transformation is necessary. This information can alert local governments to potential policy changes at higher sectors of government. Local government officials can thus act to influence policy through their knowledge and insights a priori.

PRINCIPAL FUNCTIONS OF HUMAN RESOURCE MANAGEMENT

This section provides a brief overview of the seven primary HR functions that HR systems fulfill in local government. More thorough discussion of each area is provided in Chapters 3 through Chapter 9.

Employment Opportunity Management (Chapter 3)

Employment opportunity management stands at the top of the organizational HR activities figure (i.e., in Figure 2.1). As Americans, we cherish the fact that we live in a land of economic opportunity. The belief that a person can rise through educational attainment and meritorious labor constitutes the backbone of the American dream of life, liberty, and the pursuit of happiness. This belief rests on the premise that an individual's potential for employment should not be impeded by artificial barriers unrelated to the ability to perform productively in the workplace. Thus, a person's age, race, gender, and ethnicity (among other non–work-related factors associated with demonstrated ability to perform in a job) should not influence her selection if she is capable of performing the tasks associated with the job. Chapter 3 addresses how HR systems, through the application of equal employment and affirmative action philosophies, seek to ensure the protections of and rights of individuals (as well as groups of individuals possessing the same non–work-related characteristics—like race).

Work-Life Management (Chapter 4)

The nature of America's workforce and its demographic composition are changing in dynamic fashion today. Emerging research demonstrates significant attitudinal differences across "generations" of employees in the workplace. Thus, how one manages workers and their performance will be influenced by the generational cohort of the individual. Life experiences, for example, differ significantly for a sixty-year-old individual compared with another worker in his early twenties just entering into the workplace. Employee retention and sustained work productivity of young workers, for example, will depend upon how effectively organizational management practices relate to their generation's work-related attitudes, beliefs, and values. Thus, organizations that develop and apply effective work-life balance philosophies place themselves in a competitive advantage relative to other systems that fail to do so.

Other changes in American society also place pressures on organizations to institute more family friendly (i.e., work-life balance) management practices. We are an aging society; the elderly are the fastest growing cohort in America. Increases in the aging population, coupled with greater gender diversity occurring in the workforce, create counterpressures on families to find strategies for balancing work demands with their need to provide support for both their children and often their retired parents (and even grandparents). Chapter 4 discusses what organizations can do to help their workers remain productive employees while still meeting their family role as parent, spouse, and supportive caregiver.

Talent Acquisition Management (Chapter 5)

Key HR activities depend on locating, managing, motivating, and rewarding talented workers. Broadly defined, talent acquisition management refers to an organization's strategy and ability to attract, retain, and motivate its employees. The Society for Human Resource Management (SHRM) (2002, ii) notes that "while talent management has always been part of the HR's mission, a combination of demographic and market forces will bring new urgency to cultivating a workforce that offers true competitive advantage." The future challenge for organizations is not to attract qualified people; rather it is to identify the "valued employee." SHRM identifies these as employees from all levels of the organization, not just the senior management level, meeting one or more of three key criteria. The valued employee is a person who possesses critical skills needed by the organization, exhibits high performance, and/or demonstrates "high potentials," including those that may be central to helping the organization meet its diversity objectives (2).

Talent acquisition management strategies must also focus on developing reward systems catering to the needs of each employee. This is increasingly important for younger workers. HR technology presently exists to create customized reward systems. Developing these reward structures will be a "human" challenge rather than a technical one for HR systems. This is particularly true for government, where deep-seated reliance of civil service pay grade structures based on longevity, rather than talent, has been the norm for the past half-century.

Performance Management (Chapter 6)

One of the most difficult organizational tasks involves accurately measuring employees' performance and their contributions to achieve desired outcomes. Many employees distrust their organization's appraisal process and/or their supervisor's ability to rate accurately their contribution. Too often organizational appraisal instruments are developed for all the wrong reasons: for ease of application across the workforce, for efficiency's sake, or simply because "management" requires that the annual evaluation be performed. When conducted for these reasons, the performance review process often demotivates workers rather than creating the impetus for improv-

ing employee performance and collective outcomes. This helps explain why so many employees (as well as their supervisors) view the performance appraisal process with disdain. Paraphrasing Will Rogers, an early twentieth-century political philosopher and humorist, most employees have never met a performance appraisal system that they liked. Distrust of performance appraisal systems has even led organizations to disband formal performance appraisal all together.
Good performance reviews occur for the following reasons:

- to reward individuals (or work teams) for their performance-based contributions to achieving organizational goals;
- to communicate with employees about changes in future assignments and associated performance expectations relating to these changes; and
- to identify the developmental potential of employees through assessment strategies evaluating performance associated with increasingly demanding work assignments.

Chapter 6 addresses the benefits and drawbacks of the employee performance appraisal processes as part of the organization's effort to utilize performance management systems effectively. The chapter discusses common methodologies used to assess employee (and team-based) productivity. It also identifies evaluator rating errors and why they occur. Furthermore, it discusses how to reduce rater bias errors in the performance management process, and the consequences that HR systems face when they continue to operate with flawed performance management systems.

Talent Development Management (Chapter 7)

Organizations are only as good as their employees, and organizations must maintain talent to sustain cutting-edge competency. This solidifies a firm's stance in the ever-competitive marketplace, but also it creates strength in the eyes of its workforce. Employee retention is enhanced significantly when employees believe that they work for an organization where talent abounds. The organizational culture that fosters and recognizes talent creates an environment where individuals want to belong, to contribute, and to be recognized as a part of the talent pool. The City of Phoenix, Arizona, has created this type of reputation. It is one factor that has sustained it as one of America's best-managed cities over the past two decades.
Talent development management works closely with the concept of talent acquisition management, briefly discussed above and in Chapter 5. Talent acquisition management addresses the recruitment, screening, and selection of talent for a workforce. Talent development management focuses on expanding the human capital of an organization's workforce to achieve improved outcomes through training and developmental strategies. The central focus of talent development management identifies, measures, and implements initiatives that help employees do their work better, be better prepared for the changing nature of work, and gain experiential knowledge that prepares them for tomorrow's leadership roles. This will be discussed in greater detail in Chapter 7.

Compensation and Benefits Management (Chapter 8)

Compensation management comprises the administration and oversight of compensation programs and systems to ensure equitable and legal distribution of monetary resources to an organization's workforce. Put simply, compensation matters, but many people view compensation only as its most tangible and visible element—namely, current salary or hourly wage. Individuals with this perspective likely lose out in the "money game," because compensation encompasses much more than a worker's earnings. Compensation comprises three primary elements. First, it consists of the wage or salary one receives. Next, it involves the quality and number of benefits that organizations provide for their employees and their family members. Finally, it includes other quantitative (perks) and qualitative (quality of working life) aspects associated with employment. Qualitative influences may include the existing culture within the organization, its geographic location and appeal to the employee, and the work flexibility it affords its employees. For some people, living in a warm climate year round would be a key issue in deciding on psychological factors of compensation. They might choose to live there even if it means taking a lower salary to do so. Time with one's family might also be a compensation consideration. Many talented individuals choose work with local government so they can spend more time with their families. Clearly, in many cases their skill sets could place them in better-paying jobs, but they choose to trade off additional wages for time away from work to spend with family members and/or friends. The same may apply to overtime pay; individuals might decline additional earning potential in favor of more time to spend with family or friends.

As is suggested here, wise employers envision compensation beyond its tangible (i.e., monetary) aspects. As Frederick Herzberg (1964) suggested long ago, while money is an important consideration, it is not necessarily the sole factor driving employee productivity and commitment. Social and psychological factors also play a significant role for employees. Good corporations, public and private, try their best to provide competitive compensation. Yet these organizations view compensation from a broad-based perspective rather than simply as a monetary reward. Increasingly, issues like pay equity and quality-of-life issues (both on and off the job) must factor into organizational compensation packages. Thus, individuals may choose to work for a leading-edge organization for less income (at least for a short period) in order to gain skills and experiences that will propel their career development and desirability within other organizations.

More discussion about theories of compensation, their application in government, and their importance as a competitive talent acquisition and retention strategy will occur in the first half of Chapter 8.

Benefits management comprises the administration and oversight of benefits systems that ensure equitable and legal distribution of the organization's benefits programs to its workforce. Along with compensation, benefits packages have financial, emotional, and security implications for both employer and employee. The employer's side concerns cost containment as well as the issue of balancing the burdens placed on the taxpaying public with an obligation to its workforce. Employees, on the other hand, view benefits as part of the compensation package that is (or at least should be) provided by the employer. In recent years, salary and wage increases granted by employers have been offset by employee co-payment obligations. In many instances, rapidly rising medical insurance costs have left employees in worse financial condition, with many receiving less in real-term earnings than they did in previous periods.

Benefits management is a complex task of administering, managing, and determining the allocation of organizational resources to meet the benefits needs of employees while simultaneously limiting the burdens placed on the taxpaying public. Maintaining up-to-date knowledge of existing federal and state regulations and legislation poses many challenges, especially given the exponential growth in legislative policies and regulations in recent years. Many benefits administrators earn as much as HR directors, because their decisions carry significant implications for the organization's financial resources. Realistically, selecting a medical benefits plan that saves an organization even a small percentage over a previous medical benefits contract may result in the accrual of hundreds of thousands, if not millions, of additional dollars in savings for the organization. Good benefits administrators expect to be rewarded for the value that they bring their organization. If the rewards do not meet their expectations, they will likely move elsewhere.

The second half of Chapter 8 will provide an overview of the changing nature of benefits programs in American government. In addition, it will address landmark and emerging legislation and tax policies that influence the practice of benefits administration in American organizations, including local government.

Employee and Labor Relations Management (Chapter 9)

The last "management activities" chapter (Chapter 9) focuses on employee relations, labor relations, and collective bargaining in the context of local government. America's labor policy in the public sector is exceedingly complex, because no unifying legislation exists guiding its practice, as is the case in the private sector. Whereas the National Labor Relations Act and its National Labor Relations Board (NLRB) have oversight responsibilities of labor policy in the private sector, state governments dictate, through legislation, what and who will be allowed to bargain collectively in their state and local governments.

Generally speaking, labor relations participation has eroded significantly over the past half-century. For example, participation rates in the private sector today remain below 10 percent. If government employee participation is included, this figure jumps to 12 or 13 percent of the nation's existing workforce. Nevertheless, even with declines in participation among the workforce, labor relations and collective bargaining continue to be important aspects of the relationship between those directing an organization and those producing goods or services within it.

Chapter 9 will discuss labor relations in the context of their historical, legal, and economic impact on local governments and the services they provide. Furthermore, it will address best methods for enhancing relations between management and labor. Hardball bargaining tactics, as historically common during twentieth-century collective bargaining, have lessened value in today's labor environment. Formulas for

Table 2.1

Human Resource Management Levels

HR level	Time frame	Responsible officer	Type of activities
Strategic/Executive	3–5 years	HR director (executive)	Oversight of all HR activities/accountable HR officer
Tactical/Middle-level management	1–2 years	HR manager (generalist)	Coordination over several functional areas
		or HR manager (specialist)	Direct management responsibility of key functional areas
Operational/Administrative	Current activities	HR technician and HR clerk (entry-level or nonsupervisory HR specialist)	• recruitment officer • trainer, training coordinator • compensation analyst • benefits coordinator • job analyst • HR information technician

successful collective bargaining, at least as they relate to union interests, have moved away from bread-and-butter (i.e., wage and salary) conditions toward the broader needs of the union membership. Examples include cost-containment of benefits packages, retention of jobs for union members, and quality-of-life benefits, including safer working conditions, flexible working schedules, and better day-care provisions.

HUMAN RESOURCE SYSTEM MANAGEMENT LEVELS

James D. Thompson, in his seminal work *Organizations in Action* (1967), classified organization levels within three categories. Thompson suggested that all organizations have strategic, tactical, and operational responsibilities. Each of these levels serves specific purposes. Table 2.1 provides a breakdown of general responsibilities of HR systems based on Thompson's organizational typology.

STRATEGIC HUMAN RESOURCE MANAGEMENT

The strategic level ranks as the highest organizational level. Executives serving in leadership capacities at this level are responsible for the oversight of all HR organizational activities. In addition, they determine the organization's human capital direction through a review of internal organizational needs as well as through assessment of demands placed upon the organization from its task environment. Figure 2.1 provides examples of external pressures that influence internal organizational policies, practices, and activities.

Typically, an HR director serves in this capacity for large city governments (municipalities with 2,500 employees or more). In very small municipalities (with less than 150 employees), much of this responsibility falls on the city manager or a selected representative. Strategic decision-making time frames are long-range in scope. Thus, the HR director, along with his executive staff, considers the needs of the organization over a period of three to five years. Strategic HR focuses on questions such as:

- How will the nature of technological change affect the composition of our existing workforce over the next five years?
- Can we prepare our employees (through training and development strategies) to plan for the emerging technology and emerging jobs? If not, what transition strategies should we employ to maintain seamless services for our citizens?
- How do we contain health care and pension costs in an era of out-of-control cost increases? How much of these costs can (or should) be passed on to our employees? What will be their reaction? What impact will health care and pension cost shifts to employee have on labor relations with existing collective bargaining units?
- How do we continue to provide quality services in an era of reducing revenues? If cuts in the workforce must be made, who should be retained and who should be terminated? How do we implement such reductions in force without destabilizing work performance and employee morale?

These questions illustrate just a few of the myriad issues that strategic-level HR decision-makers must consider when taking action and anticipating employee and union reactions.

TACTICAL HUMAN RESOURCE MANAGEMENT

Tactical (often referred to as middle-level management) HR takes the policies and plans determined at the strategic level and oversees their implementation by lower-level operational personnel. Tactical-level managers serve as a buffer between the strategic and operational levels. As such, they must interpret policies from above and work with operational personnel to put these plans into action. Some tactical-level managers serve as HR generalists, others as HR specialists. Typically, HR generalists have broad job responsibilities with overall coordination over several different HR functions. HR specialist managers, on the other hand, have specialized training in key and complex areas of HR management. HR specialists often can be found in benefits, EEO/AA, employee relations, and HR information systems units. The critical success of both the HR mission and operations depends on HR generalists and specialists. Often, these individuals serve in a "management by exception" capacity, addressing complex problems that their operational staff cannot answer or that consume too much of the operational unit's time to address. Tactical-level managers typically confront issues affecting the organization's success at achieving near-term (up to two years) goals.

OPERATIONAL HUMAN RESOURCE MANAGEMENT

HR personnel in these positions are involved in the daily operational and administrative activities of their organization. Table 2.1 provides examples of the types

Table 2.2

Competing Human Resource Paradigms

	Traditional HR	Progressive HR
1. Structure	Hierarchical	Organic
2. Management focus	Internal HR process orientation, with primary emphasis on administrative tasks and regulations	HR as consultant orientation, with emphasis on operational performance improvements
3. HR leadership style	Transactional and administrative	Transformational and entrepreneurial
4. Risk intensity	Low to risk-adverse	Moderate risk-taking
5. Problem-solving style	Reactive orientation	Proactive and preventive orientation
6. Human capital orientation	Employees are labor costs to be cut	Employees are an investment that should be nurtured and protected
7. HR culture	HR's interests first	Outcome achievement first

of position titles often associated with individuals employed at this level. Generally, this level is responsible for current HR activities. Much of the scope at this level involves administrative duties. As will be seen below, much of the work currently being handled will either be outsourced over the next decade or will be self-administered through web-portal structures by employees or their department supervisors. Operational-level HR is often labor-intensive and not easily seen by top-level leaders as adding value to the outcomes desired by the organization. Whether this perspective is correct or not is debatable. Nevertheless, the perception persists, and thus career opportunities at the operational HR level are likely to diminish over the next decade.

HUMAN RESOURCE MANAGEMENT PARADIGMS

As noted in the first chapter, worker distrust and disdain for HR operations can be high in some organizations. Often, the style of HR management practiced in these agencies creates this problem. Two models (i.e., paradigms) of HR management style are discussed in this section. One is referred to here as the traditional HR paradigm. The other is referred to here as the progressive HR paradigm (see Table 2.2).

Utilization of the traditional HR approach fosters the continuation of HR's past with attempts to control HR practices through a highly centralized structure. This approach to HR is dominated by administrative tasks and regulatory oversight. HR units that practice this paradigmatic approach will lose credibility and influence in their agencies, especially in organizations where adaptation is necessary and resources are constrained.

David Ulrich, a University of Michigan management professor, proclaims, "HR is dead. Long live HR" (Bates 2002). His comment reflects the point that the old ways of practicing HR (like the continued utilization of traditional HR) are dead, but the appreciation and need for HR live on when more progressive HR practices are adopted.

Small-size local governments, especially municipalities with fewer than 500 employees, are likely to practice traditional HR. In smaller local governments the HR function typically falls on the shoulders of the chief executive or an assistant. Traditional HR systems place emphasis on administrative responsibilities, with much less emphasis on long-term goals and outcomes. Here the primary goal of the department is to comply with external regulatory reporting obligations and to provide basic services (e.g., recruitment, operational training, benefits coordination) to operating departments and personnel. Cities using traditional HR are also likely to have staffs with small professional education, and they tend to follow blindly (without questioning) the will of their municipal councils. The chief executive, often city or town manager, serves mostly in an implementation capacity, carrying out the wishes and whims of the council or commission. These systems typically lack future vision. They continue to practice government by "doing what we always have done best." These systems tend to be risk-adverse and unwilling to perform routine administrative tasks using advanced technology, which, if used, could ease the administrative burdens placed on the HR staff. Surprisingly, these systems are still excellent candidates for progressive HR application, but moving in this direction will be painful, as their primary means for getting there will be through the outsourcing of most HR administrative and operational responsibilities.

On the other hand, the practice of progressive HR is driven most often by a strong executive or an HR visionary. Clearly, the transformation from traditional HR toward progressive HR is occurring. This is particularly the case in private sector HR systems. Systems using progressive HR have greater future focus and directed purpose than do systems using traditional HR.

The progressive HR visionary wants the HR systems to contribute to the overall success and goal attainment of the organization. These systems strive to provide consultative support to advance the cause of their operating units in the achievement of desired unit and organizational outcomes. Progressive HR systems are less turf-oriented in comparison to traditional HR systems. Who receives the credit is not as important in progressive HR systems as long as they meet their customers' needs and have a seat at the "decision-making table." As noted in Table 2.2, progressive HR is more interested in facilitating organizational outcomes, through supportive consultation with operating units. It seeks to align programs to achieve an organization's mission, goals, and aspirations. Furthermore, it addresses HR problems and issues using a proactive and preventive approach. Thus, rather than reacting to the need for a new employee (as often would be the case with traditional HR), it advises executive decision-makers of staff changes that might be considered as new positions emerge and as other positions become obsolete or better served through outsourcing strategies.

HUMAN RESOURCE MANAGEMENT AS A PROFESSIONAL CAREER

Careers in HR management can be financially rewarding, professionally enhancing, and personally challenging. Over the past two decades, HR has been in transition, moving from traditional HR management, with its heavy emphasis on administrative processes, toward progressive HR activities. Progressive HR increases emphasis on consultative partnering with operational units for improved performance outcomes. Clearly, future HR departments will be smaller than in the past. HR's reduced size, however, does not necessarily mean that its significance will diminish.

The time-honored career path for HR personnel has been to gain progressive exposure to a variety of organizational HR practices. Future HR careers are likely to favor individuals with specialized skills as well as broad knowledge of organizational activities beyond the specific realm of HR. They will understand organizational operations and practices almost as well as line managers with oversight responsibilities. Many future HR practitioners will have advanced education in business, public administration, or related fields. Knowledge of IT, marketing, financial administration, and the like will be the norm for future HR leaders who will understand professional organizational practices and participate in the organization's strategic decision-making process based on this knowledge.

As noted previously, careers as HR generalists will decline, especially for those practitioners overseeing administrative-level activities. Many of these positions will become functionally obsolete as HR information technology advances and as organizations outsource these activities to HR vendors who can provide services seamlessly for a lower cost to the organization. In the wake of these changes, the number of HR specialist positions will increase. Steve Bates (2002) offers examples of HR jobs of the future:

- The chief financial officer of HR will apply metrics to demonstrate the inherent economic value of HR through analyses of the cost-effectiveness of its proposals, policies, and practices.
- The internal HR consultant will facilitate operational units' personnel in the application of HR practices. Examples include improving departmental recruitment and selection strategies and developing motivational and retention strategies for sustaining valued employees. The consultant also will provide advice and assistance about HR-related legal questions and ethical issues facing management.
- The talent manager will be responsible for locating, developing, and retaining the employee talent pool. Responsibilities will include talent acquisition strategies (e.g., do we hire, contract through outsourcing, or "rent" new workers) as positions change. In addition, the talent manager will hold key influence in developmental strategies necessary to keep talented employees performing up to their potential in the job.
- The vendor manager will work closely with outside vendors providing HR and related services. Maintaining close relationships and knowledge of outside vendors and service providers will allow the vendor manager to determine which vendors best suit the firm's HR service needs. Furthermore, the HR vendor manager will monitor quality and cost closely to ensure that the organization receives an excellent return on investment from selected vendors.
- The HR self-service leader will interface directly with information technology specialists, ensuring high-quality employee access to web-portals. This allows

employees to update personal information as well as access information online about their own benefits and pension plans.

Excellent growth potential will exist for those candidates possessing the desired skill sets needed in the future HR department. However, this scenario means that HR students and practitioners must think differently about their educational preparation and work experiences. Clearly, graduate education in the fields of business administration, public administration, or information technology (depending on the student's sector and skill interests) will be a necessity for aspiring HR careerists. For example, Dave Kieffer, an HR consultant working for William M. Mercer, Inc., suggests "Get thee off to business school. Study finance" (Bates 2002). Paraphrasing this advice, for those interested in public service, I would suggest, "Get thee enrolled in a NASPAA accredited program in public administration or public affairs."

CHAPTER SUMMARY

This chapter began by discussing six influences that increase the potential for organizational success. Among the most important forces are strong leadership, professionally capable and talented HR practitioners, and the cooperation and commitment of all in achieving desired outcomes for the community served.

HR systems help achieve these desired outcomes by effectively planning and implementing a variety of HR activities. The chapter identifies seven primary functions that HR systems perform to assist their organizations in attaining their mission and other primary goals.

The chapter further identifies three different levels of HR management, using Thompson's organizational model: strategic, tactical, and operational. Each level serves a distinct function while working simultaneously with other HR levels to facilitate desired outcomes.

Chapter 2 also distinguishes between two paradigmatic models of HR available for practice by organizational HR systems: traditional and progressive HR management. This chapter identifies the benefits when cutting-edge HR systems (in the form of progressive HR) applications are utilized. Unfortunately, many municipal HR systems, especially in small cities, continue to practice elements of traditional HR. The chapter warns of the consequences when HR systems continue to implement the traditional approach.

This chapter concludes with a brief discussion about future career opportunities in HR management. HR systems are in transition (from traditional to progressive HR). The next generation of personnelists will need new knowledge, skill sets, and innovative thinking to remain relevant to their organizations. The chapter identifies the decline of administrative- and operational-level HR career opportunities as a result of both advancing information technology and the privatization of HR activities. Individuals seeking future careers in HR management will need to be college-educated, have broad work experiences outside of HR, and understand organizational operations from a broad, holistic perspective. Knowledge of HR will be required, but candidates will also be trained in fields like information technology, social marketing, and finance and budgeting.

KEY CONCEPTS AND TERMS

Employment Non-Discrimination Act (ENDA)

environmental factors

environmental scanning

human resource generalist

human resource management levels: strategic, tactical, and operational

human resource specialist

progressive human resource management

six key leadership factors

systems theory

traditional human resource management

PRACTICAL LEARNING ACTIVITIES

1. Identify an organization that you are familiar with or have worked at. Review the six key leadership factors identified near the beginning of this chapter. Assess how well your organization achieves each of these goals. Where organizational shortcomings involving one or more of these six factors exist, identify strategies that might be used to enhance employee performance and strengthen an existing employee's future leadership potential. Be prepared to discuss your assessment and the strategies for change that you recommend.

2. Using Figure 2.1 in the text, review the environmental pressures that organizations face when implementing HR management. Select one of these environmental factors (i.e., economy or technology) and determine how recent changes here impact and influence HR practices and policies in the American workforce.

3. Table 2.2 identifies two distinct HR management approaches—traditional and progressive. Typically, an organization, based on its culture and values, practices one approach or the other. Identify two organizations, one that practices traditional HR and a second closer to progressive HR. Compare the strengths and weaknesses of each system's approach to HR management. Which one of the two organizational systems would you prefer to work with? Why?

REFERENCES

American Federation of Labor and Congress of Industrial Organizations (AFL-CIO). 1998. Professional and technical employees in the labor force: An overview. www.dpeaaflcio.org/pros/workplace/labor_pro&tech.htm.

Bates, S. 2002. Facing the Future. *HR Magazine* 47, 7 (July). http://findarticles.com/p/articles/mi_m3495/is_7_47/ai_89025017/?tag=content;col1.

Easton, D. 1957. An approach to the analysis of political systems. *World Politics*, 9, 4, 393–400.

Herszenhorn, D. 2007. House approves ban on anti-gay discrimination. *New York Times*, November 7. www.nytimes.com/2007/11/07/washington/07cnd-employ.html?ex=1352091600&en=b8b4428 60813be06&ei=5088.

Herzberg, F. 1964. The motivation-hygiene concept and problems of manpower. *Personnel Administration* (January–February), 3–7.

Human Rights Campaign. 2010. Employment non-discrimination act. www.hrc.org/issues/workplace/ enda.asp.

Schweitzer, A. n.d. www.randomterrain.com/quotes/success.html.

Society for Human Resource Management (SHRM). 2002. *The Future of the HR Profession*. Alexandria, VA: Society for Human Resource Management.

Tempest, R. 2004. The hidden cost of Iraq war. *Los Angeles Times*, May 23. www.latimes.com/news/ local/state/la-me-guard23may23,1,7374685.story?coll=la-news-state.

Thompson, J. 1967. *Organizations in Action*. New York: McGraw-Hill.

3 Employment Opportunity Management

I will feel equality has arrived when we can elect to office women who are as incompetent as some of the men who are already there.

—Maureen Reagan

After reading this chapter, you will

- understand the distinctions between equal employment opportunity and affirmative action as applied in the workplace;
- gain a historical perspective of employment policy initiatives and how these new laws and regulations have shaped recent employment opportunity management;
- understand the mechanisms that government employs to create equal employment compliance among public and private employers;
- acquire knowledge of key legislative, executive, administrative, and judicial decisions and policies that have shaped employment equity management; and
- enhance your perspective of the future of employment opportunity management in the United States as we move into a global economic environment.

Americans take immense pride as citizens in the "land of opportunity." As the Declaration of Independence indicates, each person has the right to life, liberty, and the pursuit of happiness. As individuals, we marvel at people who ascend from relative obscurity to positions of prominence in the U.S. workplace. Corporate leaders in recent years who have gained fame include Bill Gates (Microsoft), Sam Walton (Wal-Mart), Dave Thomas (Wendy's), Jack Welch (General Electric), and Ray Kroc (McDonald's). Each of us probably knows a story about one of these men, as they have become legendary icons in our society.

One noted observation about the list above: almost all of our multinational corporate heroes are men. This should not come as a surprise, as most of the executive leaders in American industry are males. In a typical calendar year, one can count the number of women leading Fortune 500 corporations on his (or her) hands, and still not run out of fingers. At the end of 2005, Fortune 500 companies utilized the expertise of female chief executive officers (CEOs) in only seven corporations. This accounts for less than 2 percent of these companies, even though females constitute about half of the total American workforce today (Jones 2005). On a more positive note, as of September 1, 2010, the number of female CEOs in Fortune 500 companies (now thirteen) had almost doubled. In America's Fortune 1000 corporations, twenty-seven women (or 2.7 percent of the total number of CEOs) served as their organization's chief executive (Catalyst 2010). We still have a long way to go.

Equality in governmental leadership appears no better, especially at the state and national levels. For more than two centuries (i.e., for 219 years until Barack Obama's presidential victory in 2008), leadership of the federal government's executive branch had been the exclusive domain of white males serving as president. Representative balance at the state and local government level had not been much better. Research reported by Riccucci and Saidel (1997, 429) indicates that "in most cases, women and people of color are not well represented in top policy making positions in state governments across the country." The point made here is that often the rhetoric of equality in both American industry and government is not matched by the reality of the facts, especially in executive-level leadership positions.

Historically, as will be noted in this chapter, American public policy often has been employed to sustain preferential employment opportunities for specific interest groups (such as America's veterans, who tend to be predominantly male) at the expense of other qualified and, in some instances, better applicants. For example, Dresang notes that preferential treatment for American military service members is as old as the republic. As he states, George Washington "was the first to give special recognition and job preferences to military veterans" (Dresang 1998, 23). Veterans' preference, which provides hiring advantages for qualified veterans, continues to be a significant selection factor, especially in governmental civil service systems.

EMPLOYMENT OPPORTUNITY MANAGEMENT IN THE AMERICAN WORKPLACE

This section discusses two of the prominent employment opportunity management philosophies that influence equality considerations in government. These two philosophies are equal employment opportunity (EEO) and affirmative action (AA).

Many Americans believe that EEO and AA programs are indistinguishable. In reality, they differ: EEO prohibits discrimination against any individual when making or implementing policies affecting job-related decisions, such as hiring, promotion, training and development, and employee discipline. By comparison, AA policies seek to remedy past discrimination by granting flexibility in decision-making that affects job-related considerations for protected class members, such as females, African-Americans, Hispanics, and disabled individuals. AA proponents suggest, however, that AA policies should not favor or protect unqualified candidates, when making or implementing these job-related decisions. Part of the reason for this confusion about the differences between EEO and AA policy relates to employers' application forms, which often note that their organization is "an equal employment opportunity/affir-

Figure 3.1 **Zone of Equality**

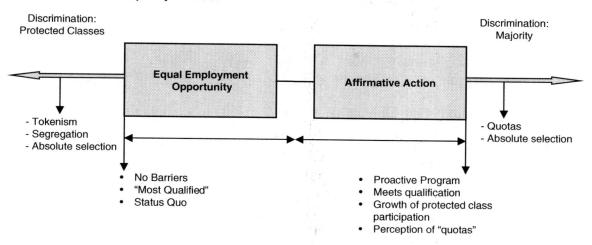

mative action employer." Applicants, reading this, frequently believe that these two separate concepts are one and the same. Both employment philosophies influence organizational employment practices. Often the culture of the organization dictates the dominant utilization of one philosophy over the practice of the other.

Literally, EEO and AA compete for control and influence in most workplaces. Primarily, they influence and affect the organization's selection, promotion, retention, and development practices and patterns. The application of EEO and AA is influenced also by environmental pressures beyond the organization's culture. Public policy initiatives resulting from new legislation, executive orders, administrative regulatory actions, court outcomes, union influence, and citizen feedback influence the pendulum of control over which of these two philosophic perspectives dominates at any one time.

One external pressure affecting employment opportunity practices involved the growing application of AA standards beginning in the late 1960s and early 1970s. Demands for action by civil rights groups, as well as increased legislative interventions, led to new laws supportive of AA policies. This resulted in significant growth in the application of this philosophic approach, especially from 1963 through 1972.

Figure 3.1, titled Zone of Equality, provides insights about the competing nature and distinctions between EEO and AA programs. I contend that societal forces continuously influence shifts toward, and away from, each employment opportunity perspective (i.e., EEO or AA). Often, movement toward one employment philosophy's application occurs at the other's expense. Both employment philosophies, however, are acceptable legal approaches (as defined within U.S. employment legislation) for the practice of workplace equal opportunity. Organizations, however, can and sometimes do move beyond acceptable ranges of this EEO-AA continuum, thereby discriminating illegally against the individual (or groups) in society by unlawfully favoring other interests.

Public opinion polling typically indicates that most Americans favor the application of EEO standards. Americans, correctly or not, often perceive AA as being driven by "quota system" practices. To this end, the Civil Rights Act of 1991 outlaws the use of "quotas" in the determination of job conditions (such as the hiring or promotion of employees). With few exceptions, individuals want to be treated fairly and want to be selected based on their skills, knowledge, and abilities rather than personal characteristics, such as skin color or gender, unrelated to job performance.

DISTINCTIONS BETWEEN EEO AND AA

EQUAL EMPLOYMENT OPPORTUNITY

EEO consists of public policies formed by legislative actions, regulatory decisions, executive orders, and judicial outcomes designed to provide equal potential for access to employment in American society. It serves as a mechanism for arbitrating disputes over issues of employment discrimination when disagreements about job decisions and conditions arise. A key quality of EEO philosophy is that the individual who demonstrates the strongest set of skills, knowledge, and ability should be selected for the job. Thus, individuals identified as most qualified according to valid and reliable performance predictors should not be excluded from employment based on non–job-related factors. A worker's personal attributes that are deemed unrelated to job performance (e.g., one's gender, race, religion, age, national origin) should not factor into employment (or promotion) decisions unless some compelling reason justifies their inclusion, Typically, such characteristics are allowed for only the most compelling reasons.

In human resource (HR) management parlance, authorized job discrimination is permissible when bona fide occupational qualifiers (BFOQs) are identified and allowed as part of the employment determination process. BFOQs grant the exclusion of otherwise qualified individuals from employment, due to some personal characteristic (like age, gender, or religion), even when the applicants can prove their ability to perform the job responsibilities. One highly visible example of a BFOQ, applicable in the American workplace, now requires America's commercial airline pilots to retire at the age of sixty-five years. On December 13, 2007, President George W. Bush signed Public Law 110–135 (Aviation Online Magazine n.d.), the Fair Treatment of Experienced Pilots Act, allowing an additional five years of flight service by pilots (GovTrack.us n.d.). Prior to this law's passage, for more than half a century, pilots had been required to retire at the age of sixty years. This BFOQ is justified for safety reasons—as a means of minimizing health-related safety accidents—as a consequence of concern for pilots' declining health beyond this age. The likelihood of a pilot having a heart attack or stroke (among many other age-related illnesses that could impair ability as a pilot) increases with age. Society has determined that the rights of employment for airline pilots diminish when compared to the protection of airline passengers, thereby mandating forced retirement when an airline pilot now reaches the age of sixty-five. In the case of applying a religious BFOQ, a denominational bookstore seeking to hire a sales representative may consider religious background as a hiring factor (based on needed for specific religious knowledge and belief) to represent its products. On the other hand, if this bookstore were hiring a cashier the BFOQ would probably not be allowed to stand. Finally, gender-based BFOQs would result with male models being disqualified for employment consideration as women's clothing models, even with past experience as professional male clothing models. In this example, clothing designer sales likely would suffer with men modeling women's clothing, so the disqualifier would be allowed for a justified business reason.

EEO supporters reason that the best-qualified applicant should be selected based predominantly on job-related factors. To do otherwise would be irrational. They argue, "Why select a less qualified applicant over a stronger candidate who exhibits greater productivity potential?" Clearly, EEO-based decisions favor candidates with greater past employment experiences as well as requisite skills, knowledge, and abilities (SKAs) gained through past educational opportunities and professional experiences. Thus, EEO proponents believe that selection should remain a value-neutral process determined solely by factors associated with productivity outcomes and benefits to the organization. Therefore, to hire a less qualified Caucasian candidate over a more qualified protected-class applicant (or vice versa) would be discriminatory as well as economically irresponsible. EEO goals view selection from a neutral perspective, "colorblind" to race, gender, religion, age, and so on.

ADVANTAGES AND DISADVANTAGES OF EEO

There are a number of advantages and drawbacks to the utilization of this philosophy.

Advantages of EEO Utilization

- Higher general public acceptance compared to affirmative action. Most Americans perceive EEO as the most appropriate basis for employment-related decisions (including hiring, promotion, training and development, demotions, and downsizing).
- Potential decrease in work disruptions, as internal candidates promoted to higher positions will have greater awareness of the existing organizational culture and work climate, as well as greater familiarity with the needs of both their superiors and fellow workers.
- Greater cost efficiencies through decreased training costs for both entry-level hires and promotional hires. Internally promoted candidates already have the advantages of insider knowledge about the position and its needs. Nevertheless, under almost all circumstances, the candidate selected based on predictive job-related performance characteristics will require less technical training than will other less-qualified applicants.

Disadvantages of EEO Utilization

- EEO maintains a population's status quo as far as societal group representation is concerned. Thus, if 5 percent of college graduates in the field of accounting are African-American, this "most qualified" group will gain employment access due to its advanced educational attainment. Educated African-Americans will benefit, but African-Americans as an ethnic group (constituting approximately 13 percent of the nation's population) will remain underrepresented in the accounting field.

- Growth toward greater workplace diversity and representation may be stunted by the use of EEO. Effective HR systems strive to attract well-qualified minority candidates as part of the competing candidate pool. To do so might require increased recruitment costs, targeted marketing strategies, and greater creativity and innovation.
- Non-selected internal candidates' resentment might intensify if they believe that greater consideration should be given to those "loyal" incumbents in the organization.
- Non-selected internal candidates' morale and work productivity may decline. In such cases, further negative consequences might occur over time, including increased conflict, poor work attendance, lower quality and quantity of work outcomes, and increased direct costs associated with increased disciplinary actions against "errant" employees.

Many organizations favor internal promotions for good reasons. However, such a strategy, designed to reward existing employees as well as contain negative behavioral consequences resulting from external hiring, literally counters the strict adherence of an EEO philosophy.

AFFIRMATIVE ACTION

The term "affirmative action" first appeared in President John F. Kennedy's 1961 Executive Order 10925. In this document Kennedy called for federal agencies to use "affirmative action" when reviewing their employment practices and policies during recruitment efforts on black college campuses and while developing employment strategies for change (Sylvia 1994). AA is employment policy designed to enhance hiring and promotional opportunities for groups in society that previously have been the recipients of discriminatory employment practices. These groups, termed protected-class groups, include women and racial minorities (i.e., African-Americans, Hispanics, Native Americans). Protected-class categorization allows the U.S. Equal Employment Opportunity Commission (EEOC), the primary U.S. employment regulatory body, to monitor and act on workplace discrimination. Similar regulatory agencies exist in state governments to ensure compliance with their state statutory employment policies.

AA diverges significantly from EEO. It seeks to broaden the hiring (and promotion) of individuals from societal groups that historically experienced employment-related discrimination. AA derives from a concept known as representative bureaucracy. J.D. Kingsley's 1944 study of employment in Great Britain (Dresang 1998) first coined this term. Meier (1993) suggests that representative bureaucracy illustrates a government's level of openness to employment of persons of all backgrounds. Representative bureaucracy holds that the demographic composition of government (i.e., the bureaucracy) should strive to mirror the demographic composition of society. Thus, if women constitute half of the eligible workforce participants, then they should also occupy half of all civil service positions in government. In circumstances where less than population parity exists, "affirmative efforts" should be made to promote greater participation for the affected group—in this instance, women. Moreover, truly representative bureaucracies are those that strive for equal distributions of positions based on demographic group composition across all levels of government (i.e., at the executive, middle, and entry levels of the bureaucracy). In its broadest, most ideal application, representative bureaucracy should permeate all organizations, not just government, with employment statistics approximating the demographic characteristics (i.e., its percentage of the population) of each group in society. Attaining population parity outcomes is unlikely, but serves as a target that AA proponents suggest society should aspire to realize.

AA initiatives view strengthened workplace minority representation as necessary in society. Access to work serves as a key means of improving social power and economic wealth that result through representational employment parity. Thus, inclusion of individuals previously locked out of employment creates strengthened democratic societies. Nevertheless, as might be expected, AA also creates considerable potential for conflict and raises questions concerning the legitimacy of its application, especially among a population's majority class (in the United States, primarily Caucasians and/or males). Often, majority-class members contend that selection should be based on value-neutral characteristics such as employment testing that demonstrates performance-related abilities.

AA proponents claim that government specifically, and society in general, have an obligation to right the wrongs of past job-related employment discrimination through public policy that promotes greater minority-based representation in America's workplace. They claim that artificial job testing methodologies often work against fair and balanced consideration of minority applicants, many of whom have not had the same educational opportunities as other individuals in society. In place of "most qualified" applicants, selection systems should allow for greater consideration of minority job-applicants who have the abilities to perform effectively the demands of the job but may not receive the highest test score. Adherence to the "most qualified" standard, they contend, maintains the status quo with regard to employment representation in the workplace. Thus, proactive initiatives that provide greater access to employment are needed to rebalance past discrimination in employment practices. Reaching population parity, AA proponents claim, can only occur with the utilization of AA initiatives.

ADVANTAGES AND DISADVANTAGES OF AA APPLICATION

The advantages and disadvantages of AA are as follows.

Advantages of AA Programs

- Enhances the growth of minority participation in the American workplace.
- Offers people of color, and women, role models and mentors with the same or similar cultural backgrounds and life experiences.

- Creates the potential for greater understanding between majority and minority employees through increased awareness of diversity and cultural distinctions.
- Promotes stronger linkages between the organization and the society it serves, due to increased diversity within the organization that reflects the diversity of the community.

Disadvantages of AA Programs

- Many Americans perceive AA programs as being "quota" systems. This may adversely affect qualified minority candidates who may unjustly receive hostile treatment from fellow employees and/or subordinates.
- In some instances, qualified but less experienced candidates will require additional training to gain knowledge that other, nonselected qualified candidates might already possess. In these instances, training costs and productive losses, at least in the short term, may increase.
- Increased recruitment and selection costs also may result from increased efforts to identify and recruit qualified minority candidates to apply for employment within the organization.
- Resentment may increase and morale drop among qualified existing majority employees bypassed in favor of protected-class applicants.

EEOC AND DISCRIMINATION: MEASURING EMPLOYMENT UTILIZATION LEVELS

No matter which approach dominates, EEO or AA, organizations should anticipate challenges to their selection and promotion practices. Clearly, systems with employment records reflecting robust hiring across all demographic segments of the local labor market have a better stance. The EEOC employs labor market availability analysis and utilization analysis techniques as part of its assessment process. Availability analysis determines the number of protected-class members available for employment within a local labor market. Utilization analysis measures the number of protected-class members employed within an organization in comparison with local labor market availability analysis statistics. Organizations with an approximately equivalent or better utilization record comparable to availability statistics reflect evidence of equal employment practices. In this case, the employer demonstrates strong efforts to hire minority candidates. Utilization analysis statistics that fall below market availability indicate that an organization's employment practices exhibit an underutilization of available protected-class participants within the local labor market. This may signal discriminatory selection practices on the part of the employer.

ASSESSING DISCRIMINATORY PRACTICES

The EEOC's 1978 Uniform Guidelines on Employment Selection Procedures serves as the selection bible for employers, through its recommendations about the process and steps to be taken when making job-related employment decisions (EEOC 1978).

This document discusses actions associated with hiring, retention, promotion, transfer, demotion, dismissal, and referral practices. The EEOC Uniform Guidelines also plays a key role for regulatory agencies like the EEOC, Office of Federal Contracts Compliance Programs (OFCCP in the U.S. Department of Labor), U.S. Office of Personnel Management (OPM), and U.S. Department of Justice when they are contemplating actions based on employment discrimination claims.

These agencies consider two primary categories of discrimination in employment: cases of disparate impact and cases of disparate treatment. Disparate impact refers to cases where protected-class members, as a group, are significantly underrepresented in the workforce due to an organization's employment practices. In these instances, determination of underrepresentation is based on two indicators: (1) internal selection decisions and (2) an assessment of the organization's utilization statistics in comparison with local labor market availability (as determined through availability analysis). Judgment about whether or not an organization complies with the law in its selection practices is determined in part through the use of the EEOC's 4/5th rule. This is discussed in greater detail below.

The second major category of employment discrimination is disparate treatment. While disparate impact refers to discrimination of protected-class groups, often based on group aggregated statistical observations, disparate treatment refers to cases where protected-class members (i.e., individuals) are treated differently from others. Organizations may demonstrate selection outcomes in compliance with local labor market utilization statistics. They may still be guilty of employment discrimination, however, if their policies, practices, or actions treat an individual candidate differently from others based on personal attributes like race, color, gender, age, religion, national origin, and so on. Organizations must maintain vigilance to ensure that they train their staffs about practices that might result in discrimination claims. Employee education and training beyond the HR unit should be provided, as actions outside of HR may create questions of a biased selection process. For example, an organization's receptionist, when asked about position openings by applicants, may inadvertently create difficulties for the organization by providing varying information to job applicants. Advising inquiring males about fire service position openings while failing to provide similar position opening information to inquiring females could result in increased charges of gender discrimination. Claims of "steering" protected-class candidates to certain position openings may also result in disparate treatment charges. Operational-level interviewers (e.g., the immediate supervisor in the hiring operating department) also can create litigation challenges if the supervisor is untrained or poorly trained in "fail-safe" hiring techniques. Requesting information relating to personal characteristics, rather than job qualifications, of applicants can create perceptions of hiring bias in the selection process. For example, interviewers should be trained to avoid asking questions relating to future family plans, marital plans or status, and childcare arrangements, as they do not relate to individuals' job-related qualifications or abilities to perform in the job. HR talent acquisition experts must effectively train and thoroughly educate all employees who are involved, even remotely, in the selection process. Doing so will reduce potential discrimination litigation as well as sustain the organization's public persona as a good employer.

EEOC's 4/5TH RULE AND EMPLOYMENT DISCRIMINATION TESTS

The EEOC's Uniform Guidelines employ the 4/5th rule as a measure to determine if disparate impact in employment exists for protected groups. Typically, an organization must demonstrate that it meets the 4/5th standard in both internal hiring practices and in comparison with the labor composition currently available in the external local labor market. Violation of the 4/5th rule points to prima facie evidence that employment discrimination occurs within an organization:

- Internal equity practices: when the organization's internal hiring practices and selection rate levels for protected groups fall below four-fifths (80 percent) of the hiring and selection rates for a majority group (i.e., Caucasians and/or males). This measurement refers to the internal hiring practice of the organization.
- Labor market representation comparisons: when the employer's workforce composition, as compared with labor market availability for each protected group, falls below an 80 percent ratio of the majority group's (Caucasian and/or male) local labor market rate. In these cases, the organization's hiring practices appear to exclude female and minority group participation at rates higher than would be anticipated.

The 4/5th rule is a standard method for measuring if employment discrimination practices exist within an organization. Two test approaches help determine if disparate impact discrimination is present.

Test 1 (Internal Equity Check): Organization Selection Practices

Discriminatory selection practices potentially exist whenever the selection rates of protected group members (including women) fall below the 80 percent selection rates of the majority group members (Caucasians or men).

Reviewers typically compare minority group selection rates with Caucasians' selection rates as well as selection rates for women compared to those for men in order to determine if violations of the 4/5th rule have occurred.

Internal Equity Check Example. In the City of Sunnydale, Florida, the selection rate (i.e., the percentage of those hired from the applicant pool) for men (the majority group) seeking position openings in the past year was 30 percent. During this same period, the selection rate for women (the protected group) filling position openings was 18 percent. Has the 4/5th rule been violated, thereby suggesting evidence of disparate impact employment discrimination?

A 4/5th rule violation occurs when the protected group's selection rate varies from the majority group's rate by more than 20 percent (i.e., falls below the acceptable 4/5th rule threshold range). In this case, the majority selection rate × 4/5 = 30 percent males × .80 = 24 percent. This means that, according to the 4/5th rule, the threshold rate for women should be 24 percent.

Conclusion. The City of Sunnydale's internal selection practices should be reviewed. Outcomes from city hiring practices signal disparate impact, because its selection rate for women (18 percent) falls below the 4/5th rule's threshold rate, which in this case is 24 percent.

Test 2 (External Equity Check): Labor Market Representation Comparisons

The organization also must review the composition of its workforce in comparison with the supply of available protected-group workers within its relevant labor market. If the composition of protected-group members employed by the organization is lower than the 4/5th rule standard (80 percent) of available talent from that protected group externally, then this indicates prima facie evidence of disparate impact.

External Equity Check Example. The following table compares labor market availability with the City of Sunnydale's employment statistics.

Protected group	Labor market availability	4/5th rule threshold	City of Sunnydale's utilization
African-Americans	16 percent	12.8 percent	14.3 percent
Hispanics/Latinos	10 percent	8.0 percent	6.2 percent
Asian-Americans	4 percent	3.2 percent	5.2 percent
Women	50 percent	40.0 percent	32.0 percent

Conclusion. Comparison of the City of Sunnydale's workforce with labor market availability indicates that the city is within acceptable ranges of protected-group participation for African-Americans and Asian-Americans, but it underutilizes available Hispanics/ Latinos and women in its workforce. Consideration should be given to determine what factors may limit participation of these underrepresented groups in the city's workforce.

A prima facie violation of either internal or external measures signals that the organization's selection practices may be flawed, thus resulting in the underutilization of minority group members or females available in its relevant local labor market. Such underutilization outcomes indicate a need for the organization to examine its selection practices to ensure that its recruitment and selection procedures provide reasonable opportunities for all applicants. Reviewing processes and practices, at a minimum, must determine that job-related tests used to select candidates exhibit both statistical validity and reliability. Job-related validity refers to the accuracy of a test (in this case, any hiring practice used as a part of the selection process) to identify correctly what it intends to measure. Job-related reliability indicates consistency of the measurement (test) results over time. Both validity and reliability are critical in determining whether or not job-related employment discrimination is present when selection decisions are made.

EMPLOYMENT LAW

The second half of the twentieth century witnessed significant increases in public policy designed to enhance and protect the employment rights of American protected-class members. Organizations today, large and small, respect the potential consequences associated with employment discrimination litigation. Their HR policies and training programs increasingly have been implemented to mitigate the potential for discrimination challenges by both employees and job applicants. Such efforts occur for good reason; litigation costs can chew up hundreds of thousands of dollars (or more) of scarce resources whenever business or government is sued for employment discrimination.

The growth of employment legislation places HR units in a difficult position. They dually serve the needs of management while simultaneously acting to ensure their organization's compliance with federal, state, and (in many instances) local employment law. HR units are in an unenviable position of enforcing employment laws and policies against other organizational units. Thus, HR managers must act delicately by convincing units to use sound (and legal) judgment when making employment decisions while working closely with them to create innovative, value-adding strategies that enhance the units' productivity and mission attainment.

EARLY PRESIDENTIAL INTERVENTION VIA EXECUTIVE ORDERS (1940–1961)

The momentum to improve employment opportunities among American minorities began in the early 1940s. In reality, President Franklin D. Roosevelt's executive decisions initiated a means to move antidiscrimination policies forward when congressional approval was virtually impossible.

Executive orders grant a sitting president the opportunity to approve policies that affect operations in the federal government. Executive orders can also apply to those organizations, public or private, that receive funds from federal contracts and federal grants. These orders remain in effect as long as a sitting president desires. They can also be rescinded at any time by the current (or future president) simply by approving a new order that cancels an earlier presidential act. The benefit of the executive order is that the decision to act is made by one individual, as opposed to laws that require approval of identical legislation in both houses of Congress. This advantage also is its own disadvantage, as the action remains in force only for as long as a sitting president desires.

Executive Order 8802. In 1941 President Roosevelt signed Executive Order 8802 prohibiting government contractors from employment discrimination based on race, color, or national origin. This order constituted the first presidential action taken to prevent employment discrimination by private employers holding government contracts. Its impact, however, was limited as no enforcement authority or sanctions were included in its approval (EEOC n.d.a).

Executive Order 9981. President Harry S. Truman's signing of Executive Order 9981 mandated the integration of the U.S. armed forces. Up to this point, segregation of military units had been the norm. Truman's order required also that there be "equality of treatment and opportunity for all persons in the armed services without regards to race, color, religion or national origin" (EEOC n.d.b). It should be noted, however, that the integration of American soldiers did not become a reality until 1952 with the country's entry into the Korean War. This executive order, however, was silent on the issue of equality in opportunity based on gender.

Executive Order 10925. In March 1961, President John Kennedy's Executive Order 10925 further strengthened employment discrimination policies by establishing the President's Committee on Equal Employment Opportunity. This committee could now impose sanctions on those government contractors determined to discriminate in employment on the basis of race (EEOC n.d.c)

CONGRESSIONAL EQUAL EMPLOYMENT LEGISLATION (1960s)

The 1960s was a period of significant economic growth and social transition. The civil rights movement that began to take shape in the mid-1950s had matured, was gaining organizational strength, and increasingly called for public laws granting greater protections against employment, voting, and educational discrimination. In August 1963, more than 200,000 civil rights protesters—about one in four of them white—converged on the nation's capital. The March on Washington included numerous civil rights activists' speeches, including Martin Luther King Jr.'s famous "I have a dream" speech at the Lincoln Memorial. Such mass protests, along with the increasing potential for civil unrest, led to congressional intervention in the form of a number of new protections against discrimination. Key legislation passed during this era included the Equal Pay Act of 1963, Title VII of the Civil Rights Act of 1964, the Voting Rights Act of 1965, and the Age Discrimination in Employment Act of 1967. Three of these four acts have direct impact on the treatment and protection of America's workforce. The Voting Rights Act does not have direct linkage to employment discrimination. Its significance should not be diminished, however, as it outlawed the use of poll taxation as part of the voter registration process. It also prohibited the use of literacy tests as a means for excluding minority voters, and it granted the federal government the authority to administer state and local voter registration processes where deemed necessary. Political empowerment of America's minority population through increased voter participation was, and continues to be, a significant factor in ensuring that society meets the needs and interests of its minority groups.

The Equal Pay Act of 1963. The Equal Pay Act, approved in June 1963, was the first national civil rights legislation addressing employment discrimination. It prohibits discrimination in pay on the basis of gender, when men and women perform similar work utilizing similar skills, effort, and responsibility for the same employer and when working under similar working conditions. It should be noted, however, that the law allowed for pay variances based on merit considerations and length of service (seniority). Furthermore, employee discrimination awards factored in discrimination only over the previous two years and only provided adjustments for the differences between what the individual was being paid and what she should have been paid.

These limitations seriously hindered early litigation efforts, as the cost of litigation in many instances would be greater than the award received even in the most serious gender-in-pay discrimination cases.

Title VII of the Civil Rights Act of 1964. On the evening of June 19, 1964, the U.S. Senate passed the Civil Rights Act of 1964 by a vote of 73 to 27. To reach this consensus required the longest debate in the Senate's nearly 180-year history, with 534 hours of debate in Congress (both Houses) and the inclusion of more than 500 amendments to the original bill (EEOC 2004).

Title VII of the Civil Rights Act of 1964 specifically addressed employment discrimination issues. It applied to most private sector employers with fifteen or more full-time-equivalent employees. Subsequently, amending legislation has resulted in the inclusion of most non–agricultural-based organizations today, including state and local governments, labor organizations, employment agencies, schools, and all branches of the federal government.

Title VII prohibits employment discrimination based on a person's race, sex, color, religion, and national origin. It prohibits discrimination in all job-related conditions, including recruitment, selection, wages, work assignments, promotions, benefits, discipline, discharge, and organizational downsizing. The legislation also established the EEOC, a five-member bipartisan commission serving five-year terms. New members are selected by the president, when vacancies arise, and are confirmed by the U.S. Senate.

Among all federal employment legislation, the Civil Rights Act of 1964 serves as the foundation for EEO legislation. It is a landmark act and one of the most significant documents in American legislative history.

Age Discrimination in Employment Act of 1967. During the decade of the 1960s, issues relating to age discrimination and forced mandatory retirement also became prominent. The Age Discrimination in Employment Act of 1967 (ADEA), whose monitoring and enforcement oversight resides with the U.S. Department of Labor, provides protection from job-related age discrimination for workers age forty and older.

Prior to the passage of this act in 1967, federal laws provided few job-related protections for workers based on their age. The original ADEA outlawed age discrimination by private sector employers engaged in interstate commerce. Subsequently, Congress's passage of the ADEA of 1974 extended protections for government employees at all levels. It also shifted retirement from age sixty-five to seventy years. Finally, during Ronald Reagan's presidency, Congress authorized the ADEA of 1986, which dropped mandatory retirement at any age for most employees.

Today, employers can no longer force employees to retire from their jobs (with the exception of those positions with BFOQ age provisions or executives in policy-making positions) simply on the basis of their age. Thus, individuals whose work performance continues to meet organizational standards cannot be forced into retirement against their will, as was often the case prior to 1967. Note, however, that a worker's age alone will not protect against being terminated if achievable levels of performance cannot be demonstrated.

OTHER SIGNIFICANT EMPLOYMENT PROVISIONS (1970–PRESENT)

A number of significant employment laws, policies, and outcomes beyond the prolif-eration of actions during the 1960s also have been enacted during subsequent decades of the twentieth century and into the new millennium. A brief review of some of the most significant actions is offered below.

Equal Employment Opportunity Act of 1972. The Equal Employment Opportunity Act (EEOA) of 1972 extended provisions of Title VII of the Civil Rights Act of 1964 to cover most U.S. employers with fifteen or more workers. Discrimination in em-ployment legislation as a result of EEOA of 1972 now mandates that state and local governments, public and private employment agencies, public and private educational institutions, and labor unions also provide fair employment practices as determined by the 1964 Civil Rights Act. EEOA also strengthened greatly the EEOC enforce-ment powers, including requiring many public and private employers to implement affirmative action plans that stipulated future protected-class employment goals as well as a timetable documenting a strategy for achieving these outcomes.

Pregnancy Discrimination Act of 1978. The Pregnancy Discrimination Act of 1978 requires any employer with fifteen or more employees to treat pregnancy as a medically covered benefit provided medical benefits are offered to employees. It also mandates that maternity leave be treated the same as other personal or medical leaves.

Civil Service Reform Act of 1978. The Civil Service Reform Act (CSRA) of 1978, sup-ported by President Jimmy Carter's administration, disbanded the U.S. Civil Service Commission, which had been in effect since 1883, replacing it with the newly created U.S. Office of Personnel Management. The OPM director, under the newly enacted law, reported directly to the president. CSRA, among other things, streamlined the recruitment and selection process within federal organizations by granting greater decentralized decision-making control to personnelists in federal regional area offices. In addition, it established the Senior Executive Services, to allow government greater flexibility in moving government's most talented civil servants when their skills were needed in other agencies. It also instituted a merit-based performance system to reward employees for their work productivity. In many instances, however, the legislation's intended outcomes were never achieved, in part as a result of Carter's presidential defeat by Ronald Reagan in the 1980 presidential election.

Americans with Disabilities Act of 1990 and Amendment of 2008. The Americans with Disabilities Act (ADA) of 1990, which provides protection against discrimination in employment due to a person's disability, significantly strengthened disability dis-crimination legislation. Before this date, the Rehabilitation Act of 1973 only provided protection for disabled individuals seeking federal employment. The Rehabilitation Act of 1973 is still in force in federal government. It did, however, serve as a model for ADA of 1990, with much of the same wording applied to the new law. ADA of 1990, under the auspices of the U.S. Department of Labor, extends protections to disabled American job applicants and employees seeking employment opportunities and job protections in state and local government as well as in the private sector. In 2008, Congress approved the Americans with Disabilities Act Amendment (ADAA) (PL110–325), which took effect on January 1, 2009. This act restored ADA of 1990 disability protection rights lost through two Supreme Court decisions, *Sutton v. United Air Lines*, 527 U.S. 471 (1999), and *Toyota Motor Manufacturing, Kentucky, v. Williams*, 534 U.S. 184 (2002) (ADA Amendments Act 2008).

Civil Rights Act of 1991. The Civil Rights Act of 1991 applied a number of amendments to strengthen Title VII of the Civil Rights Act of 1964, which had been significantly weakened by three key U.S. Supreme Court decisions during its 1989 term:

- *Patterson v. McLean Credit Union*, 491 U.S. 164 (1989), in which the Court held that an employee could not sue for damages caused by racial harassment on the job;
- *Martin v. Wilks*, 490 U.S. 228 (1989), which allowed City of Birmingham Caucasian firefighters, who had not been party to the establishment of a prior consent decree establishing rules governing the hiring and promotion of black firefighters, to file suit challenging the decree; and
- *Wards Cove Packing Co. v. Atonio*, 490 U.S. 642 (1989), in which the Court's decision substantially shifted the burden of proof from employer to employee for disparate impact discrimination disputes by now requiring the plaintiff to identify and prove the particular policy or action that produced the inequity.

Congressional passage of the Civil Rights Act of 1991 reestablished the Griggs standard, placing the burden on the employer to provide justification for its actions as a business necessity. The Supreme Court did add that the "mere existence of a statistical imbalance in an employer's workforce on account of race, color, religion, sex, or national origin is not alone sufficient to establish a prima facie case of disparate impact violation" (Perritt 2001, 285).

The Civil Rights Act of 1991 also strengthened civil rights protections for employees in the following ways:

- It required the same protections under Title VII and ADA for U.S. citizens employed in foreign countries by American-owned or American-controlled employers.
- It amended section 703 of Title VII outlawing the use of "race norming" techniques in the selection or promotional process. Race norming allows the adjustment of a candidate's test score on the basis of candidate group characteristics (race, sex, national origin, or other criteria).
- It granted, for the first time, the use of juries in employment discrimination cases, if requested by either party to the litigation.
- It allowed plaintiffs to recover monetary awards for emotional distress and punitive damages based on cases of gender and religious discrimination. Prior to this point, only more traditional awards (e.g., reinstatement of back pay, lost benefits, and position, and recouping of attorney fees) had been authorized in the Civil Rights Act of 1964.

Family and Medical Leave Act of 1992. The Family and Medical Leave Act (FMLA) provides covered employees unpaid leave to care for their own or for family members' medical needs. The U.S. Department of Labor specifies that "employees are eligible for leave if they have worked for their employer at least 12 months, at least 1,250 hours over the past 12 months, and work at a location where the company employs 50 or more employees within 75 miles" (U.S. Department of Labor n.d.a). All qualified employees must be allowed leave, when warranted. It should be noted, however, that FMLA's "key employee exemption standard" does allow employers sparingly to refuse to reinstate key employees (typically, high-echelon salaried employees) to their positions if such leave creates "substantial and grievous economic injury" to the organization's operations (U.S. Department of Labor n.d.b).

FMLA allows qualified employees up to twelve weeks of unpaid leave in the following situations:

- the birth and/or care of a child, including permanently adopted or foster children in the family;
- the care of an immediate family member (e.g., spouse, child, or parent) suffering from a serious health condition; or
- care of one's own serious health condition (including pregnancy and maternity leave).

During the period of FMLA leave, the employee is protected against adverse job treatment (such as dismissal). Furthermore, employer medical benefits must be sustained during the leave period, although these medical and insurance costs may be recouped should the employee fail to return once FMLA leave is expended.

EFFECTIVENESS OF EEO

The previous sections demonstrate significant federal intervention over the past forty years to provide protections for protected-class members of society. Examples of federal legislation such as the Equal Pay Act of 1963, Title VII of the Civil Rights Act of 1964, and the Civil Rights Act of 1991 instituted policies designed to create movement toward equal treatment in employment for societal members whose gender, race, ethnicity, or religion, among other personal characteristics, would be significant factors. Thus, over time, we would expect to see a narrowing of the gaps in income and unemployment between men and women and between Caucasians and minorities; that is, women's pay would come to approximate men's pay, and work opportunities for minority members would reflect work opportunities for whites. If these policies were effective, we would expect to see a narrowing of the gap in unemployment between African-Americans and other minority groups in comparison with American Caucasians.

Figure 3.2 reports U.S. Bureau of Labor Statistics (2010) unemployment statistics. It provides insights relating to unemployment by race in five-year increments from 1975 to 2005, with the addition of the latest published data of 2009. Figure 3.2 reviews unemployment trends over time to determine if equal employment strategies have

Figure 3.2 **Unemployment by Race, 1975–2009**

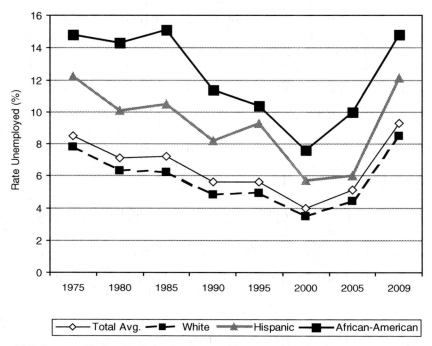

Source: U.S. Bureau of Labor Statistics (2010).

allowed greater equality in employment opportunities for women and other protected groups. The results demonstrate that the United States is still challenged to provide employment opportunities for all. One rule of thumb that unfortunately appears to continue in the American workplace is this: Take whatever the unemployment rate is for Caucasians and double it. The result should approximate the level of unemployment experienced by the country's African-American and Hispanic workforce. The trend analysis from 1975 through 2009 appears to confirm the continuation of this rule of thumb, especially for the African-American workforce. One note of caution should be mentioned here. Employment legislation over the past fifty years (i.e., from 1960 to the present) has created increased opportunities for minority participation in the American workforce. Highly qualified minority job applicants now have access to employment that their equally qualified grandparents might have been locked out of before the civil rights movement in the 1960s. Individual access and growth potential has improved over time. Yet, in the aggregate, opportunities for minorities as a group still lag behind similar opportunities for American Caucasians, especially males.

Figure 3.3 offers data compiled by the Institute for Women's Policy Research (2010). These data provide median weekly earnings for females by race as compared to earnings for white males during 2009. Aggregate pay inequity persists for women of all racial and ethnic groups, possibly with the exception of Asian-American females, based on median weekly pay as shown in Figure 3.3.

Figure 3.3 **Female Wage Group, 2009**

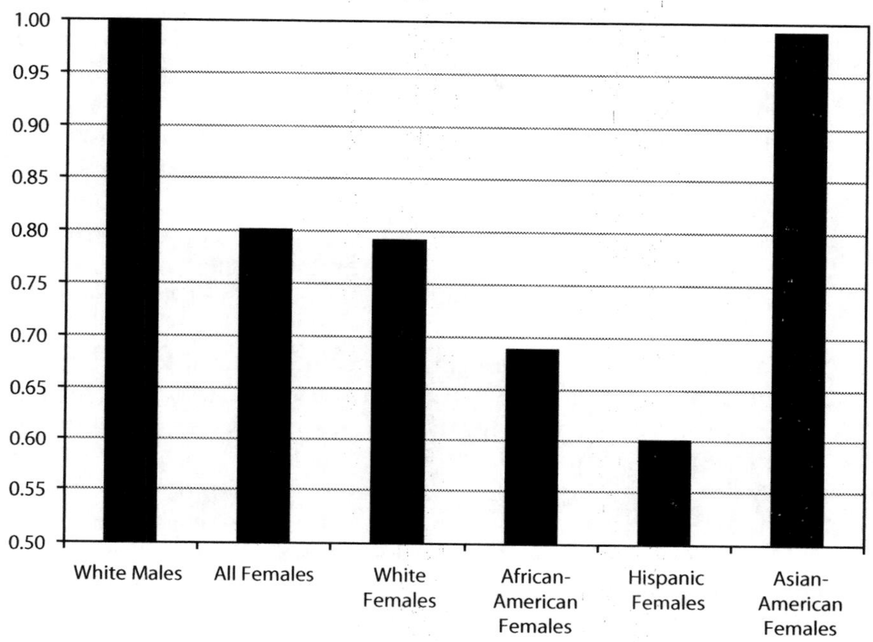

Source: Institute for Women's Policy Research (2010).

Figure 3.3 answers the question: For each $1.00 earned by the median-earning white male in the American workforce today, what pay rates are provided to females of various racial and ethnic groups? The latest comparison as of 2009 presented this wage gap pictorial. The earnings comparisons were .802 for all females, .792 for white females, .689 for black females, .602 for Hispanic/Latina females, and .992 for Asian-American females. Caution is advised, however, when comparing aggregated data as it has its limitations. Individual pay comparisons for those in the same job and with similar job experiences, education, and skills will show much lessened pay differential, typically on the order of 10 percent variance. Also, a high percentage of women being employed in traditionally low-paying service-related positions (e.g., entry-level clerical and secretarial positions, dental assistants) accounts for a partial explanation for aggregate wage gaps. In addition, some wage differential also occurs because women often accept existing wage offers while men tend to negotiate for higher pay.

Clearly, a number of factors play a part in pay differentials between white males and others based on their gender, race, or ethnicity. Nevertheless, Figure 3.3 does suggest that U.S. wage equity challenges still exist and are likely to continue for some time to come.

EQUAL EMPLOYMENT PROTECTION IN A GLOBAL SOCIETY

The world today, in both developed and developing nations, moves at lightning speed toward the integration of information technology within one global-based information-sharing structure. Banking illustrates this point. In 1998–1999, during my first overseas Fulbright experience in Swaziland, my wife and I conducted all our stateside banking in the blind. At that time, our American-based bank did not have online accessibility. Consequently, we had to pay our bills and balance our accounts without even the most remote access to our monthly bank statements. Often, we were forced to call our grown children in Tampa, Florida, in order to figure out where things stood. Fast-forward just seven years, when we returned to Swaziland on another Fulbright grant (2005–2006). Not only did we have online access to our banking accounts, but also we paid all our bills online 10,000 miles away from home in one of the most remote corners of the world. Our experience demonstrates the forces of change as global societies move toward a global economic system.

Advances in telecommunication and information technology will alter how the United States fashions EEO considerations. As a society, American business and government will become "meaner and leaner" systems. They have no choice, if we hope to remain an international economic force. Business, government, and public policy decision-makers will decline continuation of policies that provide protections for those less talented in our economy. Even the most talented in our society will face the heat of world competition for jobs, especially as China and India's educational and economic systems advance relative to America's. Many of the public policies enacted in the 1960s and beyond will become outdated as existing jobs in America are outsourced to the reliable and cost-effective service providers in other nations. Government employees will not be spared from the potential bloodletting that will occur between now and 2025.

Early retirement buyouts and reduction-in-force options will proliferate in U.S. organizations over the next quarter-century. Governmental accounting processes—for example, accounts receivable like water, electric, gas, and other similar utility bills—will become seamless through online information processing. Disputes over service account billings likely will also occur via online and telecommunication systems, with resolution coordinated either through regional centralized dispute centers or even via other nations' referral centers. Detractors suggest that this can never happen in America, but in reality it already has in the private sector. For example, much of Dell Computers' technical assistance is provided through overseas operations—such as in India. A computer problem arises requiring assistance. The computer user calls Dell's U.S. toll-free telephone number for technical support. This call is transferred to India, where twenty-four-hour operational assistance is provided at a tenth of the labor cost for the same staffing operation in America.

The tidal wave of change approaches in EEO protections, and it will alter the terrain of current needs being provided to America's protected classes. AA programs, for example, whose legitimacy was significantly challenged by *California Board of Regents v. Bakke* in 1978, subsequently received progressive challenges, with significant judicial attempts to dismantle AA impacts in the late 1980s. American public opinion with regard to AA initiatives has turned increasingly negative since the early 1980s. Recent efforts in California, Texas, and Michigan, among other states, have weakened AA applications in many governmental settings. Within increasingly competitive global markets, continued adherence to sustained AA philosophies and standards will likely diminish.

Age discrimination laws afforded in the U.S. workplace also may become an increasing challenge as American employers struggle to transform their organizations in increasingly competitive global work environments. American workers, private and public, undoubtedly will have to work harder and possibly work for less pay in order to retain their positions, as temptations (and economic reality) of shifting work to offsite international settings. With significant advancements in global worker skills occurring, especially in China and India, American workers must continuously develop advanced skill sets to sustain employability and global economic competitiveness. Such pressures to remain economically competitive in global markets may lessen protections for older, and often more expensive, employees as U.S. organizations seek ways to remain competitive.

Government service departments, such as police and fire, are less likely to be affected than other governmental functions like finance and accounting, utilities, library services, HR management, public works, and recreation, which will face growing efforts to outsource services. Nevertheless, the demands on police and fire personnel will increase with greater selectivity of personnel based on desired skill sets. One example of this trend already occurring in government is the requirement that firefighters seeking entry into fire units must also hold paramedic certification. Also, in Florida, many governments now require that police applicants have police academy training before applying for local law enforcement openings. In both instances, the path to employment now requires training and skill sets that were not required of entry-level personnel a decade ago. Growing competition for limited opportunities will shift American governments toward increased usage of the EEO philosophic standard—as even the best and brightest may not be good enough in comparison with other service provision alternatives (i.e., usage of other outsourcing providers anywhere in the country or globally). The challenges ahead will be immense and dynamic, uprooting paradigms of the past as a result of enormous global changes.

CHAPTER SUMMARY

U.S. public and private employers face a broad and complex array of employment laws and public policies protecting their employees and job applicants against adverse job treatment. A historical review and discussion of key EEO policies has been provided in this chapter. This book, like other HR management texts, can provide only an introductory glimpse of what is covered. This chapter reviewed primarily federal employment legislation and policies. Nevertheless, it is important to realize that state and local government policies also have influences, and their policy mandates also deserve the attention of HR managers (or operational managers). Good HR specialists keep this point in mind and familiarize themselves with policies from all jurisdictions that may have an effect on their organization.

KEY CONCEPTS AND TERMS

affirmative action (AA)

Age Discrimination in Employment Act (ADEA) of 1967

Americans with Disabilities Act (ADA) of 1990

Americans with Disabilities Act Amendment (ADAA) of 2008

availability analysis

bona fide occupational qualifier (BFOQ)

California Board of Regents v. Bakke

Civil Rights Act (CRA) of 1964 and 1991

Civil Service Reform Act (CSRA) of 1978

disparate impact

disparate treatment

Equal Employment Opportunity Act (EEOA) of 1972

Equal Pay Act of 1963

executive orders

Family and Medical Leave Act (FMLA) of 1992

Pregnancy Discrimination Act of 1978

protected-class groups

Rehabilitation Act of 1973

reliability

representative bureaucracy

Uniform Guidelines on Employment Selection Procedures

U.S. Equal Employment Opportunity Commission (EEOC)

utilization analysis

validity

veterans' preference

4/5th rule

PRACTICAL LEARNING ACTIVITIES

1. Review the table of data presented below. Determine the 4/5th rule threshold rates based on this information. Once completed, make an assessment

about where the City of Citrus, Florida, currently stands in terms of labor market participation rates for protected groups in its local government's workforce.

Protected group	Labor market availability	4/5th rule threshold	City of Citrus' utilization
African-Americans	22.0 percent	___ percent	17.7 percent
Hispanics/Latinos	12.5 percent	___ percent	8.7 percent
Asian-Americans	4.8 percent	___ percent	5.2 percent
Women	55.2 percent	___ percent	47.3 percent

2. The Age Discrimination in Employment Act provides protections against mandatory retirement for most employees in the American workforce. Individuals today, no matter how old, cannot be forced out of the workforce for age-related reasons, provided they can still adequately perform in their jobs. Should America again impose mandatory retirement at sixty-five years of age as was the case before 1967? Why? Why not?
3. In this chapter, we discuss two EEO philosophies, EEO, and AA. Which approach do you think should be used in the American workforce? If you select EEO, identify who benefits most from its application and who benefits least. By the same token, if you select AA, who do you believe would benefit most, and at whose cost?
4. Discuss the significance and impact of civil rights legislation in light of Figure 3.2 (unemployment rates by race/ethnicity) and Figure 3.3 (gender wage differentials) in this chapter. Is progress being made in improving employment equality, based on your observation of trends in these figures, as a result of civil rights legislative policies? If so, where is progress being made? If not, what do you believe should be done (including consideration of dropping these legislative acts) to improve employment equality in the American workforce in future years?

REFERENCES

ADA Amendments Act of 2008. Public Law 110–325.

Aviation Online Magazine. n.d. Fair Treatment of Experienced Pilots Act (The Age 65 Law). http://avstop.com/Legal/fair_treatment_of_experienced_pilots_act.htm.

Catalyst. 2010. Women CEOs of the Fortune 1000 (September). www.catalyst.org/publication/322/women-ceos-of-the-fortune-1000.

Dresang, D. 1998. *Public Personnel Management and Public Policy*, 3rd ed. New York: Longman.

GovTrack.us. n.d. H.R. 4343: Fair Treatment for Experienced Pilots Act. www.govtrack.us/congress/bill.xpd?bill=h110–4343.

Institute for Women's Policy Research. 2010. The gender wage gap: 2009 (data from Table 1: Median weekly earning by race/ethnic background, 2009). www.in.gov/icw/files/fs_mar_2010.pdf.

Jones, D. 2005. Not-so-good a year for female CEOs. *USA Today*, December 22. www.usatoday.com/money/companies/management/2005–12–22-women-ceos-usat_x.htm.

Meier, K. 1993. Representative bureaucracy: A theoretical and empirical exposition. In *Research in Public Administration*, ed. J. Perry, 1–35. Greenwich, CT: JAI Press.

Perritt, H. 2001. *Civil Rights in the Workplace*, 3rd ed. New York: Aspen.

Reagan, M. n.d. www.wisdomquotes.com/000743.html.

Riccucci, N., and J. Saidel. 1997. The representativeness of state-level bureaucratic leaders: A missing piece of the representative bureaucracy puzzle. *Public Administration Review* 57, 5 (September–October), 423–430.

Sylvia, R.D. 1994. *Public Personnel Administration*. Belmont, CA: Wadsworth.

U.S. Bureau of Labor Statistics. 2010. Labor force characteristics by race and ethnicity, 2009 (Report 1026, Table 10).

U.S. Department of Labor. n.d.a. Work hours.www.dol.gov/dol/topic/workhours/fmla.htm.

U.S. Department of Labor. n.d.b. Wage and hour division. www.dol.gov/whd/regs/compliance/1421.htm.

U.S. Equal Employment Opportunity Commission (EEOC). 1978. Part 1607—Uniform Guidelines on Employment Selection Procedures. www.access.gpo.gov/nara/cfr/waisidx_00/29cfr1607_00.html.

U.S. Equal Employment Opportunity Commission (EEOC). n.d.a. Executive Order No. 8802. www.eeoc.gov/eeoc/history/35th/thelaw/eo-8802.html.

U.S. Equal Employment Opportunity Commission (EEOC). n.d.b. Executive Order No. 9981. www.eeoc.gov/eeoc/history/35th/thelaw/eo-9981.html.

U.S. Equal Employment Opportunity Commission (EEOC). n.d.c. Executive Order No. 10925. www.eeoc.gov/eeoc/history/35th/thelaw/eo-10925.html.

4 Work-Life Management

What material success does is provide you with the ability to concentrate on other things that really matter. And that is being able to make a difference, not only in your own life, but also in other people's lives.

—Oprah Winfrey

After reading this chapter, you will

- appreciate the challenges of balancing work and family roles and responsibilities;
- grasp better the types of initiatives offered by organizations with strong work-life philosophies;
- understand more fully the methods for determining those work-life initiatives that are important to employees; and
- gain an appreciation for the competitive advantages available to organizations that implement significant family friendly work policies.

Widely noted demographical and social changes over the past forty years increasingly point to the need for workplace policies (referred to here as work-life balance) that assist employees in balancing their work and family lives (Saltzstein, Ting, and Saltzstein 2001). Strategies for capturing, retaining, and sustaining today's talented worker clearly must address these changes. Twentieth-century workers' decisions, especially during the first half of the past century, were influenced primarily by bread-and-butter factors such as wages, fringe benefits, working conditions, and job security (Kearney 2001, 6). Undeniably, the most importance concern for most workers was the level of compensation granted through traditional programs. The traditional compensation factors that influenced workers' (and unions') decisions were attractive salary or wages, competitive medical and benefits packages, and generous holiday leave and vacation pay. These traditional benefits became the scorecard for assessing progressive organizations, especially prior to 1970.

The pre-1970 workforce was predominantly male, and the American family structure was typically a traditional nuclear arrangement. For example, in 1950 about one in three women participated in the labor force. By 1998 nearly three of every five working-age women were in the labor force (U.S. Department of Labor 2000a). In years past, these *Leave It to Beaver* families witnessed one spouse working (typically the male), while the other spouse (most often the female) remained in the home tending to the needs of a growing family. Since 1970 the number of families that embody this traditional structure has declined, partially due to increasing economic pressures facing American families. Rising divorce rates also have fragmented traditional family structures, increasing the demand for women to work outside the home. One benefit of the increased rate of participation among women and minority members has been the demand for, and offering of, a broader set of workplace benefits, including more diverse and more inclusive "family friendly" workplace benefits.

WORK-LIFE BALANCE

Work-life balance refers to organizational policies that seek to balance the need for worker productivity on the job with the realization that people have personal lives, family responsibilities, and interests outside the workplace that also require nurturing and attention. Organizations with successful work-life initiatives strive to promote both of these realms. Such promotion often results in strong organizational work-life programs and more positive satisfaction within the organization's culture. Positive work-life organizations arrange benefits structures and their policies, programs, and services to sustain worker productivity and increase job satisfaction while supporting personal well-being. Designing excellence in work-life initiatives requires granting employees greater freedoms to choose when and where to work as well as how best to utilize their time, both on the job and off the job. This option is not always possible, especially when direct customer service requires that individuals be on-site to provide such services. For example, enforcing a city's driving-under-the-influence (DUI) law cannot be done remotely (at least not yet) by today's law enforcement officers. Nevertheless, for many occupations, whenever the opportunity exists for greater workplace flexibility, organizations should consider greater flexi-work options. Unfortunately, many organizations' family friendly policies appear to be accommodating when in reality they exist in name only. Thus, the rhetoric of flexibility is offset by the reality of the job. For example, the utilization of vacation leave in municipal finance and budgeting units may be restricted or curtailed during the budget formulation cycle.

Work-life accommodations impose added pressures on organizations. Information obtained from employees should define their wants and needs. Organizations must determine whether the financial benefits gained from these initiatives provide sufficient payback for their implementation. Finally, human resources (HR) must specify policies, identify exclusions, and develop plans so it can launch new work-life initiatives. This takes time, resources, and money away from other activities and services. Empathetic cultures appreciate the ultimate values of work-life balance and therefore strive to mitigate family-related working conflicts and stresses. By easing work-related pressures, HR hopes that the workers will be capable of better performance on the job.

Robust work-life initiatives tend to be even more inclusive by focusing beyond the needs of the employee to address the needs of all family members. Formulating policies with employees and their family members in mind makes economic sense, as often what affects a child, spouse, or other family member has immense impact on the performance of the worker in the office. Ironically, investing in broader work-life policy vision often creates win-win outcomes, with both positive organization and employee benefits. Higher worker productivity, increased employee work satisfaction levels, reduced on- and off-the-job stress all can result from effectively designed programs. By instituting flexible work schedules, for example, United Parcel Service (UPS) reduced its turnover from 50 percent to 6 percent; by encouraging its employees to telecommute, Illinois Bell increased its productivity 40 percent (Austin 2004).

Most work-life policies do not occur by chance or through employers' workplace benevolence. Work-life initiative integration takes place whenever it makes economic sense. Hospitals and other health-care organizations frequently offer work-life programs as a means of reducing job-related stress as well as increasing their worker's parental involvement in their children's lives. Moreover, local community health facilities, especially in major urban centers, lead in the provision of child-care services. The largest of these facilities typically provide on-site childcare services for their staff. What explains such work-life accommodations? Frequently, the composition of the hospital's workforce determines work-life policies and programs. Hospitals employ significant numbers of women, many of whom have young children. Sustaining worker participation requires the employer to consider both on-the-job issues as well as other, off-the-job factors that influence the employees' ability to participate in the workforce itself. Currently, about two-thirds of working women are mothers with children under the age of six years. Thus, organizations with robust levels of female employees realistically have little option but to provide competitive childcare assistance, especially in those positions where telework (i.e., allowing employees to work off the primary worksite) is not feasible. As Becerra, Gooden, Kim, Henderson, and Whitfield (2002, 295) note, families' dependency on childcare has steadily increased over the past thirty years. Thus, organizations without policies or provisions for such services may place themselves in a less attractive position in terms of effectively recruiting or retaining employees.

TRADITIONAL BENEFITS

A significant key to work-life success is an understanding of the organization's benefits structure. The provisions and policies form the core of what constitutes an organization's work-life strategy. Researchers typically divide employee benefits into two distinct categories: traditional benefits and family friendly (also known as work-life) benefits. Caputo (2000, 422) defines traditional benefits as "longstanding and widespread benefits such as health and life insurance coverage, pension plans, and paid vacation, as well as well-established but more relatively recent and less pervasive benefits such as profit-sharing and stock options." By comparison, Caputo defines family friendly benefits as "relatively recent employee benefits including flexible time, child care, flexible work hours, and parental leave."

A comparison of the two types of benefit categories is necessary. The demarcation lines across traditional and family friendly (work-life) benefits typically are not precise, but some distinctions still exist.

Traditional benefits provide long-term security as a result of the worker's association with the organization. In many instances, the goals of traditional benefits protect the employee and his or her family in health-related emergencies (e.g., medical care in case of illness or life insurance in case of the employee's untimely demise) and during postemployment periods (e.g., pensions earned for eventual retirement). Such benefits have little to do with improving the working environment or establishing conducive settings for increased or improved worker productivity. Traditional benefits (with the exception of bonus programs and stock option programs, which typically are not offered in governmental agencies) are offered solely on the basis of time-in-service in the organization. How well or poorly employees perform is immaterial provided they obtain a minimum standard of performance on the job.

FAMILY FRIENDLY BENEFITS

Family friendly benefits, on the other hand, recognize that both working and personal life factors influence work outcomes. People find it difficult to separate home stresses from working life and vice versa. Thus, individuals experiencing personal problems will carry these problems to work, often resulting in reduced work performance and/or increased agitation in dealing with fellow workers over normal work challenges. Many organizations, realizing the work-home interlinkages, have established employee assistance programs (EAP) and employee wellness programs (EWP). Family friendly benefits work hand-in-hand with EAP and EWP programs as stress intervention initiatives. Thus, the working mother with a flexible work schedule can reduce her role conflict associated with the divided loyalties of being both a good mother and a productive worker. She can better schedule the conflicts of work with her family responsibilities, thereby reducing her stress. The most common work-life programs include

- childcare assistance
- elder-care assistance
- EAPs
- EWPs
- flexible benefit policies
- flexible work arrangements
- fitness center facilities or monetary subsidies for fitness services
- subsidized carpool or transportation programs, and
- telework facilities.

Municipal governments often lag behind the private sector in the provision of work-life benefits. In some instances, this may be the result of taxpayers' reactions to progressive programs for public employees. The author recalls one example when an attempt to create a health facility for Florida state employees received substantial negative public feedback, claiming that government employees do not deserve taxpayer-funded, country-club–like amenities.

Gary Roberts's (2003, 242) research on family friendly benefits from a sample of 358 municipalities notes the disparity of progressive programs in local government. He states that only a "minority of municipal employees and governmental units provide family friendly benefits." The U.S. Department of Labor's (2000b) research confirms Roberts's findings. It reports the current application of family friendly benefits programs in municipal governments as follows:

- childcare support (3 percent),
- long-term care insurance (8 percent),
- wellness programs (27 percent),
- fitness centers (12 percent),
- flexible workplace arrangements (less than 1 percent),
- adoption assistance (less than 1 percent), and
- subsidized commuting (4 percent).

These findings suggest that local governments may be less family friendly than their private sector counterparts. If so, municipal governments should take care to ensure that they do not lose talented employees and desirable job prospects, especially women, to other local labor market employers because of adherence to less flexible benefits provisions.

QUALITY WORK-LIFE CULTURES: WHAT DO THEY LOOK LIKE?

Strong, positive, and sustained organizational cultures do not happen by accident in most organizations. Organizational cultures serve as the major source of identity for employees, aids in guiding their behavior, helps reduce the uncertainty for their actions, and help join employees together in pursuit of common purposes (Lundberg 2003). Thus, they require strong and unselfish leaders who envision organizational outcomes resulting from collective, as opposed to individual, achievement. Moreover, they underscore that desirable results can occur when organizations create cultures supporting both developmental and social needs. Great city managers understand that the values and commitments held by "street-level bureaucrats" (i.e., first-line service providers) are as significant to the achievement of the city's mission as are the efforts of executive-level leaders.

Talented individuals want to work for family friendly (i.e., work-life focused) organizations. Recruiting and retaining talent in local government already is challenged by local labor market competitors seeking to steal away a city's human capital investment. Providing a positive working culture is a vital strategy for protecting against other cities or private corporations pilfering an organization's most valuable asset (i.e., its talented workers). In reality, strong work-life cultures facilitate both recruitment and retention efforts, because word of mouth spreads like wildfire within the community. Happy employees become organizational ambassadors promoting the benefits of working for the city.

One question often asked by individuals seeking placement in a work-life work setting is "How can I identify a family friendly organization?" Currently, few good quantitative models or simple formulas exist to provide a reasonable solution to this question. The *Orlando Sentinel* (2006) newspaper, however, conducts a qualitative yearly assessment of the top 100 companies for working families. It examines the following five factors to determine a company's family friendly score:

1. Core benefits such as health and life insurance, flexible spending accounts, and 401k programs.
2. Family-related benefits such as childcare, maternity/paternity leave, and elder-care programs.
3. Work environment benefits such as flextime, employee rewards, and dress policy.
4. Communication within the company—things like a company newsletter, Intranet, and suggestion boxes.
5. Training and planning information about continuous training for employees and tuition reimbursement benefits.

Applicants should also ask the following questions in order to determine the family friendly scope of a local government:

- Is the organization committed to offering high-quality and diversified EWPs?
- Is it willing to allow nontraditional working schedule flexibility?
  - Does it allow for flexible work schedules?
  - Are job sharing and cosharing of occupational positions offered, and do employees share work benefits (e.g., 20/20 hour workweeks for two employees)?
- Does the municipality allow for the utilization of nontraditional worksites?
  - Can qualified employees use telecommuting to work from home?
  - In large cities, are satellite offices and alternative telework site options available?
- Are career sabbatical programs offered?
  - Can workers take paid time off to gain significant knowledge and new insights through focused studies and research into an existing or emerging professional interest?
  - Does the city allow community service sabbaticals, thereby allowing workers to give back to their (or another) community through volunteer services and "full-time" assignments to the community service organization or project?
- Are municipal programs designed to facilitate family enrichment and development? (In this case, the concept of family takes on many forms, not just traditional or nuclear family structures.) Examples of programs include elder-care planning and crisis interventions, or parent-child job sharing and parental participation at school "teach-ins."

The nature of work-life offerings provided by a municipality will be influenced by many factors, including the size of the city, the organizational philosophy of the city leaders, the existing culture within the organization, the wealth and revenue base of the community, and the demands of employees and/or their union representatives. Clearly, limits exist as to what can and should be offered. Decisions about work-life needs should be analyzed based on the needs of the workforce and the benefit-cost factors associated with the inclusion as part of the benefits that the city provides its staff. The next section discusses how such an analysis can be designed and conducted to determine which work-life benefits a city can and should offer.

DETERMINING WORK-LIFE NEEDS IN THE WORKPLACE

The Center for a New American Dream recently observed that three out of five Americans feel pressured to work too much, while more than four out of five workers wish they had more free time to spend with their families (Alati 2003). Progressive work-life policies influence workers' feelings and will continue to influence employee attitudes, especially with the changing demographic composition of the American workplace. Presently, female employment nearly matches the participation rates of males. Moreover, over the next quarter century, societal aging will force greater employee involvement in elder-care issues, as workers increasingly bear the burdens of caring for their retired parents (and even grandparents) while caring for their children. Changing attitudes toward work also will create increasing demand for flexible working hours that better fit the individual worker's lifestyle. Younger workers will be especially resistant to rigid 9-to-5, forty-hour weekly work schedules.

WORK-LIFE NEEDS ASSESSMENT

Needs assessment is a process of discovering deficiencies within an organization that could be remedied in order to improve performance outcomes. In a classical management context, this process involves identifying work-related skills deficiencies and then offering training as a corrective intervention for performance improvement. Work-life needs assessments seek to identify programs, policies, or initiatives that, if introduced, would strengthen the attainment and achievement of desired organizational outcomes. The assessment takes into consideration means for fortifying the importance of families and off-work life activities. Work-life needs assessment recognizes that workers regard-off-the clock desires as important as the development of their on-the-job skill sets. For example, introducing day-care subsidies or placement assistance does not enhance the employee's skills base, yet, when provided, sets the stage for improved working conditions and thus increased worker productivity.

Every three to five years, HR should conduct a work-life needs assessment. Why conduct a needs assessment when HR can simply adapt other agency policies? Clearly, this would be a parsimonious means of saving fiscal resources! Doing so would rob the organization and its employees (and their families) of benefits that fit their particular needs. It should be noted here that each organization possesses its own unique characteristics, so family friendly policies and programs vary considerably across organizations. Clearly, when determining progressive benefits, a one-size approach does not fit all. Thus, monies spent up front on a needs assessment will, in most instances, pay dividends when work-life programs and policies are instituted.

Figure 4.1 **Work-Life Needs Assessment**

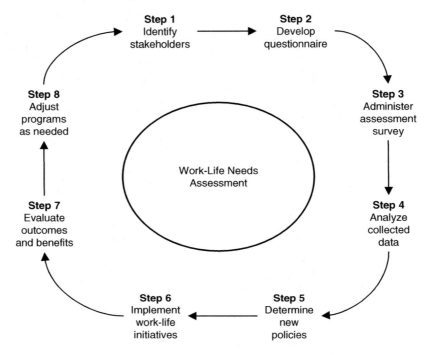

Figure 4.1 provides a graphic representation of the work-life needs assessment process. A brief discussion of each step is provided below.

Step 1: Identifying Stakeholders and Needs Assessment Planning

Each workforce possesses its own unique characteristics based on its demographic composition. HR systems need knowledge about a wide variety of work-related characteristics as these factors influence program design of work-life initiatives. HR should review the following aspects before formulating its needs assessment questionnaire:

- Family household characteristics: e.g., number of preschool children, single versus multiple heads-of-household, level of elder-care obligations.
- Ethnic and racial diversity of the workforce: the needs of a homogeneous workforce may be considerably different from the needs of a diverse workforce. One would anticipate a broader scope of offerings for a culturally diverse workforce.
- Median age of workforce by department: the age composition of the workforce also may shape program initiatives. Older workers might not have the same level of childcare needs as younger ones but may have greater need for elder-care assistance.

- Workforce gender composition: female-dominated workforce needs, especially when most of the women are working mothers, are likely to differ from systems with limited numbers of women and/or working mothers.

Knowledge of the workforce's composition is important, especially for the development of a work-life survey. Survey analysis helps, as it verifies that HR properly identifies its workforce needs and desires rather than making assumptions about these needs. Employee needs and desires should be determined based predominantly on their feedback.

Step 2: Developing the Survey Questionnaire

Employee feedback is critical to the identification of work-life initiatives. Survey questions should seek feedback on current benefits as well as others that might be introduced. Knowledge gained through survey feedback may reinforce or refute the demographic data collected in Step 1. In either case, identifying employee needs through their feedback will allow the organization to determine, formulate, and implement new and better initiatives.

In developing the survey, researchers should seek a level of information that allows for the determination of employee needs, but ask for no more! Lengthy questionnaires that require significant time to complete reduce an individual's willingness to respond; they will be ignored (or put off to a more convenient time—which often is never). Under most circumstances, surveys should require no more than ten or twelve minutes to complete. Researchers should also remember to employ the KISS method: "Keep it simple, stupid!" Finally, surveyors should make sure that individual respondent results are kept confidential, yet summary results are reported back to all employees whether or not they participated in completing the questionnaire.

Step 3: Administering the Survey Questionnaire

The size of one's organization influences the administration of an organizational needs assessment. For example, in large cities like New York City, the HR unit does not have to survey the total workforce in order to gain reliable insights into the needs of its employees. In this case, random sampling (or other reliable sampling techniques) may be employed. As city size decreases, the application of survey responses of all employees becomes feasible and desirable. Cities with under 500 employees should request information from all staff members. They must realize, however, that not all employees will respond under the best of circumstances.

One caveat about survey analysis warrants mention. When conducting questionnaires in municipal government, surveyors should not assume that all employees can read and write at a sufficient level to respond to the survey, especially workers in unskilled positions like garbage collectors and public service workers. In these cases, assistance with the questionnaire is appropriate. Furthermore, individual responses should be sought as opposed to collective feedback from the workforce. Group responses may create greater potential for skewed and biased results. Surveyors should encourage respondents to talk with their families before responding. This will increase the likelihood that the needs of extended family members will be captured. Privacy of responses may be desired among municipal workers. For this reason it is often wise to seek methods for ensuring as much confidentiality as possible when obtaining data. In past instances, I have employed secured municipal voting boxes strategically placed in city office locations to collect employee feedback. Locked ballot boxes remove the potential for tampering with survey results as well as increasing employee confidence that their feedback will remain protected.

Step 4: Analyzing Collected Data

Generally, good analysis flows from well-designed survey instruments. Thus, the design process for the analysis begins before the collection of the data. Surveys should be pretested to ensure that the respondents understand the questions. This minimizes questionnaire ambiguity, controls survey fatigue (when surveys are too long), guarantees survey completeness, and maximizes the efficient collection of information in a reasonably short period.

Once the survey has been designed, implemented, and collected, the results can be analyzed. A number of very good statistical packages available in the marketplace can be employed to identify trends in survey results. Large cities often have SPSS™ or SAS™ available for such purposes. Smaller cities may not possess these statistical programs but will probably have Microsoft Excel™ available for such analysis. For most purposes, it will provide sufficient levels of descriptive statistics to determine employees' work-life needs.

Step 5: Determining New Policies

The results of a work-life needs assessment may confirm that the city is on the right track in designing its work-life service strategies or may suggest the need for policy and provision modifications. Unfortunately, identifying the options that employees want is often easier than providing them. HR units must be careful not to create too many expectations among employees when conducting a work-life needs assessment; some identified needs may still be out of the financial reach of the city.

The first step is to compare the assessment findings to the choices that are currently provided to municipal employees. Along these same lines, HR specialists must consider the circumstances of offering work-life policies across work units. For example, flexible working hours may be easily implemented in a city's utilities unit but might create chaos within the police or fire units. Issues of equity may prove significant under these circumstances should the city decide to implement varying work-life benefits across employees or across work units. Decisions like these will vary across cities based on the city's organizational culture and prior benefits provisions. Some cities, for example, are more rigid than others in requiring uniformity of benefits across all employee groups. In addition, provisions may vary based on whether or not the city has existing union contracts in force. In these instances, varying benefits may already exist due to collective bargaining agreements. Thus, offering varying work-life provisions may possibly be granted to nonunion employee groups while remaining a negotiable bargaining element among unionized units.

HR units should also consider both the benefits of offering new provisions and the costs associated with offering these provisions. Benefit-cost analyses can help determine whether or not new policies should be integrated within the benefits structure, and if so, what other benefits may have to be dropped or reduced to allow for the new provision inclusions. Clearly, decisions of this nature must consider the financial ramifications in determining what the new policy packages should include.

Step 6: Implementing Work-Life Initiatives

At this point, the city has conducted its needs assessment, evaluated employee feedback, and made decisions about additions and modifications to be made in its new benefits program. The new plan of action has been approved by city leaders and now is ready to be implemented within the workforce.

Successful implementation will require the following:

- the modification of existing employee personnel policies handbooks;
- active communication within the city, informing employees of new benefits;
- brief orientation sessions for supervisors and employees to educate them about new benefits; and
- the creation of supportive structures to minimize barriers to entry among employees who seek to use such benefits.

Step 7: Evaluating Outcomes and Benefits

Step 7 (evaluation of outcomes) and Step 8 (making adjustments) often go hand in hand when implementing new policies. Typically, new program offerings require modifications and adjustments following their introduction. HR units should identify the reaction of employees and pay close attention to issues of ambiguity that arise among staff when they enact new policies. In some cases, there may be different interpretations related to benefits of new policies. In these cases, HR may have to serve in an adjudicative capacity. If unions are involved, negotiations may also be required prior to adjustments.

HR units, serving as the watchdog to these policies, should allow time for implementation of new policies (when permissible) before considering any major modifications. Evaluation of outcomes should be conducted six months to one year after initial implementation. Waiting this long will allow everyone to work out the minor glitches associated with new programs, making evaluation of the outcomes more accurate and more easily accomplished.

Step 8: Adjusting Programs as Needed

A frequently overused phrase, "If it ain't broke, don't fix it," applies here. Make minimal adjustments to policies, especially if the new system is well received by the staff. In some instances, policy adjustments will be required, especially when driven by new external legislation and/or judicial outcomes. One example might be changes within a state's existing family and medical leave legislation. When new laws or mandates warrant revisions, make the changes and be sure to communicate these changes to workers with the rationale for the adjustments.

CHAPTER SUMMARY

There is growing evidence in the American economy that work-life balance is increasingly important to American workers. Municipalities are not immune from this trend. Thus, they must create attractive work-life packages if they seek to remain competitive in recruiting and sustaining quality workforces capable of meeting human capital needs within increasingly competitive local labor markets. Work-life needs planning, as discussed in this chapter, offers essential strategic advantages that produce heightened performance outcomes for municipalities. They also facilitate sustained health and well-being for their workforces. Traditional benefits programs are not sufficient in today's increasingly competitive and diverse work environments. Thus, utilizing work-life needs assessments to determine and to introduce family friendly work environments can provide handsome returns on investment. Strategic-thinking, progressive municipal human resource systems use these tools to provide work-life cultures that benefit and are valued by their workers and their workers' families.

KEY CONCEPTS AND TERMS

family friendly benefits

flexi-work options

needs assessment

organizational culture

telework

work-life balance

work-life initiatives

work-life needs assessment process

PRACTICAL LEARNING ACTIVITIES

1. Discuss with class members an occasion when you felt your employer cared only about work output without much consideration or concern for employees or their lives outside of work. In these cases, was there resentment toward the organization and its approach to work-life balance? If you personally were in an organization that cared little for you as an individual and only sought methods for increasing your work productivity, how did this affect your job satisfaction or interest in sustaining long-term employability with this organization?

2. Think about the changing nature of demographic characteristics in today's evolving organization. How might changes in organizational demographics such as gender, age, and diversity differences influence HR policies and practices?

3. As the benefits director for your local government, you are responsible for sustaining a competitive benefits program in your organization. Upon review you determine that your plan is financially generous to employees, but it predominantly focuses on providing only traditional benefits as opposed to offering a balanced mix of traditional and family friendly benefits. Discuss your concerns about this lack of balance in meeting your employees' needs. Also, consider how this imbalance might affect the hiring of future employment prospects. What changes in policies and/or program initiatives would you recommend?

REFERENCES

Alati, D. 2003. It's all relative. *Merchandise* (December), 23–24.

Austin, N.K. 2004. Work-life paradox. *Incentive* (September), 18.

Becerra, R., S. Gooden, D. Kim, T. Henderson, and C. Whitfield. 2002. Child care needs and work-life implications. *Review of Public Personnel Management* 22, 4 (Winter), 295–319.

Caputo, R. 2000. The availability of traditional and family friendly employee benefits among a cohort of young women, 1968–1995. *Families in Society: The Journal of Contemporary Human Services* 81, 4, 422–453.

Kearney, R., with D. Carnevale. 2001. *Labor Relations in the Public Sector*, 3rd ed. New York: Marcel Dekker.

Lundberg, C. 2003. Organizational culture. In *Encyclopedia of Public Administration and Public Policy*, ed. Jack Rabin. New York: Marcel Dekker.

Orlando Sentinel. 2006. Top 100 companies for working families. https://extra.orlandosentinel.com/Secure/top100/guidelines.shtml.

Roberts, G. 2003. The association of needs assessment strategies with the provision of family friendly benefits. *Review of Public Personnel Administration* 23, 3 (September), 241–254.

Saltzstein A., Y. Ting, and G. Saltzstein. 2001. Work-family balance and job satisfaction: The impact of family friendly policies on attitudes of federal government employees. *Public Administration Review* 61, 452–467.

U.S. Department of Labor. 2000a. Changes in women's labor force participation in the 20th century. February 16. www.bls.gov/opub/ted/2000/feb/wk3/art03.htm.

U.S. Department of Labor. 2000b. Employee benefits in state and local government, 1998. Bulletin 2531, December. Washington, DC.

Winfrey, O. n.d. Woopidoo Business and Financial Quotes. www.woopidoo.com/business_quotes/authors/oprah-winfrey-quotes.htm.

5 | Talent Acquisition Management

Great things are accomplished by talented people who believe they will accomplish them.

—Warren G. Bennis

After reading this chapter, you will

- recognize the critical significance of recruiting and selecting high-quality employees in local government;
- be able to identify the three key phases of the talent acquisition process—talent recruitment, talent screening, and talent selection;
- understand key laws and court decisions that affect the hiring of new employees; and
- strengthen your knowledge of techniques, strategies, and methods for improving the recruitment, selection, and retention of employees within an agency.

Over the next two decades more than 60 million baby boomers (individuals born between 1946 and 1964) will transition to senior citizen status. Great concern exists in many organizations, including governmental human resource (HR) departments, that insufficient talent will be available to replace long-term retiring employees (Carroll and Moss 2002). Leadership grooming is among the most critical need facing organizations today (Adler and Mills 2008). Survey research, conducted by Aon Consulting in its 2008 Benefit and Talent Survey, reports that 56 percent of respondents expressed concerns about experiencing organizational shortages of qualified leadership talent (Adler and Mills 2008). Ashford and DeRue (2010) also report almost 60 percent of companies today face leadership talent shortages that are impeding performance outcomes, with many of these companies expecting leadership talent shortfall over the next several years.

These findings, coupled with a Council for Excellence in Government study may create concern among local governments. It found that "only 27 percent of young people said they had been asked by their parents, teachers or others to consider government as a job option, down by 11 percentage points from two years earlier" (Barr 2006, D04). Strategically minded local HR leaders realize that increased workforce shortages and ferocious competition for workers await them. Action is needed now to ensure their human capital remains competitive.

Progressive municipal HR systems are contemplating adaptive strategies now for the eventuality of such shortages. Brown and Williams (2003, 21) recommend that HR units develop talent acquisition management strategies in order to recruit and retain the best. They suggest that "staffing departments that transform into mini-search firms, conducting name generation, identifying key talents outside their organization, building 'passive networks' (to be called on in the future), and building contacts and goodwill by themselves will outdistance more traditional competitors."

Adaptation of HR systems, especially in the public sector, is not an easy process. Civil service systems further complicate this transition. Often they resist change and impede practices that allow greater managerial decision-making control, especially for actions related to workforce staff adjustments. Furthermore, unions hinder organizational transition by requiring labor-management discussions and the renegotiation of contracts prior to change efforts. Significant resistance to change unfortunately confounds effective talent acquisition. These challenges are more common in traditional HR systems.

Lengthy and slow acquisition times, often the norm in government, create lost opportunities to capture the best candidates. Highly marketable candidates frequently have multiple job offers and limited patience with organizations unable to make quick hiring decisions. The Illinois City/County Management Association's (n.d., 3) research of selection durations for acquiring new city managers reflects this situation. It estimates that the hiring duration to acquire a new chief administrative officer (city manager, village manager, chief administrative officer, or county administrator) is between seventeen and twenty-two weeks. This length of time does not account for labor supply shortages. When such shortages exist, the hiring duration may be even longer.

In Florida local government, some leadership positions have required more than a year to fill, due not to budget shortages, but rather to the inability of the city to identify qualified staff for vacant positions. Delays are the result of poor hiring processes and/ or the inability of elected officials (i.e., the council or commission) to make prompt decisions. Under these circumstances, talented and highly qualified candidates simply cannot (or will not) wait for slow systems to make decisions.

THE THREE PHASES OF TALENT ACQUISITION MANAGEMENT

Effective hiring is among the most important decisions that organizations make. A survey conducted by RewardsPlus of America found that 52 percent of employers cite recruitment and retention as the number one issue they face (Langan 2000, 461). This section discusses three phases of talent acquisition management: recruitment, screening of candidates, and selection interviews. Figure 5.1 offers a visual summary of these three phases of the talent acquisition management process. These are the pri-

Figure 5.1 **Phases of Talent Acquisition Management**

Recruitment	Screening of Candidates	Selection Interviews

• Position review
• Recruitment strategies
  • Scope of search: national, regional, or local
  • Recruitment methods: newspaper, Internet, "word of mouth"
	• Application review
	• Application testing and evaluation
	  • Skills testing
	  • Aptitude testing
	  • "Honesty" tests
	  • Work eligibility
		• Interview techniques determined
		  • Structured
		  • Nondirected
		  • Stress
		  • Panel
		  • Assessment center
		• Assessment of:
		  • Skills
		  • Behavior predictors
		  • Unit/team fit

↓	↓	↓
Identify talent	Identify best candidates	Select best candidate

mary elements of the recruitment and selection process. When performed correctly, selection strategies lead to an improved talent base for the organization.

Successful orchestration of these three phases requires current knowledge of the skills, knowledge, and abilities (SKAs) necessary for an opened position. Thus, effective hiring requires a well-developed, planned process before conducting the talent search. Effective acquisition is also a shared process between the human resource department and the operation unit. HR's role is to filter out unqualified candidates, leading to a refined talent pool. Ultimately, the most desired candidate is granted a contingent offer (i.e., a job offer pending the successful passage of drug screening, security, and reference checks).

Planning between HR and the "selection" department involves close communication among team members. They will discuss the skills needed to perform well in the position as well as the behavioral characteristics desired in the ideal candidate. The goal here is to identify a strategy for generating and securing a talented candidate pool. The team will discuss the following questions:

- Where should the position be advertised?
- How should information about the job opening be disseminated?
- In prior searches, what strategies have proved successful?
- How much time and money can and should be invested in securing candidates for this position?
- Can or should the candidate required for filling this position be gained from the local labor market or should a more extensive search be conducted?

Discussion about these questions with operations personnel is critical. This staff often is keenly aware of market and compensation pressures relating to the position under consideration. Thus, they may confirm whether or not the compensation level planned is sufficient to attract a qualified applicant pool.

PHASE I: THE TALENT RECRUITMENT PROCESS

Recruitment is the process of identifying and securing a pool of qualified job candidates for employment consideration. This phase requires much more than simply advertising for job applicants. A number of considerations must be thought through prior to the development of an applicant pool for screening.

A good recruitment process begins with an analysis of the position to be filled. This is important, especially in light of the 1990 passage of the Americans with Disabilities Act (ADA). ADA requires candidates' selection based only on the essential job functions. Thus, work aspects considered to be minor, rarely performed, or having insignificant impact on work outcomes should not be the central issue when hiring new employees. For example, an applicant for an administrative assistant position who will be expected to pick up office supplies once a month should not be excluded from consideration based on the fact that he does not have a driver's license. If the applicant is disabled and unable to drive, the expectation would be that the organization can make a reasonable accommodation, requesting another individual to retrieve the necessary supplies (since this is not a regular function of the position).

FACTORS INFLUENCING RECRUITMENT STRATEGIES

A good job analysis provides the HR specialist with a better understanding of the specifications required to perform the job successfully. This enables the HR specialist, responsible for the recruitment process, to target the recruitment process based on a number of considerations. Knowledge of the job specifications enables the recruiter to decide whether the candidate pool can be sufficiently generated from the area's local labor market. Determination of the recruitment scope will be influenced by the importance of the position to the ultimate success of the organization. Thus, recruitment of additional administrative support staff would occur through local labor market recruiting, while the selection of a new city manager would likely result in a search for qualified candidates on a nationwide basis.

The recruitment process also will be influenced by current equal employment opportunity (EEO) utilization standards within the city. If a municipality's employment records and practices indicate underutilization of minority and other protected-class candidates, HR should target its recruitment strategies to secure a more robust pool of candidates from diverse backgrounds. In this case, a more expansive search (e.g., using a greater variety of media sources, including online recruiting) or more innovative recruiting methods (e.g., greater recruitment efforts at minority colleges and universities) might be required. In addition, a city lacking diversity in the local labor market may need to broaden its recruitment scope, using either national or regional recruitment strategies, as opposed to relying simply on the local labor market, to secure a more diverse human capital workforce.

RECRUITMENT METHODS

The growing sophistication of the Internet and the rapid growth of organizational websites have had profound effects on recruitment strategies in both public and private organizations (Williamson, Lepak, and King 2003). E-recruiting, as it has been referred to, according to the Boston-based Aberdeen Group (2001), witnessed a doubling of its market size each year between 2001 and 2003. Undoubtedly, this growth has continued.

E-Recruiting Over the Internet

Today, many local governments have websites that announce new position openings, and progressive systems offer online application processing. A review of Florida municipal government websites using Florida's League of Cities, Inc., municipal directory (www.floridaleagueofcities.com/Directory.aspx) indicates that most Florida city websites list jobs. Most, however, do not yet offer job prospects the ability to apply online (or to submit their professional résumés online). This is probably the case for many local governments today. One example of an innovative local government using effective Internet technology to recruit competitively is Riverside County in California (Mooney 2002). A Riverside County job applicant has to submit only one résumé to be considered for multiple positions. Riverside County's Job Match system identifies skills and abilities enumerated in the candidate's résumé and compares for matches with all open county jobs. This allows the county to identify quickly potential talent with existing openings. In addition, Riverside County utilizes online Internet-based testing to expedite its selection process. This technology is not perfect, but it has allowed Riverside County to identify talent more quickly and make offers in a matter of weeks as opposed to months. Technology places Riverside County on par with other progressive local area employers. The use of HR Internet-based recruitment and online testing structures is likely to increase in local governments over the next decade, as local governments seek strategies for becoming more competitive with the private sector to secure their share of limited labor market talent.

Internet-based recruitment and selection are growing in popularity. Online job services on the American Society for Public Administration (ASPA) (http://PublicServiceCareers.org) and the International City/County Management Association (ICMA) (http://jobs.icma.org) websites, for example, offer specific information about public service career openings. In addition, many career websites provide on-site résumé posting, giving job applicants the opportunity to share their talents virtually for potential employers' review.

Speeding up the hiring process and broadening visibility of job announcements are increasingly critical factors in the employment talent acquisition process. Nevertheless, some cautions still exist when establishing steps and implementing a process for generating an applicant pool. Organizations must be careful not to violate U.S. Equal Employment Opportunity Commission (EEOC) guidelines by asking inadvisable recruitment questions that seek information about candidates' personal characteristics rather than their qualifications to perform the job. Questions about the candidate's age, future marital or child-rearing plans, and country of origin fall into this category. Research by Wallace, Tye, and Vodanovich (2000, 497) indicates the extent of the problem even within government. Their research findings from forty-one state Internet-based online application systems indicate that 97.5 percent asked at least one inadvisable question. State online application forms on average revealed that 4.2 potentially illegal questions were asked, with application forms from heavily populated states containing significantly more problematic questions. These findings indicate that the most common ill-advised questions occur in the areas of past salary history, age of the candidate, and driver's license information.

With the passage of the Genetic Information Nondiscrimination Act (GINA) of 2008, employers must make sure that they do not seek information related to private genetic information from job candidates during the postoffer stage of employment. Thus, questions about whether relatives have mental disorders, cardiopulmonary disorders, or other conditions that might have genetic component linkages to the candidate, through family lineage, should be avoided as they are likely to violate current employment law (Smith 2010).

Recruitment Advertising in Local Newspapers

The most traditional method of announcing job openings involves the use of position announcements (i.e., advertising) in local newspapers. This method has been particularly common in the Sunday classified sections of many newspapers. Employers have used the classified section of newspapers, in part, because newspapers are accessible to everyone, thereby avoiding criticism relating to potential discrimination against less advantaged members of society. However, newspaper job postings continue to diminish with the upswing in E-recruiting and with increased telecommunication affordability and public accessibility. Most of the nation's largest newspapers that advertise openings in their Sunday classified sections also use online job announcements via their newspaper websites. Newsprint advertising as a recruiting tool continues in use today, but its application may be more for maintaining a perception of the organization's viability as a potential future employer in the public's eye than as the primary mechanism of recruiting new staff.

Recruitment Advertising via Professional Association Websites and Trade Journals

Potential applicants often identify opportunities through professional association websites and trade journal magazines. This approach is particularly helpful when dealing with highly competitive or difficult-to-fill specialized municipal professional positions, such as city and county management and administration, urban planning, HR management, civil engineering, and public financial administration. For example, position openings for city managers are frequently placed in the ICMA's job announcement bulletins. Since ICMA has an international circulation, those seeking new opportunities in professional administrative positions often review these announcements.

On-Campus College Recruitment and Job Fairs

On-campus recruiting and the emergence of community job fairs, which have gained growing popularity over the past decade, attract potential recruits. Many large American universities provide placement services through their "career centers." These centers connect employers with upcoming graduates and alumni hoping to secure new opportunities for starting or redefining their careers. Yet HR units must consider carefully if this strategy bears fruit for the organization. As San Francisco State University's management professor John J. Sullivan (Taylor 2006, 3) notes:

> The first rule of recruiting is that the best people already have jobs they like. So you have to find them; they're not going to find you. It's amazing that so many companies still use job fairs to recruit talent. Who goes to job fairs? People without jobs! All you get are worthless résumés and lots of germs. Recruiting has to be a clever, fast-moving business discipline, not a passive, paper-pushing bureaucracy.

Employment Agencies and Headhunters

Employment agencies and headhunters, who are paid a fee for locating candidates for employment consideration, are rarely used in the public sector, especially by local governments. The one exception to this rule, however, may be cities seeking new city managers. Fees for these services in moderate-size cities can range anywhere from $15,000 to $35,000.

Employee Referrals and Word of Mouth

One of the most successful means of attracting new employees involves asking current employees about people they know who might be qualified and interested in employment. Some organizations provide referring employees a modest bonus for recommending candidates who ultimately join the organization. At Quicken Loans in suburban Detroit, 64 percent of new hires begin as referrals from current employees. The company has a team of full-time talent scouts whose sole job is encouraging employees to refer friends, classmates, and others in their personal networks and following up on these referrals. According to Quicken's Director of Talent Acquisition, Michael G. Homula, "We've turned 3,400 people into a massive recruiting force" (Taylor 2006).

Caution is warranted, however, regarding the use of word-of-mouth techniques in organizations experiencing EEOC utilization standards imbalances. If an organization's employees, for example, are predominantly male Caucasians, the friends they recommend are likely to be male Caucasians also. In such a case, the talent acquisition specialists should avoid this approach or, at best, use it sparingly.

Contingent Workers as a Recruitment Technique

All recruitment techniques identified above assume that the organization will be hiring new employees. Ultimately, the organization's concern is to have qualified workers capable of performing desired tasks in an efficient and effective manner. With increased frequency, organizations use contingent workers (i.e., contractual employees, temporary hires, part-time employees, or leased employees) in place of new hires. Utilization of members of this "workforce" expands or shrinks as workforce demands change. Presently, approximately 20 percent of Americans work as contingent employees.

Borowski (2006) suggests the following organizational benefits associated with the use of contingent workers: (1) It increases cost savings because the organization usually does not provide contingent workers with holiday pay, sick benefits, or medical and/or life insurance benefits and is not responsible for paying taxes for independent contractors—for example, withholding payroll, social security, Medicare, and unemployment contributions. (2) It improves efficiency because contingent workers can be scheduled when needed, thereby saving labor costs and allowing greater workforce flexibility. (3) It enhances administrative savings since many of the administrative burdens and record-keeping associated with regular employees are not required with contingent workers. (4) It provides better job security to "core" (regular) employees since workforce smoothing will occur with contingent workforce adjustments. (5) It facilitates recruitment and talent identification since employers can evaluate the performance of contingent workers and, if desired, hire them as core employees; furthermore, the workforce resources of outside vendors may also broaden the scope of talent available to employers.

However, as Borowski (2006) also notes, the use of contingent workers has some disadvantages: (1) It can lessen productivity since contingent workers are not dependent on one employer and thus may be less loyal and less committed to the organization and the attainment of its goals and mission. (2) It creates status differences; contingent workers may feel like second-class citizens compared to regular workers, feeling that their work is neither recognized nor appreciated to the same degree. (3) It may promote resentment between core employees and contingent workers; such a "we" vs. "they" attitude can be particularly problematic if core employees believe that contingent workers are "robbing" them of possible overtime pay. (4) It raises confidentiality concerns, since there are no guarantees that contingent workers will not move on and establish employment with a competitor. Fortunately, this is less of an issue for municipalities than it is for organizations competing in the private sector. (5) It might boost training costs since turnover of contingent workers may be higher than that of regular employees. (6) It increases liability if contingent hires should have been classified as regular employees. Tax implications result including potential legal penalties for violation of income tax, FICA, and FLSA standards.

In most instances, courts hold both the vendor (i.e., the source supplying the contingent worker) and the employer responsible as joint-employers. This holds particularly true when issues of employment discrimination arise. Thus, employers seeking contingent workers' services must carefully weigh both the benefits and disadvantages prior to taking action.

PHASE II: THE TALENT SCREENING PROCESS

The second phase of talent acquisition management, screening the pool of job applicants generated through recruitment techniques, most frequently falls within the domain of the HR unit. Reviewing applicant files and résumés, conducting appropriate testing, and separating promising candidates from marginal ones take both time and expertise. Generally, as the position's responsibilities increase, so will the involvement level of the operations unit. HR can anticipate greater screening for candidates interested in a department head's position than for an entry-level position within the same department.

Screening can be time-consuming, so departments often defer this responsibility to the HR expert. This preserves time for operational responsibilities and goal attainment. Active participation of the operating unit at this stage varies based on the size of the organization, the level of rule rigidity of its civil service unit, prior perceived successes with the current selection process, and the level of trust the operating unit has for its HR department.

The screening process consists of three primary components, each designed to narrow the candidate pool to a group of usually three to five finalists, one of whom will ultimately emerge as the new employee. The primary components are screening the applicant pool and testing the applicants.

SCREENING OF THE APPLICANT POOL

Applicant screening is designed to reduce the pool of candidates to a manageable size so that the best individuals can receive further consideration. In recent years, many organizations have begun using artificial intelligence and text scanning software to identify keywords in candidates' résumés and application forms in order to match applicants' skill sets with job specifications. The HR unit must identify quickly competent talent for further verification of job fit, using a battery of preemployment tests to verify that the applicants have the SKAs needed to succeed and the personality to work well with others in the job setting.

The Job Application Form

Among the first documents used to screen the candidates' qualifications for employment is the job application form. The content of a city's application form is influenced significantly by federal and state law, local government ordinances, judicial decisions, and EEOC regulations. Many common elements exist across all application forms. These commonalities will be discussed below.

Variations in the content of application forms do occur. These differences principally are influenced by added mandates imposed at the discretion of the organization or through enacted state or local municipal employment laws and/ or regulations. For example, the EEOC (2001) "does not enforce the protections that prohibit discrimination and harassment based on sexual orientation, status as a parent, marital status and political affiliation. However, other federal agencies and many states and municipalities do." This point demonstrates the challenges of HR management compliance. HR systems are required to consider federal, state, and local government laws when performing their duties. This can be a daunting challenge given the propensity for rules and regulation adaptation at all three governmental levels, as well as other judicial decisions that also affect HR policy and actions.

Application forms are still extensive in content, but they are being streamlined through the use of online submission processes as compared with past paper application practices. In years past, federal job applicants frequently complained about the extraordinary length and extensiveness of the Office of Personnel Management's Form SF-171 (i.e., the federal government's standard application form). Generally, as concerns for security and safety increase in public sector jobs, so might the length and intrusiveness of the application process. This is particularly true for law enforcement positions. Online applications are still lengthy thanks to increased policy mandates (at all levels of government) in employment law regulations and discrimination protections. Civil rights and equal employment protections, pregnancy discrimination, immigration status, age discrimination protections, disabilities rights, veterans' preferences, credit disclosure protections, and privacy rights relating to confidential information are some (but not all) of the factors that have helped create these application "monsters."

Application forms, nevertheless, still have a basic structure that appears consistent across most application forms. The common elements are discussed in the following section.

General Applicant Information. The General Applicant Information section provides basic information relating to the identity of the applicant, with address and contact information, as well as an indication of the position(s) for which the candidate seeks consideration.

Educational and Skills Attainment. Job application forms request information relating to applicants' educational attainment, professional licensure and/or certification, and other skills that qualify a candidate for additional consideration. Care should be taken not to require information that can identify the applicant's age. Job application forms can request information about the candidate's level of educational attainment, but should not specifically ask for the date when the education was received. By collecting information this way, the organization demonstrates its interest in understanding how much formal education candidates have received rather than their current age.

Employment History. Organizations collect employment history from candidates to gain information about their previous work experiences and how these experiences might relate to the position. In addition, screenings will look closely at the level of progression in terms of responsibilities acquired in previous organizations. This information may also provide a basis for judging behavioral characteristics of the applicant. For example, extensive job-hopping (i.e., moving from one job to another frequently), especially among mature job applicants, may be of concern to the application screener, as organizations seek high-quality candidates with potential for employment stability. Organizations often invest substantial financial sums in the training and development of new employees. If a candidate exhibits brief tenure with numerous past employers, the HR screener may fear that the organization will not recoup a return on the investment equal to the individual's time in service.

Military Experience/Veterans' Preference. Since the founding of the nation, governments have given special employment consideration to individuals who have honorably served their country (Dresang 2002). This is particularly true if veterans have been disabled while in the service of their country. Those who qualify as disabled veterans frequently are granted generous consideration, provided they are qualified to perform the position's essential job functions. Should a veteran die in the service of the country, the unremarried spouse also qualifies for veterans' preference consideration.

Other Application Elements

EEOC Applicant Tracking. Employers with 100 or more employees (with the exception of state and local government) are required to submit annually employment characteristics of their workforce to the EEOC. Financial institutions and federal contractors with fifty or more employees also must submit annual reports if they do business with government. Private organizations file the EEO-1 Report form. Slightly different report forms must be filed biannually by state governments and local governments (EEO-4), local unions (EEO-3), and school districts (EEO-5) (EEOC n.d.).

Tracking of job applicants is also significant. Organizations, including municipal governments, request applicants to provide voluntarily demographic information pertinent to their race, ethnicity, gender, and disability for EEOC tracking purposes. In other cases, information will be requested separately from applicants, frequently through a mailed questionnaire asking that they (again, voluntarily) provide such information. Smaller organizations, generally those with less than fifty employees, often are not required to submit information pertinent to the makeup of their workforce or applicant pools but should still maintain such records, as the EEOC can ask for such data, often as a follow-up to an applicant's complaint. At a minimum, all records pertaining to employment, including job applicants and applicant pool characteristics, should be maintained for at least three years.

Applicant Signature Validating the Accuracy of Information. The job application is the primary legal document attesting to the qualifications of the candidate. Statements like this one (from the job application form of the City of Brooksville, Florida) generally appear near the end of an application form:

> I certify that all statements made by me on this application are true and complete. I understand that should I be employed, any omitted, false, misleading, incorrect, or incomplete oral or written statements made in connection with my application may result in my dismissal.

As demonstrated by the Brooksville disclosure statement, falsification of the information on the job application form can, and frequently does, result in employee termination, even after many years of service to the organization. Job applicants had better be truthful in the application and interviewing process and lose the job rather than live with the stress of lying on the application and the repercussions that can result years later.

Employment Eligibility Verification. While generally not a part of the application process, candidates are required by law to demonstrate their eligibility to work in the United States, prior to beginning employment. The Immigration Reform and Control Act of 1986 and its corresponding I-9 (Employment Eligibility) form are used for this purpose.

Many employers must now also use E-Verify. Using the Social Security Administration and Department of Homeland Security databases, E-Verify allows for the online verification of worker employment authorization. In 2008 President George W. Bush signed Executive Order 12989, requiring federal contractors awarded grants or contracts of $100,000 or greater to adopt the E-Verify system. In addition to validating the eligibility of new hires to work in America, covered contractors must validate that existing employees working on covered contracts also meet employment eligibility standards. New qualifying contractors have thirty days to adopt this system and within ninety days must have it fully functioning for all covered employees. After the start-up implementation stage is complete with the E-Verify system fully functioning, future hires also must be validated through E-Verify within three business days.

Résumé versus Application

An important observation relates to the use of résumés in place of application submission. The application is the legal document in which candidates validate the accuracy of information submitted about their qualifications for a position. It should be required of all candidates. Résumé submissions, however, should also be encouraged as supportive information. Résumés allow the screener to compare information content against that provided through the application. Many résumés include false information; they often overstate a candidate's qualifications, work history, past compensation levels, and/or skill sets. Kinsman (2006), writing in the *California Job Journal*, reports that

> the resumes of American workers are filled with lies. Estimates are that 30 to 40 percent of resumes contain flat-out falsehoods. When you add in exaggerations of authority or taking undue credit, some say that as many as two-thirds of all resumes could be misleading.

Paradoxically, such résumé data can still be valuable to the screener. Box 5.1 demonstrates the value of accepting the candidate's résumé and comparing it with information provided in his or her submitted application. Gaps in the application relative to the résumé provide opportunity for clarification about the candidate's experiences, knowledge, background, and possibly honesty prior to making decisions about which candidates should be the finalists for selection interviews.

An example related to me by an employment screener demonstrates how valuable résumés can be in identifying a candidate's qualifications and honesty. An applicant seeking a child counseling position with the state's Department of Children and Family in central Florida submitted her professional résumé. The résumé indicated that she had eighteen years of relevant child counseling experience. In this case, the agency required applicants to complete its employment application form. The HR screener reviewing the applicant's information noticed that while the résumé indicated eighteen

---

Box 5.1
Use of Job Application Form versus Résumé

HR screeners should accept résumés, but require the completion of an application form too! Why?

- Résumés often are inflated, misrepresenting the applicant's talent.

- The authenticity of a résumé may be questionable, since the HR screener has no way of verifying who produced the résumé.

- Comparison of the résumé and the application form often indicates inconsistency in the candidate's account of the work record.

- Application forms (especially those completed on-site) attest to writing skills and often provide insight on grammar and spelling skills better than do résumés.

- The application is the legal document of record.

---

years of child counseling experience, the application employment history section documented only three years of prior employment as a child counselor. He contacted the applicant for clarification. After a period of silence, the candidate confessed that she had a fifteen-year-old child and that she had reported her child rearing as part of her professional "child counseling" experience. It should be noted that the screener did not immediately disqualify the candidate based on this deception, but asked her to justify how this experience enhanced her qualifications for the position. Ultimately, another candidate was selected for the job opening.

Screening Application Forms: What to Look for in the Application

Application screening is not generally considered an element of applicant testing, which is discussed below. Nevertheless, like testing, screening often provides valuable candidate information. Completed applications should be scrutinized in the same fashion as other tests, as this review affords additional information about the person under consideration. Keep in mind, however, that uses of some of these "tests" may be limited for Americans with Disabilities–qualified applicants, such as candidates with some forms of learning disabilities, if such disabilities have been disclosed to the organization. When examining applications, the employer looks for the following.

Sloppiness and Spelling Errors. In the era of online application completion and submission, it is more difficult to identify sloppiness and spelling errors when compared with on-site handwritten application submissions. In fact, with online applications the employer does not know if the candidate solely completed the application without the help of others. Thus, it may be necessary to require candidates to demonstrate their writing ability through simple on-site individual "memo" writing tests. An assessment of this information will indicate how well and how quickly a candidate can communicate with others through a written medium. Application forms serve this capacity provided that they are completed on-site without the assistance of others or error-correcting word processing software. Generally, a candidate whose writing exhibits multiple spelling errors, poor grammar, and poor sentence syntax should be downgraded relative to other candidates with better writing skills. Likewise, text with numerous scratch-through marks might indicate a lack of confidence in one's writing abilities.

Education: Attended versus Graduated. HR screeners must look closely for closure in educational achievements. For example, does a candidate who earned an MPA degree also provide the date of graduation? Degree indications with graduation dates in the future indicate progress toward completion, not attainment of the degree. In addition, how long has the individual been seeking the degree? A candidate seeking a bachelor's degree in planning who has been in school since 1988 is likely no longer actively pursuing the completion of the degree. Follow-up screening may clarify the candidate's ultimate potential. Valuable insights result when asking job candidates about the dates of most recent course completion, current grade point average, active academic standing, and the amount of coursework remaining to complete their degrees.

Completeness of the Application. Did the applicant complete all questions or leave unexpected blank spaces on the application form? If using online applications, gaps may not be problematic as application submission often is contingent upon answering each specific application question. Blank spaces on application forms (when accepted) may signal attempts to avoid or to bypass sensitive questions. Examples of question avoidance might be a candidate's unwillingness to report past felony convictions, DUIs, or firing from previous jobs. Screeners should note these gaps and seek follow-up information if they intend to forward the candidate's application to the next step.

Employment Gaps. Employment lapses should be investigated by HR screeners. Employment gaps may be explained, and queries should be made to ascertain reasons for employment inactivity. For example, a candidate may have returned to school to gain new skills for added employability. An applicant may have lapses in employment while caring for an ill family member. Military spouses often have gaps due to their spouse's overseas duty and a desire to keep the family intact. The key point is not that employment gaps exist, but rather to identify what factors explain the gaps as well as what activities the candidate might have been involved in during these gaps. For instance, someone who has experienced a period of unemployment but has continued to offer voluntary service to the community might well have additional work experience not identified in the application.

Job-hopping Trends. Screeners generally view job-hopping (i.e., frequently moving from one job to another) negatively, especially for candidates with a decade or more of work experience. For employees new in their careers, some job-hopping might well be anticipated as the individual seeks to define a chosen career. To be fair to the candidate, screeners must also seek to understand why the individual has left prior employment. Two examples come to mind. First, candidates who have been laid off from work in economically depressed labor markets may have had no choice in the matter. In these instances, if the candidate's work performance record consistently has been strong, then fears of job-hopping should diminish. The second case involves the candidate whose spouse is career military. Such a candidate's work history is likely to reflect significant job-hopping, possibly every two to three years, as the military spouse moves from post to post. In this case, the candidate's diverse locations of employment (in all likelihood worldwide) should signal a query from an experienced applicant screener.

Reasons for Leaving Previous Jobs. As indicated above, knowing why the individual left previous employment is an important screening issue for judging the candidate's employment potential. Screeners often look for candidate behavioral cues. For example, applicants indicating dislike for or personality differences with previous supervisors may create concern about the applicant's ability to work well in any work setting. Termination from a previous job, when discovered, should also be explored carefully. A candidate who has been fired for stealing from a prior employer probably would be evaluated more negatively than the applicant terminated for missing too much work to care for an ill parent or child, provided that the issue of illness has been resolved.

Availability Date for Employment. Screeners often ask candidates to indicate their earliest date of availability for employment. In this instance, if the candidate is currently employed, immediate availability should be a negative factor. Good applicants will want to treat their current employer fairly, so some lag in availability should be expected. Depending on the level of the recruited position, the lag in availability for an employed candidate may range from two weeks to two months. A sitting city manager might well need to offer generous notice prior to departure. In these infrequent instances when giving notice results in the employee's immediate termination, every possible effort should be made by the hiring employer to offer immediate employment to the new recruit.

TESTING OF APPLICANTS

Screening candidates through tests helps determine a candidate's skill sets and fit to the position opening. In some instances, testing occurs before reviewing a candidate's application in order to screen out applicants who do not possess the ability to do the job and/or the personality characteristics to work well in the organization. In other instances, the application is assessed before the testing. The test costs and the ease of conducting the tests can influence when test administration occurs. As test costs increase, so will the likelihood for testing to occur after the initial screening of job applicants. As an example, testing to screen for the selection of a new police helicopter pilot is likely to occur following the review of candidate applications due to the costs associated with such tests. On the other hand, typing or word processing tests for administrative staff hires might well be conducted of all applicants as a means of reducing the numbers of candidate applications to review. In this instance, testing could be conducted quickly, possibly even online, at relatively modest costs.

Ability Testing

Ability tests combine methods that screen for specific skills as well as knowledge that predicts a high likelihood for performance on the job. The best tests sample portions of the job tasks the candidate would perform if selected for the opening.

Assessment Center Testing

One excellent testing methodology that cities sometimes employ to determine promotion potential to leadership positions in police and fire departments is assessment center testing. Assessment center testing challenges candidates with a series of work-related exercises. These include individual writing sample tests, dynamic group decision-making exercises, and individual presentation or public speaking exercises based on a problem scenario provided shortly before the applicant's presentation. Assessment center testing exhibits high job content validity and thus proves to be a very good predictor of future on-job performance, but these tests are expensive to conduct. Assessment center reviewers often require specialized training and, preferably, are selected from outside of the organization in order to limit self-interest or rater selection bias. Thus, reviewer expenses such as per diem costs (e.g., travel, lodging, and other incidentals) limit their applicability in local government settings.

Ability and assessment center tests, whenever feasible, should test the individual's capability to perform critical tasks associated with the position. For example, if a city is hiring a fleet mechanic, it can create a scenario that asks applicants to diagnose a disabled vehicle and repair it. In this situation, the city should pay the candidate a reasonable honorarium to take the ability test, provide the tools and parts that will be needed to diagnose and fix the vehicle, and obtain insurance to protect the city in case an accident occurs. The mechanic applicant that accurately diagnoses the car's problem and provides an effective repair of the vehicle should be given further consideration for hire.

Knowledge Testing

This type of test often is used in place of ability tests due to lower costs for administrating tests. For example, in the case above, screeners would first determine if the mechanic has the appropriate licensure or certification (where appropriate). The remaining applicants are asked to take a written test demonstrating their knowledge of vehicular mechanics and their diagnostic troubleshooting abilities. Knowledge tests demonstrate that individuals understand concepts about the subject under exam. This generally is a good predictor of on-the-job performance but not as valid a predictor as an ability test, since an applicant may understand mechanical principles well but still have limited talent when it comes to repairing the vehicle.

General Aptitude Testing

Organizations also can gauge applicants' cognitive strengths through the use of general aptitude testing like the Wonderlic Personnel Test or the General Aptitude Test Battery. These tests measure factors such as the applicant's reasoning, thinking abilities, memory, and recall skills. Candidates' verbal and mathematical skills often are determined through general aptitude testing. Aptitude testing is popular due to its relatively low costs and ease of administration and assessment.

When considering the use of ability versus aptitude testing, organizations preferably should employ work sample testing based on the vital tasks that the candidate will perform. This approach offers a more predictive measurement of expected on-the-job work performance. It should be noted that if testing is to be developed in-house, the HR staff must have an expert (either in-house or hired contractually) to validate test reliability and validity before putting such tests into practice.

Physical and Dexterity Testing

Physical and dexterity testing frequently is used for those positions requiring levels of agility, significant hand-eye coordination, and body strength and endurance. Police and fire departments, for example, often require applicants to pass minimum physical fitness standards to qualify for employment consideration. In these instances, as a means for minimizing potential discrimination charges, appropriate standards must allow for adjustments based on factors like gender and age variances.

Behavioral Testing

Ability tests determine whether candidates possess the SKAs to perform the position's key duties. This information is necessary, but not sufficient, to determine which candidate to hire. The candidate's behavioral characteristics also influence work performance. The most talented applicant may still be an inappropriate hire if his or her personality or behavioral tendencies create problems within the unit. For example, the organizational whiner, who constantly has a complaint about something or other, creates challenges for organizational performance as well as significant frustrations for the immediate supervisor and fellow workers. Furthermore, this behavior often damages the whiner's personal credibility and individual productivity and increases social isolation since coworkers simply wish to avoid communicating with the whiner.

Another approach of behavioral testing occurs when the screener seeks to identify troubling trends in the candidate's work history. Do past comments, written or verbal, about an applicant's work record signal less than average commitment to work? Documentation of excessive absences, frequent tardiness, or aggressive behavior toward coworkers potentially signals troubling past behavior.

Unfortunately, in-depth behavioral insight about job applicants may not be easily obtained. Thus, organizations often employ formal behavioral testing methodologies (such as psychological, personality, and honesty testing) to establish when behavioral tendencies and applicant personality traits may not fit within the job context. Among the personality tests in wide use today are the Myers-Briggs Type Indicator (MBTI) and the Minnesota Multiphasic Personality Inventory (MMPI) tests. Although these tests remain popular, some members of the academic community have expressed concern about the validity of their application, especially when used for candidate screening.

PHASE III: TALENT SELECTION INTERVIEWS

In an ideal world, at least from the applicant's perspective, all job candidates would be interviewed for job openings. Unfortunately, this is not always practical due to limitations of time and resources. Selection costs can be enormous, forcing organizations to limit the number of final candidates personally interviewed for potential hire. In the public sector, for example, historically the federal civil service system and many other governments have employed the "rule of three" as their limit. This approach requires managers to select new employees from among the three most highly rated available candidates. In the federal government, however, evidence shows that rigid application of the rule of three has been eased in recent years (U.S. Merit Protection Board 1995). A similar trend exists with other governmental bodies. For most searches, between three and five finalists are interviewed for position openings, but governments demand selection flexibility, especially when they believe that an ideal fit does not exist within the finalists' candidate pool.

The third and final phase of the talent acquisition management process involves establishing an interview methodology, conducting interviews of the finalists, and administering postinterview testing. For example, drug screening, medical and physical exams where warranted, and security and reference checks may occur once a final candidate has been determined and the organization has secured the commitment of that candidate.

INTERVIEWING APPROACHES

Structured Interviews

A variety of methodological approaches can be used to glean information about the skill sets, qualifications, and behavioral tendencies of job finalists. The determination of the method (or combination of methods) employed will vary across organizations. The approach selected can be influenced by cost, face validity, potential for avoiding adverse impact, and the method's legal defensibility in court (Dixon et al.), where concern for volatile legal risks is paramount. Systems that have been sued for discriminatory interviewing practices are likely to use safe interview approaches like the structured interview, which is more resilient to legal challenges. Structured interviews employ a uniform battery of questions asked of each candidate, without follow-up queries from the interviewer. The interviewer asks only these questions, noting key aspects of the candidate's replies. Using this strategy ensures that interviewers ask the same battery of questions of each candidate. This approach reduces the potential for a less experienced interviewer, like a candidate's potential supervisor conducting the interview, from asking illegal or biased questions of the job candidate. Providing each candidate an identical set of questions serves to protect the organization better in case legal challenges arise. Generally, HR creates (or reviews) the questions to be asked beforehand, thereby decreasing bias due to inappropriate wording. Questions asked must be directly related to the job qualifications, rather than to personal characteristics, of the candidate. Structured interviewing provides the most fail-safe approach for avoiding the pitfall of interviewer bias.

The strengths of structured interviews also introduce their greatest weaknesses. Questions that come to the interviewer's mind during the interview might have high relevancy to the candidate's qualifications to perform the work, but these questions should not be asked. Potential loss of valuable information may result as the trade-off for making better hiring decisions against lessened legal liability due to interviewer error or question-set bias.

Semistructured Interviews

Semistructured interviews incorporate aspects of structured interviewing, but they allow greater probing through the addition of free-flowing follow-up questions. Semistructured interviews commence with a planned set of questions to be asked of all candidates, but the interviewer can also ask follow-up questions in order to clarify the candidate's responses. Semistructured interviews should be employed only by seasoned and experienced interviewers who understand interviewing techniques and those interviewing errors that can create legal challenges for the organization. These professionals know how to frame follow-up questions that seek strengthened information about job-related aspects of the candidate's qualifications. Always keep in mind that interview questions asked of each candidate must directly relate to the job, not the candidate's gender, ethnicity, age, background, or other irrelevant personal characteristics.

Stress Interviews

Stress interviews seek to determine how candidates react when placed in stressful or psychologically uncomfortable situations. As noted earlier, performance success is influenced by both the employee's ability and work behavioral responses. Some jobs require greater emotional and behavioral fortitude than do others. Law enforcement officers, for example, frequently are placed in stressful situations that can mean the difference between life and death for themselves as well as the public they serve. Thus, a screener may attempt to ascertain how a candidate acts under stress, through stress-induced situations and questions. For instance, an interviewer who comments negatively about a candidate's education or degree ("Do you really believe that your MPA is as good as an MBA?") or disputes the candidate's writing ability ("I have reviewed your writing samples and they are marginal!") might be interested in determining the applicant's behavioral responses under stress. How does the candidate react? Does he become angry or argumentative? What does his body language say about his ability to remain calm when placed under pressure?

Panel Interview

A panel interview is an interview conducted by a team of interviewers (typically three to five) who query the candidate in the same setting, then combine their ratings into a final panel rating (E.C. Mayfield, cited in Dixon et al. 2002). Good panel interview teams will make every effort to include minority- and gender-based diversity on the panel interviewing team. However, a downside of panel interviewing is its cost, which often is more expensive—in terms of staff labor costs as compared to the utilization of structured interviewing techniques. These costs, however, might be offset by the greater predictive and face validity of panel interviews as well as increased buy-in among incumbents regarding the ultimate selection decision (Dixon et al. 2002). Panel interviews also have the benefit of limiting unilateral selection decision-making by one individual (often the candidate's potential immediate supervisor), which helps when disputes arise or end up being litigated in court.

INTERVIEWING TECHNIQUES

The skill of the interviewer influences, positively or negatively, effective hiring. A variety of steps by the interviewer can ensure maximum benefit from the time spent with job applicants. The goal of the interview should be to gain insights about the candidate that often are not measured through the screening or selection testing process. As is often the case, a candidate may look good on paper but when interviewed may become less desirable because of skill deficiencies not measured through other means. An applicant's ability to communicate verbally, for example, is not often observed until a face-to-face interview occurs. Other aspects of a candidate's previous work experiences (both positive and negative) may not surface until discussions occur at the interviewing table.

Good Interview Techniques

One of the primary goals of good interviewing is to put the candidate at ease (except when conducting stress interviewing) so that she can more easily recall and share work experiences, work achievements, and performance record. Mitigating candidate stress during the interview helps the interviewer gain fuller information from the candidate. Thus, how the interviewer approaches the process can influence the information gained about the quality of the candidate under consideration. The following recommendations provide methods for creating productive interviewing environments.

- Hold phone calls and turn off cell phones during the interview.
- Avoid personal interruptions so as to maintain continuity of the interview.

- Situate the interview, if possible, in a nonconfrontational setting. Use a conference table rather than sitting behind a desk.
- Remove distractions, such as important documents, from the interviewing table.
- Understand and exhibit positive body language when interviewing the candidate. Employ direct eye contact, position your body in a supportive (rather than defensive) position, and avoid yawning and stretching during the candidate's responses.
- Listen actively to the candidate's comments, rather than focusing on the next questions.
- Fight off any temptations to judge the candidate's merits based on early positive or negative comments, dress, or other behaviorism.
- Ask open-ended questions that require more than a simple "yes" or "no" response. Framing questions with words like "Who," "What," "When," "Why," and "How" can elicit responses in which the candidate must provide an evaluative assessment of a past work situation.

The interviewer must understand common evaluation errors prior to conducting the interview and/or assessing the candidate's qualifications for the job. Interviewer errors will be discussed later in this chapter.

Poor Interview Techniques

Poor quality interviews create barriers to effective information collection and rob candidates of the opportunity to demonstrate the merits of their talent. This cheats the applicants and in some cases influences the quality of their responses, commitment to sharing information about their work successes, and commitment to work for the organization. Poor interviewing signals to high-quality candidates that the organization may have inferior employees. First impressions work both ways in interviewing. The interviewer makes judgments about the qualification of the candidate, and the candidate makes judgments about the quality of the organization, in part, based on the professionalism of the interviewer. In this case, poor interviewing techniques rob both parties—the job applicant, who may receive less than a fair review of her job skills, and the organization, who may lose a desirable and willing applicant to work for the organization.

Some of the common poor interviewing techniques to avoid are discussed below:

- Avoid making early snap decisions about a candidate's merit near the beginning of an interview.
- Fight off first impressions about the candidate's qualifications for the work until all information has been collected. Unfortunately, many interviewers make decisions to filter out or select candidates in the first four minutes of the interview.
- Do not cut interviews short, especially when there is a battery of questions to ask all candidates.
- Do not cut a candidate's responses short. Allow the candidate to provide a full response.

- Avoid leading questions that are likely to elicit obvious responses. For example, few interviewees will admit that they do not enjoy working with others, even if they do not.

Common Interviewer Rating Errors

Assessment of candidates also may be clouded by the biases of the rater. Before conducting interviews, HR specialists should consider their own personal biases that may color the weighting of each candidate's potential. A number of interviewing rater errors can occur. Some of these have been alluded to earlier in the chapter. Avoiding these errors will reduce selection bias and grant fair consideration to all job applicant finalists.

"Just Like Me" Syndrome Error

Also known as similarity error, this occurs when the interviewer is positively predisposed to candidates with similar backgrounds, personal characteristics, or interests similar to her own. Thus, an interviewer whose graduate degree is from Harvard might tend to rate a candidate higher than candidates from other schools if the candidate also received a graduate degree from Harvard.

Contrast Error

This error occurs when candidates are interviewed sequentially (or in close time proximity to each other), and the interviewer evaluates candidates against each other rather than against job specification standards.

"Best of the Bad Bunch" Error

This error occurs when interviewers select the best candidate from an unqualified group of applicants, as none of the applicants is a good fit for the job. This error occurs frequently when departments feel pressured to hire a new employee. In university settings, academic hiring most often occurs from November through March. Thus, departments might feel the pressure to secure even an inadequate candidate rather than lose the hiring line to another department in the next year if their search does not result in a new hire.

"First Impression" Error

Many people are accustomed to making quick judgments about those they meet. This also occurs frequently in the hiring of new employees. Often, decisions to hire are made in the first four minutes of the job interview. Generally, these decisions are based on initial perceptions (good or bad) about the candidate and made with insufficient or incomplete information. Unfortunately, once this impression has been formed, many interviewers filter subsequent information to fit this impression, thereby distorting the true skill set of the candidate. Good interviewers realize this tendency and will fight off the temptation to judge the merits of the candidate until all information about the individual has been received and reviewed fairly.

"Halo Effect" Error

This error occurs when one highly desired or admired characteristic influences positively other components of the interview. For example, a police officer candidate in top physical shape may skew the interviewer's perception of the candidate's qualifications in other areas, especially if the interviewer admires individuals who are physically fit. Other characteristics, such as the candidate's ability to react under pressure, communicate well orally or in writing, or work well with others, especially if they are characteristics that are difficult to gauge by the interviewer, may thus be scored higher than warranted.

"Devil's Horn Effect" Error

This error is the flip side of the halo effect error. If the candidate possesses a characteristic or trait that the interviewer disdains, the evaluation of the candidate's skill set or abilities or test scores may result in a lowered score in other areas. Using the example above, the law enforcement candidate in average shape (that still meets the standard) may find assessment in other areas lowered by the interviewer because of lessened physical fitness.

Interviewer Stereotype Bias Error

This error occurs when personal stereotypical biases of the interviewer influence the perception of the candidate's qualification. Age, sex, gender, and race biases are among the most common stereotype biases that introduce interviewer judgment error. For example, in an occupation like auto mechanic, where males dominate the profession, interviewers must carefully judge all candidates based on qualification as opposed to gender.

CHAPTER SUMMARY

As witnessed in this chapter's discussion, selection of new hires (or promotions of internal candidates) is a complex and challenging process. HR specialists must look closely at the needs of their organization, identify the skill sets needed for the position under consideration, and effectively communicate job opportunities to the organization's workforce and the public at large. Candidate screening seeks to identify the best candidates for further evaluation through on-site interviews and skills and behavioral assessments. Ultimately, this group forms the pool of job finalists whose talents are reviewed closely through job interviewing. As seen here, a number of interviewing approaches are available to judge which finalist best fits and meets the needs of the organization. Interviewers must be sure that the questions asked directly relate to the job, not to the candidate's personal attributes. Furthermore, interviewers should make every effort to ensure that interview selection biases and errors do not distort the ultimate selection of the best candidate. HR can facilitate this concern through questionnaire clearance and/or interviewer training before meeting with candidates to judge their job worthiness. All candidates, whether a finalist or not, deserve a fair and honest assessment of their potential for the job opening. The HR unit and the department conducting the hire have an ethical obligation to every applicant, and to the city government they represent, to do all in their power to achieve this standard.

KEY CONCEPTS AND TERMS

Americans with Disabilities Act of 1990

applicant screening

applicant tests: ability, aptitude, behavioral, dexterity, knowledge, physical

assessment centers

Equal Employment Opportunity Commission (EEOC) applicant tracking

equal employment opportunity (EEO) utilization standards

E-recruiting

essential job functions

E-Verify

Executive Order 12989

Genetic Information Nondiscrimination Act of 2008 (GINA)

headhunters

interview approaches: panel, structured, semistructured, stress

interviewer rating errors: best of the bad bunch, contrast, devil's horn effect, first impression, halo effect, just like me/similarity, stereotype bias

interviewer techniques

I-9 Employment Eligibility Verification

job application assessment techniques: good and bad approaches

job-hopping

organizational whiner

reasonable accommodations

recruitment

rule of three

selection interviews

skills, knowledge, and abilities (SKAs)

talent acquisition management

word-of-mouth recruiting

PRACTICAL LEARNING ACTIVITIES

1. Word-of-mouth recruiting has proved to be a highly effective means of identifying candidates for position openings in many organizations. Under what conditions should it be used sparingly, or not at all, when seeking to hire new employees from a pool of candidates?
2. Select either the ICMA or ASPA career website discussed in this chapter. Go online and identify a position that you might wish to apply for now (or upon completion of your education). How easy was it to access this information? Would you use this website in the future for other job search information?
3. How effective do you believe the EEOC has been in its efforts to ensure equitable treatment for all job applicants seeking employment in U.S. organizations? What factors might inhibit the EEOC in its effort to protect American workers against employment discrimination during the hiring process?
4. Review the interviewer rater errors discussed in this chapter. Then think about past interviews that you have had when seeking a job or career opportunity. Do you believe that you have been the victim of any type of interviewer rater error or bias? Can you identify any occasions when an interviewer displayed discriminatory bias? Be prepared to discuss your experiences with the class.
5. Stress questions are often used to identify how candidates react to pressure. How would you respond to an interviewer who questions your SKAs to succeed in the position being offered?

REFERENCES

Aberdeen Group. 2001. E-recruitment solutions: Attracting and retaining talent via the web. www.aberdeen.com/summary/report/other/e-Recruitment.asp.

Alder, S., and A. Mills. 2008. Controlling Leadership Talent Risk: An Enterprise Imperative. *Ready* 1, 1 (November).

Aon Consulting. 2008. www.aon.com/about-aon/intellectual-capital/attachments/human-capital-consulting/Leadership_FINAL_0.pdf.

Ashforf, S., and S. DeRue. 2010. Imagining the Future of Leadership: Five Steps to Addressing the Leadership Talent Shortage. *Harvard Business Review*. http://blogs.hbr.org/imagining-the-future-of-leadership/2010/06/5-steps-to-addressing-the-lead.html.

Barr, S. 2006. 45 years after Kennedy's call, web site introduces a new generation to government careers. *Washington Post*, April 25, D04.

Bennis, W. 2006. QuoteWorld.org. www.quoteworld.org/quotes/1224.

Borowski, C. 2006. Risks, benefits of contingent workers. *Indiana Employment Law Letter* 16, 1.

Brown, J., and L. Williams. 2003. The 21st century workforce: Implications for HR. In *Human Resources in the 21st Century*, ed. M. Effron, R. Gandossy, and M. Goldsmith. Hoboken, NJ: John Wiley.

Carroll, J., and D. Moss. 2002. *State Employee Worker Shortage.* Lexington, KY: Council of State Governments.

Dixon M., S. Wang, J. Calvin, B. Dineen, and E. Tomlinson. 2002. The panel interview: A review of empirical research and guidelines for practice. *Public Personnel Management* 31, 3 (Fall), 397–427.

Dresang, D. 2002. *Public Personnel Management and Public Policy,* 4th ed. New York: Longman.

Illinois City/County Management Association. n.d. *A Guide to Hiring a Chief Administrative Officer.* DeKalb: Illinois City/County Management Association.

Kinsman, M. 2006. Truth-stretching resume: Even if you get hired, fudging facts puts your job in jeopardy. *California Job Journal,* July 16. www.jobjournal.com/article_full_text.asp?artid=1752.

Langan, S. 2000. Finding the needle in the haystack: The challenge of recruiting and retaining sharp employees. *Public Personnel Management* 29, 4 (Winter), 461–476.

Mooney, J. 2002. Pre-employment testing on the Internet: Put candidates a click away and hire at modem speed. *Public Personnel Management* 31, 1 (Spring), 41–51.

Smith, A. 2010. GINA remains a "sleeper statute." Society for Human Resource Management, October 26.www.shrm.org/LegalIssues/FederalResources/Pages/SleeperStatute.aspx.

Taylor, W. 2006. To hire sharp employee, recruit in sharp ways. *New York Times,* April 23, sec. 3, p. 3.

U.S. Equal Employment Opportunity Commission (EEOC). 2001. Facts about discrimination based on sexual orientation, status as a parent, marital status and political affiliation. U.S. Equal Employment Opportunity Commission, June 27. www.eeoc.gov/facts/fs-orientation_parent_marital_political.html.

U.S. Equal Employment Opportunity Commission (EEOC). n.d. EEO reports/surveys. http://eeoc.gov/employers/reporting.cfm.

U.S. Merit Protection Board. 1995. *Rule of Three in Federal Hiring: Boon or Bane?* Washington, DC: U.S. Merit Protection Board.

Wallace, J., M. Tye, and S. Vodanovich. 2000. Applying for jobs online: Examining the legality of Internet-based application forms. *Public Personnel Management* 29, 4 (Winter), 497–504.

Williamson, I., D. Lepak, and J. King. 2003. The effect of company recruitment web site organization on individuals' perceptions of organizational effectiveness. *Journal of Vocational Behavior* 63, 242–263.

Performance Management

Performance stands out like a ton of diamonds.
Nonperformance can always be explained away.

—Harold S. Geneen

After reading this chapter, you will

- comprehend the distinction between performance management and performance appraisal;
- understand why performance management is a critical aspect of organizational management;
- grasp the problems that arise when performance is ineffectively appraised;
- gain insight about supervisory rater errors that often occur when evaluating worker performance;
- recognize different methods for evaluating employee performance as well as the benefits and drawbacks in their application; and
- understand what is required to avoid legal challenges when evaluating employee performance.

As social beings, most people desire active involvement and "ownership" of their jobs. They also need meaningful feedback about how well they are performing at work. Performance feedback serves as a powerful tool for increasing employee commitment, trust, and productivity, especially when it is practiced effectively. Unfortunately, many supervisors use performance appraisal instruments for command and control purposes. Thus, their actions discourage, more than improve, performance outcomes. Successful performance management requires conscientious supervisor assessment and appropriate and timely communication of performance outcomes. Excellent performance evaluation systems do not just happen; they require well-thought-through performance measurement processes, as well as evaluators trained in the fine art of judging performance quality.

Performance management and performance appraisal are similar but distinct concepts. The U.S. Office of Personnel Management (OPM n.d.) defines performance management as "the systematic process by which an agency involves its employees, as individuals and members of a group, in improving organizational effectiveness in the accomplishment of agency mission and goals." OPM's performance management model designates five elements:

1. Planning performance: creating work plans, establishing performance expectations, communicating expectations to employees.
2. Monitoring performance: reviewing employee and team performance periodically to assess progress and diagnose if changes are required.
3. Developing workers' capacities: focusing on training and development of employees to enhance their present performance potential and increase future skills and leadership growth.
4. Measuring work performance: reviewing periodically performance outcomes of individual employees and employee teams.
5. Rewarding individuals and teams for achieving (and exceeding) performance outcomes.

Performance appraisal, by comparison, is a key performance management component. It relates most closely to measuring work performance (#4 above). Performance appraisal measures the employee's (or team's) effectiveness at achieving desired work outcomes. Such outcomes should be directly related to the individual's (or team's) responsibilities. These goals and objectives also should link directly to the organization's mission and purpose.

Many organizations today conduct performance appraisal. Performance appraisal relates closely with the terms "personnel appraisal," "performance evaluation," and "employee evaluation," but never with "job appraisal," which is considered a separate and distinct personnel function. Far fewer organizations systematically incorporate performance management as a strategic human resource (HR) tool. Too often, too little effort is put forth to identify and measure the true performance and work contributions of each employee. In part, this may explain why many employees distrust performance appraisal practices and approaches used within their organization.

MEASURING PERFORMANCE

If performance appraisal is so poorly designed and administered in today's organization, why then should performance appraisal continue to be used? Many practical reasons constitute the need for its continued utilization, especially when effectively applied. Performance appraisal has the potential of being a valuable tool for performance improvements both in a worker's immediate duties as well as in his future career development. Thus, managers and supervisors must not become discouraged when employees disapprove of the performance appraisal process in use. Many employees dislike being evaluated, especially when they view the process as a meaningless and/or punitive tool. Evaluators have at their disposal the challenge of diagnosing true performance as well as discovering innovative ways to aid their employees at improving their performance. Effective performance appraisal promotes three desired outcomes:

- It rewards high performance: employees deserve to be rewarded for high performance. In order to reward performance outcomes, the supervisor must understand each individual's position as well as the characteristics of each position that reflect varying levels of performance achievement.
- It communicates changing performance expectations: appraisal meetings should prepare employees for changing work roles and performance expectations. Organizations have an obligation to inform their workers when performance standards change. Performance appraisal meetings provide supervisors the opportunity to advise workers of such changes so they can appropriately modify work behavior toward achieving new performance expectations and outcomes.
- It facilitates future employee potential: performance appraisal also provides a forum for discussing strategies for employee growth and skills development. Effective performance appraisal requires supervisors with the knowledge and abilities to diagnose the strengths and weaknesses of their employees and recommend strategies for enhancing future skills development.

Too often employees view performance reviews as a punitive tool enabling the boss to maintain behavioral control over their actions or as a means to punish them for failing to live up to their superiors' performance expectations. It is no wonder that many employees view performance appraisal with skepticism and distrust. Dr. Samuel Culbert (2008), of UCLA's Anderson School of Business, noted in a *Wall Street Journal* article that performance review "destroys morale, kills teamwork and hurts the bottom line. And that's just for starters." Thus, successful performance evaluations require quality consideration of performance by supervisors actively overseeing and committed to honest performance evaluations. Also required for success is the implementation of a quality performance appraisal process that truly measures and rewards people when their performance merits such consideration.

RATER ERRORS AND EVALUATION BIAS

Much of the employee dissatisfaction associated with performance appraisal revolves around rater subjectivity. The following six types of common rater errors are discussed below:

- Bell-shaped–based evaluation errors
- Recency errors
- Rater pattern errors (leniency rating errors, stringency rating errors, central tendency rating errors)
- Halo effect and devil's horn effect errors
- Contrast errors
- Personal rater bias errors

Bell-Shaped–Based Evaluation Errors

Clearly, evaluating employees can also be distasteful to supervisors who may feel constrained to conform to their organization's expectations. Evaluators may feel pressure from their own superiors to conform to bell-shaped (i.e., normal distribution) ratings of employees as a means of ensuring workforce pay increases tolerance. Fairness would suggest the application of honest evaluations for each employee's work efforts against the standards of individual job requirements. Unfortunately, organizational life is not always fair, especially when the rater's self-interest requires remaining within the budget. Thus, fairness in the evaluation process may already be compromised simply by the expectation that the rater's behavior will align with the organization's budget. This type of scenario—evaluating performance within resource constraints—can severely jeopardize the potential for appreciating performance reviews, as well as mitigate trust between employees and their immediate superiors. Simply stated, highly performing employees should be compensated better than poorer performers. Moreover, evaluation reviews should be less about money and more about performance outcomes, employee development, and strategies for improving performance in future periods.

Recency Errors

Performance appraisal affords the rater (typically the employee's immediate supervisor) the opportunity to review work outcomes and accurately judge the employee's contribution across the evaluation cycle. While performance evaluation occurs continually, formalized evaluation feedback most commonly occurs on either a six-month or annual basis. Rating inaccuracy, commonly known as recency error, occurs whenever the evaluator passes judgment on an employee's work performance based primarily on recently witnessed work results (whether favorable or not). Recency errors hinder a more balanced assessment of work performance over the "life" of the evaluation period, significantly affecting the accuracy of the rater's performance score.

Rater error occurs often as the result of poor commitment to the performance assessment process by the evaluator (and possibly by the organization). In these situations, the evaluator places little trust in the evaluation as a constructive tool for shaping future employee behavior, growth, and performance. Instead, the performance review is considered a laborious, pro forma task of meaningless value. Thus, the evaluator does little during the evaluation cycle to measure successes and/or failures unless they have personal implications for the rater's own career. An upcoming employee's annual review cues action on the evaluator's part. In many cases, raters may not even focus on evaluation until their HR department notifies them that an employee's performance review is approaching.

Unfortunately for the organization, employees learn from the behavior of their rating supervisors. If they realize, and many do, that the window of performance observation is at hand, they might temporarily increase their effort in order to garner favorable performance consideration from their rater. Thus, the error associated with this cat-and-mouse evaluation game occurs because the rater is witnessing performance closest to the timing of the formal evaluation, while prudent observations should have been taken throughout the evaluation period. Most likely, poor performance during earlier portions of the work cycle might be overlooked, with higher performance being measured and attributed to performance across time.

Typically, recency error raters begin to take performance measurement to heart when their HR unit advises them that it is time to conduct the "annual" performance review of an employee. This alert is likely to occur four to six weeks before the evaluation. At the same time, the employee, who realizes from past experience that she will be under greater scrutiny due to the upcoming evaluation, will work harder, enhancing her commitment to her job (or loyalty to her rater, or both.) Ultimately, after the evaluation, "normal" performance returns until the next evaluation cycle, when the flawed process begins again.

The rater and the organization should learn to monitor, measure, and record performance of employees frequently during all periods of the annual performance cycle. In addition, they should not wait to advise the employee about her performance. This alerts the individual that her performance is actively measured. They should also communicate means for improving performance. Finally, organizations should modify errant behavior of raters who practice recency error behavior by holding them accountable for their actions.

RATER PATTERN ERRORS

Rater patterns for evaluation also create mismatches between the rating score and the reality of performance. Three common patterns are most often identified as problematic. These three pattern errors, discussed below, are leniency, stringency, and central tendency errors.

Leniency Rating Errors

This rating error results from a rater's tendency to upgrade performance of his staff. It occurs whenever the evaluator rates employees' performance better than is warranted. Such performance inflation advantages the rater's staff at the expense of truer rating by others. This error is likely to hinder further performance improvements, as employees become accustomed to the rater's "generosity" rather than exhibiting higher levels of performance.

Why do leniency rating errors occur? Rater leniency occurs for a number of reasons. Some raters seek to avoid the challenges associated with accurate assessment, giving high ratings in order to avoid the conflict and stress associated with accurate evaluations. This may be closely related to the rater's belief that giving high evaluations, even when undeserved, will create a more trusting and family friendly feeling among the staff. In other cases, especially in governmental organizations where resources are scarce, supervisors boost evaluation scores as a means of psychologically rewarding employees in lieu of monetary rewards (i.e., providing realistic pay increases for performance outcomes).

Stringency Rating Errors

Stringency rating errors are the flip side of leniency rating errors. In this instance, the evaluator systematically downgrades the true performance of the employees. One sign of stringency among raters might be to review their ratings of their employees over time. If the rater rarely (if ever) has evaluated any employees overall as outstanding or exemplary, it is likely that the rater exhibits stringency characteristics. Again, one of the primary goals of performance reviews is to rate accurately employee (and/or team) performance in order to reward their work efforts, when warranted. Stringent rating can create a sense of defeat among high-performing employees. When employees begin asking, "What does it take to be recognized for outstanding performance in this organization?" this connotes that their rater probably practices the error of stringency rating.

A number of factors explain stringent rating errors of work performance. First, one must ask whether or not the rater has a history of rating performance harshly. If the answer is no, the rater's application of tougher standards is probably due to internal demands from higher-level authority. Pressures to conform to lowered performance standards often occur during periods of resource scarcity. Criticizing raters for not maintaining more rigorous performance standards might also influence systematic ratings of all staff, if for no other reason than fear of management retribution for not holding the line on performance assessment.

If, however, the rater has a history of stringency rating when evaluating the performance of the staff, then other factors might explain severe evaluation outcomes. Some raters believe that if they rate their employee as outstanding there will be no incentive for future improvement in his performance. Thus, they justify their severity in their own minds by arguing that no one is perfect and that all employees have room for improvement. In addition, raters may believe that performance reviews identifying potential talent may be detrimental to sustain their own leadership positions. Thus, they rate their employees harshly as a means of containing the advancement of potential future rivals. Finally, some raters learn certain behavior through their own past experiences in the rating process. If they have been the recipients of stringent performance reviews, they may believe that the organization's culture mandates tough standards when reviewing employees. They rate their workers severely simply because they believe it is expected based on their own experiences.

Again, performance reviews should accurately and fairly measure workers' productivity, not only within their unit but also equitably across all units and all employees. The stringent rater's actions unfairly hurt her employees' potential relative to others, especially in large organizations where past performance ratings may be key factors in the promotability (or in some cases, the retention) of such employees. Therefore, performance evaluation accuracy remains critical for fair treatment of all employees.

Central Tendency Rating Errors

Central tendency rating errors occur when the evaluator rates employee performance within a satisfactory range regardless of the true contributions of the employee. This lumping of all employees in a default satisfactory range ultimately results in lowered productivity among all unit employees. High performers either will choose to relocate to other units or organizations that value and reward them for their efforts or they will simply fall in line, lower their performance, and accept future satisfactory evaluations. Poor performers, who already have received the inflated evaluative benefit "satisfactory," "meets standards," or "achieves expectations," have no incentive or external pressure to improve. Ironically, their future performance may be even poorer as they test the system to see just how far their performance can slide. Central tendency evaluations lead to marginally performing units (or organizations), if the problem is systemic.

Grouping performance outcomes in the middle, "satisfactory" range occurs for a variety of reasons:

- inattentiveness to monitoring work performance, either as a result of a lazy supervisor or a disbelief in the benefits of performance management;
- the desire to avoid conflict or concerns that accurate evaluation will hurt unit cohesion; and
- disdain for having to justify performance levels during performance reviews.

Of these three types of rater pattern errors, central tendency errors are most destructive to overall unit productivity. Poor performers are rewarded while productivity is punished, but all workers witness the fact that it does not matter how well or poorly an employee performs because results are the same—"satisfactory." Most employees therefore develop the same apathetic attitude: "it does not matter how hard I work; I will still receive the same evaluation." Being given the choice of working hard while many others coast creates resentment and defeats any potential for establishing a high-performance, high-productivity culture. Granted, some employees will continue to put forth outstanding effort, but these employees are not driven by the performance appraisal process. They either have a high sense of commitment to those they serve or place high value on what they are doing.

HALO EFFECT AND DEVIL'S HORN EFFECT ERRORS

Rater halo effect and devil's horn effect are presented together in this section. They mirror each another, having opposite impacts on the evaluation process.

Performance halo effect errors result when the employee exhibits a particular performance characteristic that is admired by the rater. Such behavior significantly influences favorably the rater's performance assessment. For example, a firefighter who meritoriously risks his life to save the life of the town's mayor during a residential fire might be granted a higher rating than he deserves during this (and possibly future) performance evaluation. Thus, the rater overrates this performance factor at the expense of other work-related characteristics, leading to an inflated assessment of the employee's performance. The firefighter may have missed work, abused department policies, and failed to demonstrate respect for others, yet continues to gain the benefit of the halo earned by his lifesaving actions. In this instance, the rater's objectivity is blinded by an act, skill, or behavior exhibited by the person being reviewed.

Devil's horn effect errors result when an employee exhibits a performance characteristic detested by the rater. The employee's actions here significantly hinder the rater's performance assessment. Suppose, for example, that the outcome for the mayor in that residential fire proved fatal due to an error made by the firefighter. Thus, rightfully or not, he is blamed for the death of the beloved mayor and is held accountable at his performance review. The firefighter may have a stellar career and be productive in all phases of his work, but due to a poor decision, he is blamed for the tragic outcome. Assuming that the firefighter still has employment, he suffers immense downgrading of performance during his review. In fact, his career may be ruined; that one poor decision becomes a lasting stigma with a lifelong impact on his performance evaluation. This stigma may well follow him throughout the rest of his firefighting career.

Raters have to fight both halo and devil's horn effect errors by remembering that they must evaluate performance against standards rather than allowing their bias (pro or con) to dominate their performance assessment. This may be more easily said than done, especially when devastating instances result in devil's horn effect errors.

CONTRAST ERRORS

Contrast rating errors result when a supervisor rates one employee against another, rather than rating each individual against defined performance standards. Rating one poorly performing individual satisfactory simply because that individual performs slightly better than another poorly performing employee exemplifies the contrast error effect. By comparing both workers against established performance criteria rather than one person against another, the supervisor should evaluate both as not meeting performance expectations based on established work standards.

PERSONAL RATER BIAS ERRORS

Personal rater bias errors (also referred to as stereotype bias errors) occur when the supervisor allows his personal beliefs to affect the performance rating of the individual being reviewed. Demographic characteristics of the individual (or group of individuals with the same characteristics) may bias the rater. Some of the common characteristics creating the potential for personal bias are race, gender, sexual orientation, age, religion, and disability. An example of personal bias occurs when the evaluator downgrades the performance of female firefighters because he believes that no woman can be as effective in this role as her male counterpart. Rather than using established performance standards to judge each individual's efforts, the evaluator's bias influences the results to align with his own personal beliefs and biases.

Organizations should train their evaluators to reflect about their own potential bias and its potential impact on how they rate others. Organizations also should monitor and review supervisory evaluation practices to ensure consistency across raters and to minimize the potential for rater error occurrences. Doing this will guard against the increased potential for disparate impact discrimination charges.

METHODS FOR MEASURING PERFORMANCE

Organizations have a number of methods to gauge employee performance. The following seven common measurement approaches are discussed below.

- Critical incident
- Rating scales
- Employee ranking
- Behavioral anchored rating scales (BARS)
- Narrative or Essay evaluation
- Management by objectives
- 360° performance appraisal

Frequently, multiple techniques are used together within a performance appraisal instrument. Use of combined methods can provide fuller knowledge about the quality and quantity of work performed by employees during a given appraisal cycle, in part because supervisors utilize a standardized performance appraisal instrument across a number of different occupational positions within an organization. In these cases, standardized instruments cost less to develop and can be easier to execute. Their disadvantage, however, is that they often do not capture the unique challenges faced by employees in specific positions. Thus, their use lessens measures of true performance.

Evaluators create the best performance instruments that meet the demands and standards of each organizational position. Keep in mind, however, that in very large organizations there may be as many as 400 different occupational titles. Customized performance instruments are costly to design, so many organizations trade off the benefits of individual forms for the cost saving of uniform instruments.

CRITICAL INCIDENT

With the critical incident method of performance evaluation, the rating supervisor periodically documents in writing both positive and negative incidents of the employee's performance throughout the performance evaluation cycle. This information aids the rater in the construction of an objective review of the employee's work activities across the evaluation period.

Incident documentation should be shared with employees when recorded. This alerts employees to performance expectations as well as giving them valuable information through notification about performance successes and areas where improvements are required.

NUMERICAL RATING SCALE FORMAT

The numerical rating scale method of evaluation provides each rater with work characteristics or traits relating to an employee's job performance. Often, raters check off the appropriate anchor value that relates most closely to the quality or level of performance associated with the element under review. Common performance elements evaluated through rating scales might include the following:

- quality of work
- quantity of work
- punctuality
- job knowledge
- ability to work with others
- work safety record

These are a few samples of the types of measures of performance that performance documents utilize. In addition to defining the performance characteristic to be evaluated, numerical ranking also uses a scale to differentiate performance levels. A common example might use a five-segment measurement scale as shown in Figure 6.1.

One of the primary benefits of numerical rating is that such scores once obtained can provide a range of performance outcomes across an employee pool. This allows for a comparison across employees' performance. These scores, however, should be used with caution and care. One must keep in mind that two raters, one stringent and one lenient in their rating behavior, would view the performance of the exact same employee differently. Fortunately, statistical tools exist that HR units can employ to neutralize rater pattern differences.

EMPLOYEE RANKING

Employee ranking evaluates performance from best to worst. Thus, a supervisor with five employees could use this information to rank the employees' performances from first through fifth place (or top to bottom). Sometimes employee ranking is used to distribute merit pay increases to employees based on ranking outcomes. For example, a manager who has an average of 3 percent to distribute to his staff (all presently earning the same pay) might grant the distribution based on the ranked evaluation outcomes as represented in Table 6.1.

A review of the ranked results in Table 6.1 suggests some of the challenges when supervisors employ ranked-order evaluation as a means of distribution of compensation increases. In this case, very little difference separates the top-ranked (Employee B) and second-highest-ranked (Employee C) employees. One might argue that the additional percent increase granted to the top-ranked candidate as compared with the second-ranked candidate is not warranted. Likewise, a comparison of the evaluation scores of Employees D, E, and A (ranked third, fourth, and last) reveals negligible differences. Nonetheless, Employee D receives a 3 percent increase while Employee A receives only a 1 percent increase. Merit pay inequities can occur when increases are tied to ranked-order performance rating. Secondarily, employee ranking creates increased potential for contrast error (comparing of one employee's performance against another, rather than against performance standards). Thus, the use of employee ranking should be carefully considered before being utilized as a part of any evaluation process.

Table 6.1

Employee Ranking Example

	Employee	Rank	Rating score (100 point scale)	Percent increase
Highest rank	B	1st	98	5
	C	2nd	96	4
	D	3rd	84	3
	E	4th	83	2
Lowest rank	A	5th	81	1

BEHAVIORAL ANCHORED RATING SCALES

The BARS evaluation approach is similar to numerical scale rating. Like numerical rating, it employs rating scales (see the five-point scale in Figure 6.1) to differentiate performance quality. However, unlike numerical scale rating, it specifies performance standards on a most- to least-desired behavioral outcomes basis to measure performance quality. Figure 6.2 demonstrates an example of BARS that might be used in a local government setting for measuring managerial communication effectiveness.

Both raters and employees often view BARS evaluations positively. People seem to understand and trust performance ratings when anchors are tied to behavioral qualities associated with their work. While favorably received by many, BARS approaches often are not employed, because to be effective the behavioral anchors must relate specifically to the performance characteristics of each job title. Thus, designing BARS rating systems has high front-end development costs, so many organizations are either unwilling to invest in them or unable to commit the time needed for their construction.

NARRATIVE OR ESSAY EVALUATION

Narrative evaluation performance methods (also called essay evaluations) are also commonly used as a part of the performance review process. They often complement numeric ratings by providing detailed understanding of performance characteristics that may not be included in standardized performance instruments.

Critical incident rating exemplifies one special form of narrative evaluation. Critical incident notates both good and bad characteristics of performance during the evaluation period. The rater jots down information about performance in real time and later refers to it while preparing the formal performance review. Critical incident observations should be shared with employees as soon as possible in order to help them improve and learn in their jobs. Following this rule of earliest possible notification also reinforces desired work behavior.

Essay evaluations provide extensive feedback about employee performance. This allows the reviewer to articulate special characteristics of performance that would not normally be included in performance instruments. Thus, special employee talents, not captured through performance instruments, can still be referred to through essay feedback. In addition, poor performance characteristics that might be missing from the performance instrument can also be noted and discussed during the evaluation review.

Figure 6.1 **Numerical Rating Scale**

5 Outstanding: Individual's performance level is so high as to merit special recognition.

4 Exceeds standards: Individual's performance consistently exceeds performance expectations.

3 Achieves expectations: Individual's performance consistently falls within the range of expected performance in this area.

2 Below expectations: Individual's performance is variable and at times falls below the performance expectations. (*Note:* Retraining and/or other interventions should be considered.)

1 Unsatisfactory: Individual's performance consistently falls below the performance standards.

Note: Training and/or other interventions are warranted. Termination should follow if the individual's performance remains substandard following appropriate intervention.

The essay or narrative evaluation has an advantage because it provides individual insights into performance not normally measured when numerical rating methods are used alone. Some obvious disadvantages exist, however. The rater's writing abilities may seriously influence the perception of employee performance and achievement. Clearly, some evaluators are better wordsmiths than are others. Thus, better-developed narratives benefit the employee more than poorly written ones. Furthermore, narrative evaluations, when used alone, create challenges for comparing performance outcomes across employee groupings. Therefore, numeric and narrative evaluations often are combined in the performance evaluation process to glean both quantitative and qualitative aspects of work performance.

MANAGEMENT BY OBJECTIVES

The late Dr. Peter F. Drucker popularized management by objectives (MBO), a unique performance appraisal process. MBO provides enhanced communication between supervisor and employee, as well as improved performance outcomes. The employee's performance is based on a "goals and objectives" contract that becomes the basis for reviewing performance at the end of each evaluation cycle. The rater and employee mutually agree upon the goals and objectives that will provide the foundation for the evaluation. Merit pay increases and other rewards are determined directly as a result of achieving agreed-upon MBO defined goals and objectives. MBO strives to improve organizational outcomes through enhanced supervisor-employee communication, as well as through better-defined and understood goals-to-rewards outcomes.

Research on MBO has been a mixed bag. In some cases successes have resulted through MBO applications. In other instances, MBO has proved a miserable failure. Supervisors often become frustrated with MBO because it places heavy documentation responsibilities on them. They argue that MBO is too paper-intensive and time-consuming. MBO also has been criticized as placing handcuffs on supervisors when policies and goals change midway through the MBO contract period. Supervisors feel that they must adapt to changing priorities imposed upon them by their superiors while continuing to work with outdated MBO goals and objectives. This creates frustration for both supervisor and employee. Thus, in rapidly changing working environments, the application of MBO might not be appropriate or easily implemented.

Figure 6.2 **Behavioral Anchored Rating Scale Example**

Assessed Component: Managerial Communication

5	Outstanding	Individual is open to discussion and actively queries others for additional information and perspectives about the issue under discussion, even when she/he has taken an opposite position from others on the issue.
4	Good	Individual is open to discussion with others and listens actively to their ideas in order to show respect. She/he weighs their advice and carefully considers their input before taking action.
3	Satisfactory	Individual seeks advice from others before making a decision, but the determination of action generally is based on his/her own perspective.
2	Substandard	Individual tends to avoid seeking input and advice from others and at times makes decisions without the input of others.
1	Unacceptable	Individual withholds information and is hostile to others who might provide information that would be of value before taking appropriate action.

360° PERFORMANCE APPRAISAL

The final performance appraisal process discussed here is known as 360° performance appraisal. This performance system allows for full consideration of the employee's talents by allowing multiple raters to assess work contributions. Typically, 360° performance appraisal allows for individual self-rating, as well as assessment of the individual's performance contribution by supervisors, peer employees, customers, and clients. Thus, a 360° performance appraisal provides a more holistic review of the employee's performance than do more traditional performance appraisal systems.

A 360° performance appraisal can be difficult to implement. It requires someone to collect data from the multiple evaluators and condense feedback into usable information. Computer technology facilitates 360° appraisal systems by allowing direct input from the evaluators in many instances. This relieves some stress on HR systems as information can automatically be retrieved and tabulated.

In many instances, 360° performance appraisal is used as an advisory tool for performance reviews. It facilitates understanding areas for future development of the employee without inhibiting the oversight evaluation authority of the immediate supervisor. One primary concern with 360° performance appraisal results from the evaluation assessments coming from peers. In systems of high competition, fellow employees at one's level competing for future promotions may not provide honest or accurate feedback about the individual's performance. Thus, some organizations exclude same-level employees from the evaluation process.

LEGAL ISSUES AND PERFORMANCE MANAGEMENT

Employee discipline may result from assessment outcomes of individual performance. A number of legal issues should be addressed before applying discipline based on poor performance results. First, always apply sanctions appropriately, making certain to follow all due process procedures granted to the employee. If the employee afforded due process considerations has been terminated without granting such due process rights—like a formal hearing with the right to appeal a disciplinary decision—legal challenges may arise for unlawful termination. This becomes a particular concern when disciplining public sector employees who may be protected by civil service policies or through labor union contracts. "At-will" employees, employees who can be terminated without cause, also should be handled with care. In most instances, abiding by the following guidelines can result in lowered claims for discriminatory or unlawful actions on the part of the employer.

As noted above, performance appraisal outcomes can result in disciplinary action, up to and including employee termination. Employers should consider the following questions before acting.

Did the rater communicate sufficiently performance standards and work expectations to the employee? An employee who believes that he has been wrongfully punished or terminated may seek recourse through the legal process. When this occurs, typically following the granting of a "right to sue" permit by the U.S. Equal Employment Opportunity Commission (EEOC) or other state agency, the courts will seek to determine if a reasonable employee could have understood work expectations before disciplinary action or termination was taken. Thus, agencies must train the rating supervisors to communicate properly (and document in writing) work standards and expectations before taking disciplinary action. Evans (1991) suggests that supervisory training programs should include all of the following:

- Supervision skills
- Coaching and counseling
- Conflict resolution
- Setting performance standards
- Linking performance to pay (when "pay for performance" is in use)
- Communication employee feedback

Did the raters have sufficient contact with the employee to judge the quality of his performance on the job? Raters also must be able to demonstrate that they have sufficient contact and observation of an employee's work in order to judge reasonably the quality of performance sustained during an evaluation cycle. If this cannot be demonstrated, then others, with more direct exposure to the individual's productivity and performance outcome, should be selected to conduct the evaluation.

Were supervisors properly trained about measuring performance and avoiding rater errors prior to conducting an evaluation? Periodic training and retraining of performance evaluators serve as good "affirmative defense" for employers. Training helps ensure that raters understand techniques of performance measurement as well as the pitfalls of rater errors. With such knowledge, raters better understand the significance of their task as well as the importance of fairly and accurately evaluating their employees.

Did more than one person evaluate an individual's performance, thereby ensuring that one rater did not have unilateral control of the evaluation outcome? Discrimination investigators and courts are sensitive to evaluations where one rater has total control over the assessment of an employee's work performance. In these instances, concerns arise from the fact that the individual's rating cannot be validated (i.e., confirmed) by a second independent source. Thus, common practice calls for at least two evaluative sources to provide input into the ultimate performance review scores. In some instances, separate evaluations will be conducted by two sources. In other cases, the rater's evaluation will be submitted to an "endorser" (in most cases, the rater's supervisor) who will review and comment.

When observations of performance indicated poor outcomes, was the employee informed that her performance was below standards? Employers have an obligation to inform an employee when her work performance falls below standards or work-related quality levels. To do otherwise unnecessarily disadvantages the employee and her ability to make improvements based on timely feedback. In the American workplace, employees interpret the lack of supervisory feedback as a sign of satisfaction with their work effort or quality (Boice and Kleiner 1997). Here the impetus for communication of less than satisfactory work performance resides with the supervisor. He should indicate flaws in performance at the earliest possible point following such observations. Failure to do so leads to increased conflict and reduced trust on the part of the employee following the delivery of bad news during the annual evaluation. Rating supervisors should avoid these types of communication pitfalls at all possible cost.

Did the organization provide sufficient warning about poor performance? Based on the communication between supervisor and employee, would a reasonable person realize that his performance could lead to disciplinary actions? As noted above, supervisors have an ethical obligation to communicate with their employees whenever performance standards (quality or quantity) are not being met.

Did the organization offer remedial assistance and retraining to bring the employee back up to an acceptable standard? In addition to alerting employees effectively of poor work performance, organizations often need to provide a remedial plan for retraining employees, at least to give them one chance to achieve performance expectations. Courts look more favorably upon employers when notification and remediation precede disciplinary actions.

Did the organization allow sufficient time for a reasonable employee to improve his performance following remediation? The determination of whether work performance behavior has improved also requires the allowance of sufficient time for new skills to be learned. For example, word-processing specialists who experience declining performance standards because of the introduction of new word-processing software should be granted appropriate training in the new software and a reasonable period to become accustomed to its new features and intricacies before employee discipline results.

Was the standard attainable for most reasonably skilled employees? Unreasonable performance expectations that cannot be achieved by reasonably talented individuals should not result in disciplinary actions. Performance measures must be based on reasonable outcomes that are attainable by most talented, trained, and skilled workers. Setting standards higher than those attainable by most employees can lead to challenges of unlawful discipline and termination. Thus, performance benchmarks should be challenging yet attainable for workers with appropriate skill sets.

Expectations of Good Performance Management Systems

This chapter's final section identifies and discusses some characteristics found in high-performing work cultures. Organizations of excellence should seek to emulate similar qualities of excellence when reflecting on the quality of their performance appraisal processes and systems. Effective performance management systems seek to do all or most of the following.

• *Identify and measure accurately critical performance benchmarks.* The core of successful performance management systems hinges on the ability to identify successfully critical performance indicators and accurate performance benchmarks for the individual or group. Performance appraisal systems that connect appropriate performance behaviors with equitable reward systems promote sustained performance excellence.

• *Link performance benchmarks with the organization's mission and outcomes.* Good performance management sees the value of coupling its performance benchmarks with its organizational mission. This strengthens the potential for achieving desired organizational outcomes as well as reinforces the organization's primary purposes.

• *Provide a nexus between performance achievements and performance rewards.* Successful performance management rewards talented individuals whose performance creates organizational value. Good systems not only connect rewards with performance but also tailor their rewards systems to consider the needs of individual employees and what they value as rewards. Thus, these systems realize that the reward provisions (e.g., money, recognition, personal growth, increased work content ownership, and so on) reside within each employee. Thus, distribution of rewards takes individual needs into consideration and is granted to reflect these individual needs.

• *Create the perception of fair and equitable treatment of all employees.* Good performance systems distribute rewards with consideration for both horizontal and vertical equity and fairness. Thus, employees with similar skill sets and responsibilities are paid similar salaries (horizontal equity). Furthermore, as a worker's skill sets and work demands increase relative to others, the individual receives increased pay increments based on advanced skills, knowledge, abilities, and risks associated with progressive work responsibilities (vertical equity).

• *Promote administrative and fiscal sustainability.* Effective performance management systems facilitate operational efficiencies as well as financial frugality. In these instances, rewards are distributed appropriately based on current revenue and budget conditions; rewards, employee training and development, and employee discipline are applied with administrative fluidity; and goal achievements are related to performance management design and implementation.

• *Minimize litigation, organizational conflicts, and employee grievances.* Successful performance systems foster trust between the organization and the employee. One measure for determining existing organizational climate can be gleaned through analyses of litigation trends and costs, conflict patterns, and numbers of grievances filed as a result of performance disputes. Often, historical tracking best reflects appropriate levels of these benchmarks.

• *Prove beneficial to organizational and individual growth, learning, and development.* Good performance structures are designed to facilitate performance now as well as in future years. They seek to prepare individuals for future leadership roles by fostering progressive growth and development of the workforce. They also recognize that the organization's long-term stability mandates that succession planning and employee development begin years before individuals assume progressive leadership responsibilities.

CHAPTER SUMMARY

It should be apparent that effective performance management remains critical to organizational success. The commitment of employees, their development, and their ability to create learning and productive organizations require astute management of strategies. Thus, efforts that identify, measure, communicate, develop, and reward employees for their talent and ability result in productive outcomes desired by organizational leaders and the citizenry they serve.

Incorporated within this strategy must be an effort to develop meaningful performance evaluation systems that make sense to employees and are viewed as legitimate mechanisms for evaluating their contributions to the organization. This goal cannot be accomplished without the development of a culture that fosters honest assessment from raters trained in effective, accurate, and equitable performance evaluation. Achieving this outcome remains challenging. When achieved, however, the evaluation becomes a powerful tool for enhancing productivity as well as for creating a culture of trust and productivity within the organization's workforce.

KEY CONCEPTS AND TERMS

elements of an effective performance management system

endorser

goals of performance management: communicating with, rewarding, and developing employees

legal considerations when disciplining employees for poor performance

performance appraisal

performance appraisal methods: beharioral anchored rating scales (BARS), critical incidence, employee ranking, management by objectives (MBO), narrative or essay evaluation, rating scales, 360° performance appraisal

performance management

performance monitoring

rater error types: bell-shaped-based, central tendency, devil's horn effect, halo effect, leniency, personal rater bias, rater patterns, recency, stringency

PRACTICAL LEARNING ACTIVITIES

1. Discuss the advantages and challenges for both the organization and the individual employee when 360° performance appraisal is used to evaluate individual performance.
2. As a supervisor considering disciplinary action for an employee exhibiting less than adequate performance, what factors would you consider before implementing corrective action? Would your decision be influenced by the fact that the individual is an "at-will" employee as opposed to one with due process rights (as is generally the case for a civil service or union-represented employee)?
3. What concerns would you have about a performance management system that evaluated employee performance through a ranking system and then used this information to distribute employee merit pay increases?
4. Review the types of rater errors identified in this chapter. Which one do you believe most commonly occurs when evaluators conduct their assessment of individual performance? How do rater errors negatively affect future performance outcomes in organizations? What can organizations do to minimize rater errors?

REFERENCES

Boice, D., and B. Kleiner. 1997. Designing effective performance appraisal systems. *Work Study* 46, 6, 197–201.

Culbert, S. 2008. Get rid of the performance review! *Wall Street Journal*, October 20. http://online.wsj.com/article/SB122426318874844933.html.

Evans, E. 1991. Designing an effective performance management system. *Journal of Compensation and Benefits* (March/April), 25–29.

Geneen, H.S. n.d. ThinkExist.com. http://en.thinkexist.com/quotation/performance_stands_out_like_a_ton_of_diamonds-non/147012.html.

U.S. Office of Personnel Management (OPM). n.d. Performance management. www.opm.gov/perform/overview.asp.

7 Talent Development Management

All that is valuable in human society depends upon the opportunity for development accorded the individual.

—Albert Einstein

After reading this chapter, you will

- recognize that training and developing an organization's workforce is a vital investment logically linked to the organization's mission and long-range performance;
- gain insights about the distinctions between orientation, training, and development as key components of an organization's human resource development strategy;
- increase your knowledge of different methods of training and development that organizations employ to sustain employee talent and productivity; and
- strengthen your ability to evaluate the benefits and costs of training initiatives to increase organizational effectiveness.

In this chapter and book, talent development management (TDM) refers to sustaining and enhancing individual, team, and workforce knowledge. Other familiar alternative titles are training and development management or human resource development (HRD). Human resource (HR) professionals prefer the term "talent development management" because it signifies that the training and professional development of the workforce remain the responsibility of both employee and employer. TDM improves existing employee performance, while preparing workers for future workplace challenges. TDM stresses that it is not sufficient to train people for today's job requirements. It demands linking training (and development) with future organizational needs so that individuals (and teams of workers) can be better prepared to serve their communities. Today, it is fashionable to outsource and privatize municipal services. Often, this occurs in the name of efficiency. Such efforts may be necessary, especially in small governments that cannot afford or sustain employees' services on a full-time basis. Where necessary, governments move in this direction in the interest of conserving taxpayer burden. With existing civil servants, however, government has an obligation to establish and implement developmental strategies that promote organizational benefits through increased human capital capacities (i.e., by investing in the promotion of new skills, talents, abilities, and leadership potential) of city employees.

WORKFORCE EDUCATIONAL ATTAINMENT TODAY AND IN THE FUTURE

Chapter 1 discusses the "quiet crisis" growing in local government. Many baby boomers (i.e., individuals born between 1945 and 1964) will retire soon. A second crisis, "the skills gap," also frustrates the sustainability of qualified public workforces in local government. This occurs when a significant gap exists between the skills required to perform the job successfully and the existing educational attainment and skill levels among young new entrants into the workforce. Skills deficiencies appear particularly acute among young males and minority youth who are, or will be, seeking employment in the next decade. To add further pressure to this situation, future jobs will require even higher-order skills and better decision-making judgment. Thus, able-bodied workers will seek jobs that they are unqualified to perform as a result of their educational and skills deficiencies, while positions remain unfilled, begging for qualified new hires.

This situation becomes significantly bleak for high school dropouts. They will lack minimum skills and credentials to work in an increasingly complex and technologically advanced economy in which a high school diploma will be the minimum requirement for most jobs (Kaufman, Alt, and Chapman 2001). The consequences of dropping out of high school include lessened lifetime median income, higher potentials for unemployment, and worsened self-reported health. A disproportionately high percentage of dropouts end up in the nation's prison systems and as death row inmates (Laird, DeBell, and Chapman 2006). Furthermore, Laird, Kienzi, DeBell, and Chapman note in their research concerning U.S. educational dropout rates that approximately 30 percent of federal inmates, 40 percent of state prison inmates, and 50 percent of persons on death row are high school dropouts (U.S. Department of Education 2007). Future job applicants, without the viable skills to gain employment, will risk a similar fate.

Employers understand the significance of training employees as a means for future productivity outcomes. Training resources, however, remain limited for many governments and must be used wisely. Today, approximately half of the American workforce needs new training or retraining in order to maintain their job competency. In 2001, *Training* magazine reported that U.S. employers spent more than $54 billion for employee training. This figure would increase significantly if the study included military-related training. Training costs may be high, but by determining work deficiencies and providing effective training interventions, for both employer and employee reap benefits. The employer gains a more valuable worker with advancing job skills.

Employees also feel a greater sense of security and accomplishment knowing that the knowledge gained enhances their standing in the organization.

TDM involves a coordinated strategy designed to prepare, sustain, and develop the skills, knowledge, and abilities (SKAs) of employees (and workplace teams) for existing and future work challenges. The three key terms in this definition—"prepare, sustain, and develop"—are critically important to successful TDM. They relate to orientation for new employees, ongoing job training for existing employees, and future skills and leadership development for workers and teams. These three areas are discussed below.

ORIENTATION

Orientation prepares recently hired employees for their new work life. The goal is to increase individual job-readiness for the challenges that employees will face in their new jobs. Orientation programs also aid organizations by

- collecting vital information about the new employee not obtained through the selection process;
- educating new hires about organizational norms, rules, and behaviors; and
- providing new employees with information relating to workplace benefits afforded them as members of the workforce.

Orientation is a specialized form of training. Its significance and benefit to work performance often go undervalued in the organization. As a result, orientation training may be poorly planned, developed, and implemented. Progressive organizations take orientation planning seriously. They know, based on firsthand experience, that properly instituted orientation training is a vital component of the effective integration of new employees into the organization. Orientation training offers a powerful tool for welcoming and educating new employees. It helps bring new employees up to speed quickly. Immediate returns on investments often occur due to the new hires' increased understanding and awareness of the significance of their work as it relates to quality public service outcomes.

Job applicants often make the decision to join a new organization with scant information about its culture and other organizational characteristics. Thus, they question (and worry about) their decision until they begin to gain experiential knowledge that comes from being affiliated with the organization. New employees experience psychological uncertainty surrounding their decision to join their new organization. Poor initial impressions may lead to the premature departure of these individuals. Employers need to help new employees validate positively their decision to join, confirming that they made a smart choice. The sage old saying "You never have a second chance to make a good first impression" fits here. In the case of new employees, their first impressions confirm or refute their decision to take a job. Thus, those who judge that they have made a mistake are likely to depart (i.e., sever their employment) quickly, costing both the organization and the departing employee lost time and resources—a lose-lose outcome.

Orientation programs, when effectively planned and presented, facilitate new employees' positive first impressions. They provide valuable information and insights into the norms, rules, and expectations that guide and shape new employee behavior. Furthermore, orientation programs help employees validate that they made a wise decision to join the organization. Emotionally, new employees feel more solidly anchored in their operating units with supervisors and fellow employees who care about their needs and want to help them succeed. As Lowe suggests, "the new recruit's orientation experience directly contributes to that individual becoming a valuable and committed employee" (2006, 67).

Good orientation programs offer many benefits:

- providing positive first impressions for new recruits;
- aiding them to overcome new job anxiety;
- resolving initial fears of not being accepted socially by creating a sense of belonging;
- strengthening the recruit's understanding of how her job meshes with other jobs, thereby providing better and more productive outcomes;
- promoting affiliation as a part of the team;
- strengthening employee job satisfaction; and
- increasing the initial recruit's productivity by providing an expectation of work performance;
- clarifying organizational policies and rules related to on-the-job and off-work behavior;
- explaining health and benefits programs offered by the organization as a means for better family (or individual) planning and health care; and
- facilitating the collection of information necessary for federal, state, and local regulatory compliance.

GAINING AND SUSTAINING WORKERS' SKILLS

Training magazine's "Industrial Report" indicates that $55.8 billion was expended in 2006 for formal training programs. This amounts to approximately $1,273 per trainee (*Training* 2006). For comparative purposes, Clark and Kwinn (2005) suggest that the training expenditure (in 2004, reported as $50 billion) approximates Bill Gates's net wealth. Instructor-led classrooms continues as the primary training method for American workers. In 2006 this accounted for 62 percent of all formal training, with online, self-study programs accounting for 15 percent, virtual classrooms reporting in at 14 percent, and other methods claiming the remaining 9 percent (*Training* 2006). The nature of sustaining worker knowledge and capacity, however, is quickly changing, with the concept of training being replaced with that of learning, and the trainer's role shifting from lecturer or teacher to learning facilitator, coach, or mentor. The shift leans from instructor-led training toward technology-based learning. Figure 7.1 demonstrates the dramatic shift occurring over the past eight years. As Littlejohn (2006, 38) notes, the age-old model of "learn-then-do" is being replaced by a newer "learn-while-doing" model.

Figure 7.1   **Comparison of Instructor-Led versus Technology-Based Learning Hours**

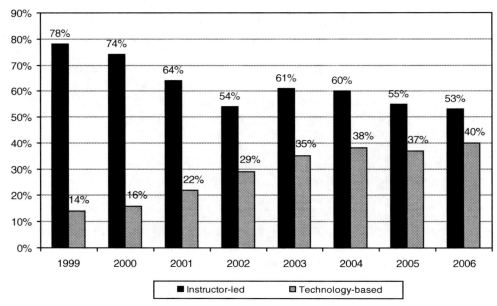

Source: Training (2006).

Training modes and methodologies adapt to take advantage of technological advancements, especially information technology via the Internet. Nevertheless, a number of traditional training approaches will continue in use even as change occurs.

TRAINING STRATEGIES AND TYPES OF TRAINING

Organizational training comes in a variety of forms. Some training styles appear formal while others provide a more individual and trainee orientation. The goal of training differs from that of employee development. Training increases individual skills, competency, and productivity in a worker's current position. Training is associated with the "here and now" scenarios that employees, as individuals and team members, face. It seeks to employ methods and identify strategies to enhance the individual's ability to function successfully in present work settings.

Development, on the other hand, is future-oriented. It seeks to grow individuals for future skills and leadership roles within the organization. Often, employee development provides individuals with a broad scope of activities. This helps determine a candidate's potential for increasingly broadened managerial challenges.

Succession planning seeks to identify talent and to prepare individuals for future organizational advancement. This helps organizations smooth out leadership transition and the vacuum it causes when leaders separate from the organization. Planning for change through organizational development makes smart business sense as it prepares tomorrow's workers to step into leadership roles when warranted. Further distinctions about development will be discussed in the next section of this chapter.

ON-THE-JOB TRAINING

On-the-job training (OJT) stands as the most common and pragmatic form of training employed in organizations today. OJT consists of the trainee working individually with a fellow worker or supervisor (i.e., the trainer) to learn by example and practice performing job tasks. Under this arrangement, the trainer works one-on-one with the trainee, demonstrating work-related responsibilities. The trainee then will replicate work under the observation and oversight of the trainer. Over time, as the trainee's skills mastery grows, the trainer disengages, allowing the trainee greater independence and decision-making discretion. Eventually, OJT ends with the now fully trained worker retaining control over task functions. In this instance, the OJT trainer continues as a source of assistance when the trainee requests advice or aid. OJT is one of the most cost effective means of training, primarily because the training involves high job content learning (i.e., training is directly associated with aspects of work). OJT also provides the opportunity for the new worker to gain significant social linkages to fellow workers through a one-on-one relationship between trainer and trainee. In many cases, OJT helps build relationships between workers, increasing social bonds and creating greater appreciation among team members.

E-TRAINING

As the technological capacities of the Internet have become more sophisticated, so has the ability of outside vendors to provide online training to U.S. organizations and their workers. In this instance, E-training refers to web-based or computer software training that workers can pursue either individually or in groups to gain new insights about their work and methods for productivity improvements. E-training specifically trains through computer programs or software that enhances worker knowledge or skills attainment.

E-LEARNING

E-training focuses on learning through a structured process via software or online training programs. E-learning occurs in a more personal, independent, and learner-driven setting. E-learners use the Internet and the World Wide Web to discover answers to their learning questions.

EMBEDDED LEARNING

Embedded learning provides answers for employees seeking to learn something specific about their work-related responsibilities or activities. With embedded learning, individuals gather Internet-based information and/or communicate with other learners (both inside and outside their organizations) to address work-related problems they face in their jobs. Embedded learning may occur through list server interaction, work-specific chat rooms, professional and job-related blogs, and/or the Internet as a means of discovering answers to pending questions. Using these sources, individuals gain new work-related knowledge and insights without the need (or costs) associated with formal training programs. Littlejohn (2006, 39) notes:

> Embedded learning is a completely different paradigm than the learn-then-do environment. It is the learning organization and leaders themselves who can have the most difficulty embracing this concept as their roles dramatically shift from content provider to content intermediary, thus ensuring access to a variety of sources in the best means possible. Now, more than ever, the learning professional has to possess a deep understanding of the work process.

SIMULATION TRAINING

Simulation training involves the use of models as a replication of working reality. Simulations of real working events can save training resources, strengthen workers' abilities, and allow for initial learning prior to tackling the actual working environment. One classic example of simulation training is flight training for pilots. Use of simulators safely allows pilots to prepare for future flights. Flight-related errors can have catastrophic consequences. Financial losses associated with plane accidents and trained personnel would be enormous. Litigation associated with flight path casualties would also be astronomical. Even with successful flight training, the overhead costs of maintaining planes as well as fuel costs for flight training are high; thus organizations seek to minimize these expenses through simulation programs. Flight simulation makes economic sense as well as constituting a socially responsible means for initial pilot preparation, training, and testing.

Another example, this one associated with local government, uses simulation training in law enforcement. Frequently, simulation assists police officers to develop safer driving skills needed when chasing fleeing suspects. Simulations associated with the use and discharge of firearms and other weapons can prepare police units dealing with dangerous criminals within closely confined areas (like housing and alleys). In this example, officers learn when to deploy (and defer usage of) firearms safely while under high personal stress.

Simulator training does not fully equate to real-life situations. Nevertheless, it often represents the next best means for training given the dangers and cost of action under true conditions. Furthermore, such training helps identify personnel lacking the emotional and cognitive makeup needed by individuals in high-stress situations. Such knowledge may allow earlier agency intervention, including the possibility of termination for those incapable of handling stressful crime scenes before they are placed in the field for action.

INTERNSHIPS

Internships serve as introductory employment training primarily for college students, nearing the end of their course matriculation, who seek entry in specific occupational fields. For example, some Florida law enforcement agencies encourage individuals seeking employment as police officers to serve first as interns. These training opportunities provide prospects increased cognition about law enforcement as a potential career choice. At the same time, it affords a potential employer the ability to assess an individual's merits for future employability. Internships most often consist of one-semester (term) working experiences that allow students to gain occupational insight and improved work socialization. Improved cognition about one's interest in pursuing a particular career often also increases as a result of the internship experience. Other student benefits derived from these programs include supplemental compensation (in many cases) while working as an intern, a strengthened network, and a potential mentor gained through the internship. Students gain valuable work experience that may place them in a more competitive position when they seek full-time employment within the occupational field. Employers also benefit from the fact that they can assess the talents and skills of the individual intern without the financial commitments and social contract considerations associated with incumbent employees. Postgraduate-level internship programs differ substantially from the internships mentioned here. In these cases, internships tend to be one to two years in duration.

POSTGRADUATE INTERNSHIPS

This specialized type of internship sequences interns through multiple functional modules: HR, finance and budgeting, planning, executive or administration. Broad-based training such as this assesses ability and prepares successful interns for fast-track integration into the intern sponsor's organization. Well-known and nationally competitive graduate and postgraduate internship and fellowship programs open to Master of Public Administration graduates include the following:

- The U.S. Presidential Management Fellowship Program (PMFP), formerly known as the Presidential Management Internship Program (PMIP)
- New York City Urban Fellows Program
- City of Long Beach, California Management Assistant Program
- L.P. Cookingham Management Internship Fellowship (Kansas City, Missouri)
- City of Phoenix, Arizona Management Internship Program
- New York State Public Management Institute (PMI) Internship Program
- City of Pasadena, California Graduate Management Internship
- Capitol City Fellows Program, Washington, DC

Internship opportunities abound for those individuals who seek to expand their horizons relating to their career field of interest. The quality of internship initiatives, however, can vary based on the quality of internship oversight and commitment of the sponsor to make the experience both challenging and educationally beneficial for the student. In far too many instances, students have been disappointed because their mentors were not fully prepared to challenge them with meaningful work. Internships should enhance the growth and understanding of functional responsibilities associated with the working environment. In addition, these experiences should provide students with a better understanding of how social and political contexts influence decision outcomes. Thus, sponsors must clearly understand their obligation and role in facilitating meaningful learning before obligating themselves as an intern sponsor.

COOPERATIVE EDUCATION

Cooperative education—as defined by the National Commission for Cooperative Education (NCCE website 2007)—is "a structured educational strategy integrating classroom studies with learning through productive work experiences in a field related to a student's academic or career goals. It provides progressive experiences in integrating theory and practice. Co-op is a partnership among students, educational institutions and employers, with specified responsibilities for each party."

Co-op training tends to last longer than internships, frequently comprising two separate periods when a student is immersed in a work setting, gaining additional knowledge about an occupational area. For example, a university industrial engineering student might spend the second semester of his second year and third year of college gaining work skills that complement his classroom training. The close linkage of education and work experience can result in synergistic gains in understanding aspects of the career he will soon enter. The transfer of classroom knowledge also is enhanced, because students understand better the relevance of the course content as applied to real-world working environments.

A number of American universities have established strong traditions of utilizing co-op education as a part of their curriculum. The University of Cincinnati and Georgia Tech, for examples, have long traditions of integrating co-op education into their students' learning process. Some institutions of higher education have made cooperative education a mandatory component of their curriculum requirements.

APPRENTICESHIP PROGRAMS

Apprenticeship programs constitute the third major form of cooperative training. Internship and cooperative education combine institutions of higher education (i.e., universities, colleges, community colleges, and vocational and technical schools) with local labor market employers. As the New York State Department of Labor (2007) notes:

> Registered apprenticeship training programs may be conducted by a single employer, a group of employers, or jointly by a union and employer(s), called a Joint Apprenticeship Committee (JAC). There are any occupations registered as apprenticeable in both construction and non-construction fields. Today, apprenticeship is expanding to health-related, new technology, high performance manufacturing, and service occupations.

In New York State, its Department of Labor apprenticeship program's website identifies more than 250 occupations where training opportunities exist. These programs offer traditional apprenticeship training for bricklayers, cabinetmakers, carpenters, drafters, electricians, heating-ventilation-air conditioning mechanics, ironworkers, machinists, plumbers and pipefitters, sheetmetal workers, welders, and many others.

Generally, wages provided to apprentice trainees fall considerably lower than journey-workers' pay, with a common range for first-year training between 25 percent and 40 percent of normal journey-worker pay. As apprentice trainees progress through the program, their pay is incrementally adjusted over time. For example, in a four-year program, the trainee's beginning pay may be 25 percent of normal pay, with increases to 50 percent in year two, 75 percent in year three, and 100 percent once certified as a journey-worker at the end of apprenticeship training.

Apprenticeship programs provide opportunities for individuals seeking occupations in vocational fields generally not offered through America's universities and colleges. These programs continue to maintain their support and popularity within occupational affiliated unions and are among the strongest justification for long-term union support within the rank and file. For individuals who do not wish to attend college, apprentice programs provide significant opportunities to gain a skill leading to a lifetime vocational career.

CLASSROOM TRAINING

This is the most traditional form of training that requires little explanation. Generally, this form of training is highly structured with an instructor (or trainer) and students. Classroom training occurs off-worksite and often may be totally separate from any employer affiliation (as is the case with formal education in schools, colleges, and universities). As noted above in Figure 7.1, instructor-led training conducted in American business and industry constituted about half of all training provided in 2006. As noted in the graph, however, the in-field training trend (which does not include, or account for, higher education classroom training) continues to lose ground when compared with technology-driven training. Some of the reasons for this drop in classroom utilization are:

- high costs for instruction;
- lost production time during training matriculation;
- costs for travel and lodging for trainee attendance; and
- concern for the merits gained through many classroom training experiences.

Increasingly, employers expect their employees to search for and discover answers to their training questions through self-discovery techniques similar to embedded learning techniques.

EMPLOYEE DEVELOPMENT

Employee development is a critical organizational investment, and one fraught with risks and losses on the return of one's investment. Moreover, employee development does not come cheaply. Thus, organizations must choose carefully about how to spend limited developmental resources. One increasingly popular approach aligns and links training and developmental strategies with the agency's mission and key goals. The Bush administration, for example, moved in this direction when Congress enacted the Federal Workforce Flexibility Act (FWFA) of 2004. This law creates greater venues for more flexible hiring, training, and developing in the federal workforce. For example, FWFA (Perez 2005)

- shifts pay request authorization from the Office of Management and Budget (OMB) to the Office of Personnel Management (OPM) as a means of recruiting and attracting high-level expertise within federal agencies;
- requires agencies to establish training programs and plans to meet strategic goals;
- mandates succession planning and managerial training for improving employee performance;
- allows agencies to compensate employees for time spent in travel;
- allows agencies to pay significantly larger bonuses and allowances for longer periods of time; and
- allows agencies to use nonfederal work experience to determine the amount of annual leave to grant an employee. For example, a desired candidate with extensive nonfederal work experience might be willing to join an agency if she would not lose comparable vacation or leave time provided by her current employer.

Employee development within local government continues to grow in importance, particularly with increasing concern about looming workforce retirements, especially among city managers. In 2007, the Florida City and County Management Association (FCCMA) launched phone-conferencing coaching sessions to mentor in-service employees and attract preservice MPA graduate students to city manager careers. As noted on the FCCMA (2007) website:

> Demand for local government talent in Florida has been growing and will continue to soar in the coming years as baby boomers retire. The FCCMA Coaching Program links volunteer seasoned professionals who are willing to share their insights and expertise with up and comers who want to learn and grow.

In 2004, 25 percent of Mississippi's Department of Employment Services 800 employees became eligible for retirement. Over the next five years (2004–2008) it anticipated that 300 employees might retire. To prepare for these losses, the department created "students of the business" training, whereby experienced employees served as facilitators, mentors, and coaches to prepare less experienced workers for future departmental leadership roles (Sussman 2006). Similar developmental training and succession planning strategies are growing in use in many state and local government agency settings.

EMPLOYEE MENTORING AND COACHING PROGRAMS

Mentoring employees through traditional coaching programs is a time-proven method to increase workers' skills and to facilitate employees' managerial leadership and development. It has become a key component for succession planning in organizations that seek to develop future organizational leaders. The strategy of matching experienced executive employees with less experienced but promising employees refers to traditional or formal mentoring. Such programs provide a number of benefits to the organization, including accelerating managerial advancement, reducing leadership learning time, and developing better decision-making skills in future leaders. In addition, mentoring facilitates improvements in the organization's managerial culture by creating dependency among more and less experienced managerial personnel.

In recent years, with the phenomenal advancement of technology, reverse mentoring has become more common. In this case, lower-level employees coach more senior-level staff. Examples of companies using reverse mentoring include General Electric and Procter & Gamble. In General Electric's case, more than 1,000 senior executives, including past CEO Jack Welch, participated in reverse training programs designed to enhance their Internet technology skills (Stone 2004). Reverse mentoring often keeps top managers and executives familiar with the latest managerial and technological developments.

Mentoring initiatives also provide organizations with the chance to instill corporate values and organizational ethical standards among the future senior managerial staff. Matching protégés with seasoned mentors provides a stronger sense of the kinds of actions and decisions that are accepted within the organization. Not only do protégés gain a better sense of strategies for efficiency and effectiveness, but also they gain insights into what is considered ethically permissible in the corporate culture.

WORKFORCE AND SUCCESSION PLANNING

Workforce and succession planning has become a more significant aspect of organizational development strategies in recent years. In part, this results from the anticipated retirement of older state and local government employees over the decades. In 1999 the Rockefeller Institute (Walters 2000) noted that 42 percent of the 15.7 million state and local employees would be eligible for retirement in the next fifteen years. Technology advances also have played a role as the job skills of today can rapidly become obsolete, forcing reconsideration of the skill sets needed for sustaining worker employability. Without planning and a strategy, public organizations fear that they will experience shortages of talent necessary to meet their missions and best serve their public.

Typically, the four primary steps of workforce planning consist of a supply analysis, demand analysis, gap analysis, and workforce strategic plan. Conceptually, the outcome of the first three steps provides a means for the development of the fourth—the workforce strategic plan. The formula is:

$$\text{Supply analysis} - \text{demand analysis} = \text{gap analysis} \rightarrow \text{workforce strategic plan.}$$

In order to develop the strategic plan, HR personnel need to identify the characteristics of the organization's existing employee pool (through a supply analysis) as compared with future needs (identified through the demand analysis). Comparisons of these two analyses result in the identification of workforce gaps, which predict areas of future workforce surplus and workforce shortages.

Supply Analysis

The supply analysis focuses on "identifying organizational competencies, analyzing staff demographics, and identifying employment trends" (Anderson 2004, 364).

Competency assessments require updated position descriptions with current job specifications. This information provides baseline knowledge of the organization and its staff. Demographic data provide key information about workforce characteristics. Does the workforce's composition provide for diversity in hiring and promotion for women and minority groups? Is the workforce aging—signaling the likelihood of increasing employee retirements? Will there be a pool of talent available to replace these retirees? Employee trends help the organization forecast such influences as employee attrition and turnover and rising human capital costs within the workforce.

Demand Analysis

The demand analysis assesses workforce needs within the organization as well as demand from other labor market competitors for workforce talent. A number of factors influence demand analysis, including increases and drops in the call for individuals with certain skill sets, replacement of human capital with technology, and generational demographics such as birthrates which may signal labor shortages. Demand analysis seeks to quantify the impact of internal and environmental changes upon the organization's future needs for talent.

Gap Analysis

The gap analysis provides information that allows HR planners to compare what exists today with what will be needed in future years. Outcomes from the gap analysis play significantly into future workforce stabilization strategies. Organizational strategic actions will be influenced by the knowledge gained in the gap analysis outcomes. Thus, when existing workforce supply exceeds projected future workforce demand, organizations can develop transition planning for the outplacement of surplus staff or retraining of employees to place them in positions of greater future need. When projected future workforce demand exceeds existing workforce supply, future shortages of staff will exist. The organization must consider strategies for retraining, hiring, or buying outside services in order to continue its work.

Workforce Planning

Workforce planning, which includes succession planning, frequently occurs when workforce gaps are identified. This type of planning strives to eliminate (or at least reduce to a sustainable level) the imbalances between labor force availability (i.e., supply) and needs (i.e., demand). As previously noted, the most common workforce planning approaches are

- planned recruitment and selection processes; and
- training, retraining, or purchasing (e.g., contractual hires or buying goods or services from other organizations) to sustain productive capabilities.

Succession Planning

Succession planning is a mitigating strategy to ease the stresses of lost leadership in an organization. It provides a venue for training today's talented individuals for tomorrow's leadership roles in the organization. Often, mentor-protégé and coaching strategies identify and prepare individuals for future leadership responsibilities.

EVALUATING THE BENEFITS OF TRAINING AND DEVELOPMENT

HR systems should work relentlessly to ensure that their training and development plans achieve effective and desired outcomes. Often this is not the case. One recent survey of new employees' attitudes indicated that "sixty-six percent of the workers think that the time spent in their last training session probably would have been spent better elsewhere." In addition, 12 percent of the respondents felt that the training was a complete waste of their time (Walsh 2006, 24). Ford and Weissbein's (1997) research found that only 10 to 30 percent of what is provided in training programs results in increased employee knowledge and skills. Similarly, Esque and McCausland's (1997) research found that less than 1 percent of trainees' new knowledge was retained following programs offered by one Fortune 500's training group.

Clearly, these types of learning outcomes are discouraging and create questions in the minds of organizational leaders about the value of training and the potential for achieving a return on their limited training and development dollar investments. As Martinez (2003) notes, in today's marketplace, training programs must demonstrate their cost-effectiveness and merits. Measuring such outcomes, however, can be subjective and often provides limited benefits in terms of training initiatives' impact on measurable performance outcomes. Examples of measurable performance outcomes include improvements in service delivery effectiveness, increased service delivery satisfaction, gains in service quality, enhanced workers' skills development, and return on investment (ROI).

KIRKPATRICK'S TRAINING EVALUATION MODEL

One of the most recognized approaches for evaluating organizational training performance is offered by Donald Kirkpatrick's training evaluation model, developed in 1959. Kirkpatrick's model measures training outcomes in four progressive levels, which are discussed below.

Level 1: Reaction

Participants rate their satisfaction with the training program, its instructional content, and/or the quality of instructional delivery. This approach serves as the most common training evaluation used to judge employee training initiatives. Its advantages include ease of implementation, with knowledge gained through participant survey feedback. Level 1 feedback also proves relatively inexpensive to acquire. Participants' reaction measured through their survey responses provides a general assessment about how pleased they were with the training and/or the trainer. Unfortunately, high subjectivity bias occurs frequently when using Level 1 evaluation. In addition, this evaluation method fails to provide information about increased participant learning or improved work performance as a result of the training provided. Without these linkages, organizations may waste resources in ineffective programs. The worst-case scenario might occur in those cases when training programs get positive feedback, yet fail to improve learning and/or performance outcomes. In these cases, HR units may exacerbate the problem by continuing highly rated training programs, believing that they have beneficial outcomes.

Level 2: Learning

This is a progressive step up from Level 1. Statistical testing seeks to determine the increased knowledge or skills that participants gained from a training seminar or workshop. Comparing test results can determine what learning (or skill) gains have resulted from the initial seminar or workshop. This testing method is frequently referred to as a pretest/posttest comparison. In many instances, test scores are compared with similar testing outcomes obtained from a group of nonparticipants (the control group) to ensure that improved learning outcomes have been derived from the training and not from other outside interventions. By measuring increased knowledge after training and comparing this with preexisting knowledge, evaluators can identify what, if any, significant learning improvements have occurred directly as a result of the training offered.

Level 3: Behavior

Kirkpatrick's Level 3 evaluation is a step up again from Levels 1 and 2 in terms of quality of measuring training outcomes. It seeks to determine if learning has been converted into practice in the workplace. As I like to say, "Knowledge for its own sake is wasted if not used to benefit individuals or achieve other desired outcomes." In the case of organizational performance, knowledge gains that are not used to provide beneficial outcomes for the organization indicate that knowledge gained through training is not being transferred into application at the worksite. Thus, learning gains that create behavioral changes in work performance will result in performance improvements and/or other desired outcomes (e.g., increased efficiency, higher quality, less waste through downtime or scrapped products, increased customer satisfaction).

The following hypothetical illustration should prove insightful. The Human Resource Department of Sunnyside, Florida, identifies an unusually high rate of back injuries in the Waste Management Department (WMD). HR determines that this high occupational accident rate results from trash collectors improperly handling rubbish and failing to use the recommended back support braces supplied by the city. The use of these back braces has resulted in decreased injuries in other cities' waste management departments. HR therefore designs and mandates training for all WMD in-field employees. HR measures participants' knowledge of safety procedures before and after the training. Evaluation surveys indicate positive feedback from the training, and tests scores show participant learning improvement. Once back in the field, however, workers do not wear their protective back braces nor practice safety standards. As a result, there is no significant decrease in the city's currently high occupational accident rate.

In this case, although participant trainees reported positive reactions to the training and although learning scores for safety procedures improved, the workers' behavior did not change, since they failed to put into practice what they had learned in the training sessions. Notably, the WMD in-field workers continued to ignore using their back braces as a means of protecting themselves against potential back injuries. Ultimately, the training was scrapped (no pun intended) as it neither changed workers' behavior nor lowered the department's high rate of occupational accidents and the health costs associated with these accidents.

Level 4: Results

Kirkpatrick's highest evaluation level measures direct work outcomes gained through the training. As Galloway (2005, 24) notes, Level 4 "provides tangible evidence that learning has occurred: it validates Level Two." Level 4 is the most valuable measurement for management "because it produces evidence that can be related to increased sales, reduced costs, increased productivity, improved quality, and lower overhead." Training outcomes that demonstrate tangible improvements in these areas strengthen HR's strategic claim to add value to organizational outcomes. Unfortunately, Level 4 measures are the most infrequently employed, particularly within traditional local government HR systems.

RETURN ON INVESTMENT EVALUATIONS

Recently, organization management, HR evaluators, and trainers have called for methodology strategies that extend beyond Kirkpatrick's four-stage evaluation model. Of particular interest to many in the field has been the increasing utilization of ROI evaluation modeling. ROI methods call for HR units to measure, in dollar terms, the benefits received against costs required to provide training initiatives. The bottom-line question for ROI training evaluation modeling is this: Do the results of training exceed the cost incurred to provide it?

The answer to this question will determine if organizations continue to direct resources for such programs. ROI training methodology in reality implements benefit-cost analysis as applied to training scenarios. Discussion about how to use ROI techniques to determine future training feasibility is presented below.

Determining Training ROI Outcomes

To evaluate training ROI, one simply collects and compares the benefits (B) derived from training against the costs (C) associated with providing such training. With this information, the ROI rate can be calculated to determine if sufficient benefits result. In addition, ROI increasingly is being used as part of cities' budgetary decision-making processes to determine which initiatives sustain funding and which get cut on the municipality's chopping block. An example of ROI is provided in Figure 7.2.

Figure 7.2 **Municipal ROI Training Evaluation**

In January 2009, the City of Sunnyside, Florida, developed sexual harassment training modules for its employees as a result of increasing litigation. HR also determined through outplacement interviews that sexually hostile working conditions directly affect the city's high turnover rates. An investigation determined that in 2008 Sunnyside had expended $350,000 for litigation settlements and associated new employee replacement costs. In early 2009, it implemented mandated sexual harassment training for all employees. The cost to provide this training, including lost worker productivity during training sessions, was determined to be $100,000. In 2010, sexual harassment litigation, turnover, selection, and new employee training costs resulting from sex harassment cases dropped to $50,000. Was the training investment worth the effort?

Answer

Losses due to sexual harassment cases (FY2008–FY2010)

FY2008   — FY2010 = litigation and other cost savings due to training
$350,000 — $50,000 = $300,000

Net benefit = $300,000 (litigation and other cost saving due to training)
Net cost   = $100,000 (costs associated with training)

ROI ratio = benefit/cost = $300,000/$100,000 = 3 to 1

Three dollars of benefit resulted from each one dollar of investment through this training.

As noted in this example, ROI analysis provides a powerful tool for managerial (and HR systems) decision-making. When used properly, it can demonstrate the merits of continued utilization of training in the organization. In many cases, ROI outcomes will not prove positive; that is, the cost of the training is greater than are the benefits obtained. This is good news, not bad news! Why spend limited resources on ineffective training outcomes? Unfortunately, many HR units shun the ROI concept because they believe that the reporting of negative ROIs will hurt their standing in the organization. In reality, this is often the case, primarily because HR systems do not view "failure" from a positive perspective. HR units need to use ROI techniques proactively to identify poor training initiatives (as based on the ROI ratio outcomes) so they can invest instead in training that adds value to their operating units. Thus, HR can report that it has scrapped ineffective training due to poor ROI precisely so it can reinvest in other training initiatives with better value. Being up-front and ahead of the game in an organization demonstrates that the HR unit values its (and the organization's) resources by making changes to enhance training-driven performance outcomes.

CHAPTER SUMMARY

This chapter has identified three primary methods—orientation, training, and development—for strategically enhancing individual, team, and organizational performance. These three components constitute the organization's TDM strategy.

Orientation programs often are the first type of training provided to employees. These initiatives prepare new workers for the challenges they face in their newly acquired positions. Orientation provides workers with a better understanding of their job roles and responsibilities and how their work fits with the organization's overall mission. In addition, orientation training grants employees a better understanding of appropriate and acceptable work behavior in their work units. Overall, this training approach helps create a sense of psychological stability for new employees as their working responsibilities commence. As shown by past research, orientation programs create opportunities for an organization to foster strong and favorable initial impressions of the working environment. Unfortunately, poorly planned and implemented orientation programs can do just the opposite, creating confused employees and increasing their concerns about their decision to join the organization. Thus, employees need effective orientation planning and well-communicated information appropriate to them. If this does not occur, the potential for the employee's premature departure will increase.

Employee training, among the most common approaches, enhances on-the-job performance of workers. As noted previously, training focuses on the immediate needs of work performance. It asks the question, "What training can we provide now that will make the employee more effective in his current position?" Many training approaches exist, with OJT training the most common form of training used in organizations today. With the advent of new technology have come high-tech methods for training employees. E-training and E-learning methods are proliferating in the marketplace and may, in the near future, be the most widely used method for employee training. HR systems must be attuned to advances in technology relating to training and, where appropriate, direct (lead) their organizations toward new training methodologies.

The final component of the TDM trilogy involves employee development. While training focuses on the here and now, development looks to the future. It seeks to answer the question, "How can we prepare today's employee for future leadership roles in our organization?" Development strategies must be tied closely to forecasted models of future workforce needs. Thus, workforce planning forecasts and succession planning outcomes often drive development efforts. Employee coaching and mentoring serve as leading methods for facilitating employee development and determining employee leadership potential.

Training employees, no matter which talent development approach an organization employs, proves expensive. Today more than $50 billion is spent annually on employee orientation, training, and development programs. Organizations need to know what works and what does not, so as to spend their limited training dollars on methods that lead to improved workforce performance outcomes. Two models are presented in this chapter: the Kirkpatrick four-stage training evaluation and the ROI analysis model. Kirkpatrick's model seeks to determine reaction to training, learning gained from training, behavioral improvements in work resulting from training, and whether or not training leads to desired work-related results.

The ROI analysis views training from the perspective of dollars invested. It asks, "Did we receive more than a $1 worth of benefits from the $1 worth of cost we spent to provide the training?" In simplistic terms, the ROI rate helps management (and HR) determine which talent development initiative should be kept versus which should be dropped.

Investing in talent development remains one of the most critical challenges for government, especially in these times of fiscal austerity. Those organizations that commit to sustaining development strategies often find their investment well worth the cost.

KEY CONCEPTS AND TERMS

employee development

employee mentoring

Federal Workforce Flexibility Act (FWFA) of 2004

Kirkpatrick's training evaluation model: reaction, learning, behavior, and results

orientation

orientation benefits

"quiet crisis" in local government

return on investment (ROI) evaluation

succession planning

talent development management (TDM)

training types: apprenticeship, classroom training, coaching, cooperative education programs, E-learning, E-training, embedded learning, internship and postgraduate internships, on-the-job-training (OJT), simulation

workforce strategic plan steps: supply analysis, demand analysis, gap analysis, workforce strategic planning

PRACTICAL LEARNING ACTIVITIES

1. Figure 7.1 reveals the changing trends in training technology, moving steadily away from instructor-led toward technology-based training. In small groups, discuss the advantages and disadvantages of each training modality. Under what conditions would you prefer to receive instructor-led training assistance as opposed to technology-based training assistance (and vice versa)?
2. Kirkpatrick's model for evaluating training, discussed in this chapter, identifies four methods for evaluating training effectiveness. In your organization (or this class when conducting teaching evaluations), which assessment approach is most frequently used? Why might this be the case? Which approach is least frequently employed? Why? What different training measurement approaches might your current employer (or course instructor) use that could result in better training effectiveness or improved performance outcomes?
3. Identify how simulation training might be used in training law enforcement officers prior to providing them with on-the-street training. In addition, what benefits might be gained for the police agency, police officer, and citizenry in using simulated training first?

4. The "quiet crisis" of local government is discussed early in this chapter. Some municipalities turn to succession planning to address this issue. Identify an organization in your local labor market and meet with its HR officer to discuss what, if any, planning it is doing to prepare for future leadership shortages. In your query, seek to determine if this organization perceives a looming crisis. Also, assess the effectiveness of its succession planning approach. Is it conducting any form of strategic succession planning? What TDM approaches does the organization use to prepare for its future leadership needs?

REFERENCES

Anderson, M. 2004. The metrics of workforce planning. *Public Personnel Management* 33, 4 (Winter), 363–378.

Clark, R., and A. Kwinn. 2005. Aligning training to business results. *Training & Development* 59, 6 (June), 34–39.

Einstein, A. n.d. ThinkExist.com Quotations. http://thinkexist.com/quotation/all_that_is_valuable_in_human_society_depends/188503.html.

Esque, T., and J. McCausland. 1997. Taking ownership for transfer: A management development case study. *Performance Improvement Quarterly* 10, 2, 116–133.

Florida City and County Management Association (FCCMA). 2007. Welcome to the FCCMA coaching program! http://fccma.org/coaching.

Ford, J., and D. Weissbein. 1997. Transfer of training: An updated review and analysis. *Performance Improvement Quarterly* 10, 2, 22–41.

Galloway, D. 2005. Evaluating distance delivery and E-Learning: Is Kirkpatrick's model relevant? *Performance Improvement* 44, 4 (April), 21–27.

Kaufman, P., M.N. Alt, and C.D. Chapman. 2001. Dropout rates in the United States: 2000. Washington, DC: National Center for Education Statistics, U.S. Department of Education. http://nces.ed.gov/pubs2002/droppub_2001.

Laird, J., M. DeBell, and C. Chapman. 2006. Dropout rates in the United States: 2004. Washington, DC: National Center for Education Statistics, U.S. Department of Education. http://nces.ed.gov/pubsearch/pubsinfo.asp?pubid=2007024.

Littlejohn, M. 2006. Embedded learning: Is it "learning" or is it "work"? *Training & Development* 60, 2 (February), 36–39.

Lowe, G. 2006. A proper welcome. *Canadian Business* 79 (July 17–August 13), 67–69.

Martinez, M. 2003. High attrition rates in e-learning: Challenges, predictors, and solutions. *E-Learning Developer's Journal*, July 14, 1–3.

National Commission for Cooperative Education (NCCE). 2007. The cooperative education model. www.co-op.edu/aboutcoop2.html.

New York State Department of Labor. 2007. Training guidelines. www.labor.state.ny.us/apprenticeship/general/TrainingGuide.shtm.

Perez, Marta Brito. 2005. The strategic value to agencies of promptly implementing the Federal Workforce Flexibility Act of 2004. U.S. Office of Personnel Management, January 25. http://spa.american.edu/isppi/documents/center_pres1_2005-01-25.pdf.

Stone, F. 2004. Leadership coaching. *Executive Excellence* 21, 2 (February), 5.

Sussman, D. 2006. Public sector training. *Training & Development* 60, 7 (July), 38–42.

Training. 2006. Industrial report. December, 20–32.

U.S. Department of Education, National Center for Educational Statistics. 2007. Dropout rates in the United States: 2005 (NCES 2007-059). http://nces.ed.gov/pubs2007/2007059.pdf.

Walsh, K. 2006. Time in training often wasted. *CIO* 19, 6 (March 15), 24.

Walters, J. 2000. The employee exodus. *Governing* 13, 6 (March), 36–38.

8 Compensation and Benefits Management

The real measure of your wealth is how much you'd be worth if you lost all your money.

—Anonymous

After reading this chapter, you will

- recognize the differences between traditional and holistic compensation;
- comprehend how both internal (organizational) and external (environmental) influences impact employee compensation;
- understand compensation and employee benefit initiatives, policy, and legislation designed to sustain physical health and mental well-being; and
- gain greater insights about mandatory and voluntary benefits that organizations offer to ensure their employees' personal security.

Compensation and benefits serve as core functions of human resource (HR) management. Both have direct or indirect implications for recruitment, appraisal, training, retention, and labor relations (Bowman 2010). Furthermore, obtaining financial security through a higher-paying job is a significant goal for young professionals entering the workforce. Sadly, focusing primarily on pay maximization is one of the most critical mistakes these individuals make when launching their careers. Referred to here as "pay tunnel vision," approaching work with only one goal in mind—maximizing entry-level pay—is a flawed strategy. In the process the individual potentially wins in the short run but often loses out on establishing a stable, solid career path in more promising organizations.

Compensation constitutes more than simply the salary workers receive for employment. If only one factor is remembered from this chapter (and hopefully this will not be the case), it should be that the wage or salary constitutes only part of the compensation provided to each employee. This point does not intend to demean the significance of receiving generous pay when joining new organizations. Clearly, that is important. What an employee receives in pay initially, when entering a career, influences future salary offers from competing organizations seeking to secure the

---

Box 8.1
Sample Case: Traditional versus Holistic Compensation

John and Jane Doe are married. Recently they graduated from college with accounting degrees. Each entered employment as a financial analyst for a different local government within the same metropolitan area. Both work in positions with relative good job security. John earns a salary of $60,000 per year while Jane's salary is $50,000. Both receive virtually identical pension plans. John's workweek averages seventy to seventy-five hours. Often he is required to work weekends with less than a day's notice. Jane works a forty-hour workweek and rarely is required to work longer hours. During her weekends she enjoys various non–work-related interests. John and Jane both have the same potential for promotion. Taking all other compensation issues as equal, which city would you rather work for if given the choice? The answer should be obvious—Jane has the better-compensated position. Her work is not all consuming as is her husband's position. Also, her organization allows her the opportunity for having a life outside of her work. Thus, the lesson to be learned is that one's compensation must be considered in more holistic terms, beyond the salary received. Factors such as workload demands, work flexibility, working relationships with superiors and peers, and better potential for balancing non–work-related activities against work demands all factor into compensation considerations. Workers should keep this point in mind when considering whether a new job offer is better than the position they currently possess.

---

employee's services. Compensation, however, involves much more than the yearly salary received in exchange for one's knowledge, skills, and effort.

The first half of this chapter discusses factors relating to the wages, salary, and work-related performance compensation. These factors of "pay" relate to tangible income received for work-related performance. For many employees, pay comes in the form of monthly or biweekly paychecks. Income through these means most closely relates to traditional (or classical) forms of compensation. The second half of this chapter addresses employee benefits and pension policies and practices that, along with pay (i.e., traditional compensation), provide an understanding of complete compensation. All of these elements considered together determine holistic compensation. Holistic compensation as a formula is expressed as:

Compensation = wages or salary + employee benefits + employee pension + perks + other quality of work-life factors

The case offered in Box 8.1 demonstrates the importance of holistic strategies when entering into compensation negotiations with prospective employers.

COMPENSATION AND COMPENSATION MANAGEMENT

Compensation management refers to the organization's efforts to sustain a competitive compensation position within its local labor market, given current and anticipated future financial resources. For governments, compensation management is complicated by the fact that while the organization seeks to take care of its employees, it also has an obligation to live within a reasonable budget so as not to overburden its citizens through rising tax burden.

The management of compensation requires financial leaders to anticipate current operating conditions based on the anticipated collections of revenues gained from year-to-year budget cycles. Municipal leaders also must take into consideration recurring debt obligations created through the approval of multiyear capital projects. Simply stated, most local governments cannot be overly generous to their employees because they do not have the benefit of deficit spending, as is the case in the federal government. Organizational leaders responsible for compensation management oversight enact and approve realistic annual budgets that support and sustain stable employment for municipal employees. Increasingly, local governments face challenges in attaining this desired outcome.

Compensation management also encompasses considerations of pay equity within and across organizational boundaries. Organizations must consider two types of pay equity when seeking to determine the fairness of their compensation plan: internal compensation equity (ICE) and external compensation equity (ECE). Both forms of equity are important to the effective distribution of compensation as well as the retention of valued employees.

INTERNAL COMPENSATION EQUITY

ICE ensures that employees possessing similar skills, knowledge, abilities, time-in-service, and responsibilities receive approximately the same wages. Also referred to as horizontal equity, ICE seeks to provide equity to others working at approximately the same horizontal level in the organizational structure. An interesting point relating to horizontal equity refers to pay offered in government relative to that offered by private employers. As Table 8.1 points out, contrary to popular belief, government service often pays competitively relative to pay offered in the private sector (Cauchon 2010).

Vertical equity, another significant compensation measure, refers to providing progressive increases in pay as an employee's level of skills, knowledge, abilities, time-in-service, and responsibilities increases in the organization. Thus, one would expect that entry-level municipal firefighters and patrol officers would be paid approximately the same (thereby maintaining horizontal equity), while entry-level firefighters would be paid significantly less than their fire chief (fostering vertical equity).

EXTERNAL COMPENSATION EQUITY

Organizations value ECE, especially in their attempt to retain highly talented employees. ECE seeks to secure approximately equivalent compensation levels with individuals who work in the same or a comparable position in other organizations. Primarily, ECE ensures that organizations pay their employees market competitive salaries as determined through comparisons with other similar local labor market positions.

Compensation studies monitor assessments of ICE and ECE. These studies help

Table 8.1

Occupational Compensation Comparison: Federal Government and Private Sector (in dollars)

Job	Federal	Private	Difference
Airline pilot, copilot, flight engineer	93,690	120,012	−26,322
Broadcast technician	90,310	49,265	41,045
Budget analyst	73,140	65,532	7,608
Chemist	98,060	72,120	25,940
Civil engineer	85,970	76,184	9,786
Clergy	70,460	39,247	31,213
Computer information systems manager	122,020	115,705	6,315
Computer support specialist	45,830	54,875	−9,045
Cook	38,400	23,279	15,121
Crane, tower operator	54,900	44,044	10,856
Dental assistant	36,170	32,069	4,101
Economist	101,020	91,065	9,955
Editor	42,210	54,803	−12,593
Electrical engineer	86,400	84,653	1,747
Financial analyst	87,400	81,232	6,168
Graphic designer	70,820	46,565	24,255
Highway maintenance worker	42,720	31,376	11,344
Janitor	30,110	24,188	5,922
Landscape architect	80,830	58,380	22,450
Laundry, dry-cleaning worker	33,100	19,945	13,155
Lawyer	123,660	126,763	−3,103
Librarian	76,110	63,284	12,826
Locomotive engineer	48,440	63,125	−14,685
Machinist	51,530	44,315	7,215
Mechanical engineer	88,690	77,554	11,136
Office clerk	34,260	29,863	4,397
Optometrist	61,530	106,665	−45,135
Paralegal	60,340	48,890	11,450
Pest control worker	48,670	33,675	14,995
Physician, surgeon	176,050	177,102	−1,052
Physician assistant	77,770	87,783	−10,013
Procurement clerk	40,640	34,082	6,558
Public relations manager	132,410	88,241	44,169
Recreation worker	43,630	21,671	21,959
Registered nurse	74,460	63,780	10,680
Respiratory therapist	46,740	50,443	−3,703
Secretary	44,500	33,829	10,671
Sheet metal worker	49,700	43,725	5,975
Statistician	88,520	78,065	10,455
Surveyor	78,710	67,336	11,374

Source: Cauchon (2010).

organizations validate whether or not their pay structures compete with other compensation programs. Many professional organizations and associations conduct annual studies for their membership. Two national associations, for example, conduct annual compensation studies. The Bureau of National Affairs (BNA) primarily focuses its attention toward evaluating compensation practices in the public sector. In like manner, the Society for Human Resource Management (SHRM) conducts annual compensation reviews for a number of private sector occupations. In addition, many local governments contract with management consulting firms to obtain neutral, objective assessments of their current equity standing.

COMPENSATION: WHY EMPLOYEES VALUE IT

Perception of the significance of pay and its ultimate purpose varies considerably among employees. For some individuals, the actual money received in their paycheck is critical for economic survival, while for others the pay received may not serve the same purpose. Nevertheless, compensation remains an important consideration for most employees, even as its meaning varies from one employee to another.

For some individuals, pay holds instrumental value. It affords the means for a desired lifestyle. Everyone needs financial resources to provide for common living expenses such as housing, food, clothing, transportation, utilities, and other life needs. Most people can recall a time when the ability to pay for these necessities went unmet with current income and savings, so it is easy to understand the value that sufficient pay holds for everyone.

For others, pay holds psychological value. It provides a means for sustaining personal and family security. In these cases, income acts as a shield to protect individuals and their family members from the stresses and discomforts associated with having too few monetary resources. With abundant resources in a savings account or other financial holdings, the individual feels a sense of financial protection in the event of personal tragedy, such as illness, loss of one's home through a natural disaster, or unexpected unemployment.

For still others, pay provides a scorecard or gauge for measuring professional growth and success in their career. For these individuals, it is important to know that they are "scoring" better than others, both internally and in comparison with others in the open market, in terms of pay received. Pay indicates relative success or failure in terms of professional growth. For others, pay serves as a means of boosting their egos. For individuals who consider pay as reflective of success, receiving less than the appropriate compensation creates significant internal stress, possibly resulting in a premature departure from their current organization.

Finally, for some, the intrinsic value they receive from work outranks the money obtained in a paycheck. For many people in the public sector, money, beyond meeting basic security needs, is secondary to other benefits resulting from work, such as the ability to make a difference in the community, serving others in need, love for the work itself, and/or a strong belief that what one does in his work adds value to the sense of community. These factors far outweigh pay as a driving force for higher performance, productivity, and continued organizational affiliation.

COMPENSATION LAWS AND ADMINISTRATION

Compensation administration involves technically complex issues, covering employee salaries, benefits, and pension laws and regulations. In this section, we will focus on some of the landmark legislation and laws that have shaped compensation practices.

Box 8.2
Wal-Mart Settles Wage Violations

Wal-Mart Stores recently announced a $54 million legal settlement for wage violations in the State of Minnesota. In doing so, it avoided potential fines of up to $2 billion. The settlement covers state law violations for mandated rest breaks for approximately 100,000 current and previous Wal-Mart employees working for the corporation between September 1998 and July 2008. In this case, Wal-Mart failed to provide mandated rest breaks more than 1.5 million times.

As a part of its settlement, Wal-Mart agreed to institute monitoring systems to ensure future compliance with Minnesota state wage laws and policies. If you think that this is an isolated incident, keep in mind that Wal-Mart currently faces more than seventy wage and salary lawsuits across America for violating wage and salary policies.

Source: Greenhouse (2008).

As will become evident from a discussion of wage and salary practices at Wal-Mart Corporation, the world's largest retailer, failure to abide by wage regulations can prove costly (see the Wal-Mart case in Box 8.2).

As observed from the Wal-Mart case, HR compensation administrators cannot simply focus their efforts on federal wage and salary policies. They also must keep in mind state compensation laws and, in some instances, even municipal ordinances that influence compensation practices. One point, however, remains constant with regard to following these laws and regulations. Organizations may face added complexities created by state and local compensation regulations, but in no instances can employers choose (at least without potential legal consequences and cost) to ignore federal wage and salary regulations in favor of state or local policies. Thus, "qualified" employers must provide covered employees a federal minimum hourly wage for work performed. Amended Fair Labor Standards Act (FLSA) legislation covers minimum wage laws. As of July 24, 2009, FLSA standards require employers to pay a minimum rate of $7.25 per hour to "non-exempt" workers (U.S. Department of Labor 2010). States can enact higher minimum wage laws, as is the case in fourteen states as of July 1, 2010 (U.S. Department of Labor 2010). Currently, Santa Fe, New Mexico, offers the highest minimum hourly wage rate in the nation, paying workers $9.85 per hour (Quick 2009).

THE FAIR LABOR STANDARDS ACT OF 1938

Virtually all aspects of workplace compensation incorporate significant discussion of the Fair Labor Standards Act of 1938. This landmark legislation provides the foundation for wage and salary administration and compensation standards and policies for most nonagricultural entities in the United States. FLSA policies protect more than 100 million workers, including full- and part-time employees in both the public and private sector (U.S. Department of Labor 2009).

The complexities of FLSA challenge even the most experienced HR specialist. Our discussion here cannot do it justice. FLSA applies to employees working for organizations engaged in interstate commerce. Typically, FLSA exempts family based agricultural concerns and small businesses with less than $500,000 per year in gross sales (when not participating in interstate trade). An example of such an exemption might be a local ice cream vendor with a seasonal business. FLSA typically does not protect individuals working as volunteers or as independent contractors. Thus, employers must determine which employees qualify for FLSA inclusion. The FLSA classification of covered individuals commonly refers to "non-exempt" employees. Non-exempt employees are protected by FLSA standards. By comparison, FLSA standards do not provide protections for exempt employees. Examples of occupations typically exempt from FLSA minimum wage and overtime pay requirements include executive, administrative, and professional occupational employees (including teachers) and outside sales employees (U.S. Department of Labor 2009). In some instances, employers may be exempt from offering overtime pay, but still may be required to provide a minimum rate of pay (or the equivalent, factoring in gratuities and tips). Occupations that exempt overtime pay but still require minimum wage payments include certain commissioned employees in retail or service establishments, railroad and air carrier employees, taxi drivers, and certain classes of auto and truck salespersons working for nonmanufacturing organizations selling items to ultimate purchasers (U.S. Department of Labor 2009). As shown here, FLSA can be position-specific. Thus, a thorough review of the regulations is required to identify whether a position falls into an exempt category. Generally, FLSA qualified organizations will have a mix of both non-exempt and exempt employees for which varying standards will be applied.

The most significant elements of the Fair Labor Standards Act address three primary areas—minimum wage standards, overtime compensation regulations, and child labor law policies and protections.

Minimum Wage

The current minimum federal wage for qualified individuals (i.e., FLSA non-exempt employees) is $7.25 per hour. Individuals receiving this wage rate will earn slightly more than $15,000 per year (excluding overtime wages), which in today's economy provides at best a modest quality of living. Almost half of U.S. states today pay more than the minimum wage mandated by FLSA. Nevertheless, the application and continuation of a federal minimum wage rate remains critical to guarantee a minimum wage "floor." Without it, there might be wide variances in hourly wage rates paid to individuals, especially in rural areas where labor needs fluctuate with economic conditions and where union representation often is minimal to nonexistent.

Overtime Compensation Regulations

Federal compensation law also requires employers to provide qualified (FLSA non-exempt) employees overtime compensation when they work more than forty hours during their weekly pay period. In these instances, employers calculate the rate for time worked beyond forty hours at one and one-half times the regular hourly wage rate. Clearly, some areas of exception exist where "comp time" (i.e., time off to balance the extra hours worked) can be provided in lieu of overtime pay. Public service positions such as police, firefighters, and public hospital nurses may work on different time schedules, as specified by FLSA. Employers must meet federal compensation laws, but once met they can provide overtime compensation of greater value than specified by FLSA. For example, it is not uncommon for employers to provide overtime for individuals working beyond their normal workday (i.e., allowing overtime for work performed beyond an eight-hour daily shift). In addition, employer overtime compensation rates sometimes climb higher (e.g., two times the normal wage rate) when employees must work on a holiday or are called into work during their vacation. Federal law does not specify extra consideration, but it may be granted based on civil service rules, union contracts, or policies specified in the organization's personnel policy handbook.

Child Labor Law Policies and Protections

Federal compensation policies under FLSA also protect children against overutilization (or outright abuse) of their labor. Fears about sweatshop abuse of children, concerns for child safety, and the desire to ensure that children have the chance to gain an education all influenced legislation designed to protect children under sixteen years old from excessive employment. Strict limits are placed on working hours when children under age sixteen work, especially during the school year. Generally, children cannot be employed in FLSA qualified organizations before the age of fourteen years. For children aged fourteen and fifteen, work permits must be completed prior to employment. During the school year, children younger than sixteen years cannot work more than three hours a day and no later than 7 P.M. States can impose stricter child labor standards. Florida serves as an example where children between the ages of sixteen and eighteen, who have not yet completed high school, face working hour limitations. When schools are in session, children in this age range cannot work more than thirty hours during the workweek. These children also cannot start work before 6:30 A.M., nor continue working past 11 P.M. when school is in session the next day. Florida's Child Labor Law provided some exceptions to this rule, primarily dropping these restrictions for students who already have married or who have served in the military (Florida Department of Business and Professional Regulations 2011).

FLSA also specifies limitations on the type of work that children are allowed to do. Individuals must be at least eighteen years old for employment in hazardous work environments. Working in a deli as a meat cutter or working as a miner are examples of occupational positions with bona fide occupational qualifiers under FLSA that prohibit children from being employed in such positions.

GENDER DISCRIMINATION IN PAY

Protections against discrimination in pay based on one's gender or ethnicity gained strengthened support with the passages of the Equal Pay Act of 1963 and the Civil Rights Act of 1964.

Nevertheless, with regard to gender-based discrimination, the Equal Pay Act (EPA) provided relatively weak protections for women in jobs of similar responsibility to men. As originally enacted in 1963, the EPA allowed for the consideration of seniority and merit-based performance factors when evaluating claims of pay discrimination. These provisions offered ample justification to continue to pay men more than women, even when performance outcomes did not justify doing so. This was especially the case when length of time in service was applied as a basis for pay differentiation.

Cases of discrimination were also limited through the EPA's regulation allowing only a 180-day filing period before imposing a statute of limitations. "Closed" pay systems do not allow disclosure of fellow employees' pay. Thus, discriminatory patterns of compensation often will not be discovered easily within the initial 180 days of employment. In these cases, there would be no legal remedy after the end of the EPA's statute of limitations. In addition, in those cases where discrimination could be proven, the law only allowed back pay coverage for the prior two years, even when the discriminatory actions occurred over much longer durations. These limitations proved to be litigation disincentives for labor law attorneys, who often chose not to take on cases of gender-based discrimination. Frequently, individuals who pushed ahead for legal recourse regarded the principle of social justice as more important than the monetary gain from their lawsuits, as the litigation costs often outstripped the awards granted through these judicial decisions.

On January 29, 2009, newly inaugurated president Barack Obama signed legislation authorizing the Lilly Ledbetter Fair Pay Act of 2009. This act amended provisions of the Equal Pay Act of 1963 and Civil Rights Act of 1964 by modifying the 180-day statute of limitations for filing equal pay lawsuits resulting from potential pay discrimination.

Lilly Ledbetter, the legislation's namesake, had worked as a production supervisor for a Goodyear Tire Company plant in Alabama. She claimed pay discrimination before retiring in 1998. In 2007—following the normal appellate process in the U.S. federal court system—the Supreme Court, finally acting on Ledbetter's complaint, denied her claim of discrimination on a 5–4 vote. The Court held that she had not filed her claim within the 180-day statute of limitations and thus ruled against her claim of pay discrimination.

The Supreme Court's decision subsequently became a polarizing issue during the 2008 presidential election. GOP presidential nominee John McCain favored the Supreme Court's decision, calling for the retention of the existing 180-day statute of limitations. Democratic presidential nominee Barack Obama favored revisions of the then existing statute. The 2008 election granted congressional control of both houses to the Democrats. Thus, it did not take long for the newly convened 111th U.S. Congress to vote favorably for revisions. Its decision, coming within a few days of Barack Obama's inauguration as president, "rectified" the Supreme Court's ruling in *Ledbetter v. Goodyear Tire & Rubber Co.*, 550 U.S. 618 (2007).

The Ledbetter Fair Pay Act of 2009 reset the statute of limitations with each new (discriminatory) paycheck, as opposed to retaining the date of the original agreed pay. Under the old law, individuals (primarily women) who had established employment years earlier and then remained with their companies and positions were prevented from claiming pay discrimination after 180 days, even though their discriminatory pay continued to the present day. Under the new Ledbetter Fair Pay legislation, individuals with years of past pay discrimination can now file suits (following the granting of standing through an EEOC right to sue permit) based on recently provided pay, no matter how long they have worked in their current positions.

Pay discrimination laws should continue to see modifications as more women enter and remain in the workplace. Generational differences will also put increasing pressure on employers to compensate equitably as younger employees—both women and men—leave organizations that do not tie income to demonstrated performance and productivity outcomes.

EMPLOYEE BENEFITS

Most individuals value compensation and consider it a significant employment factor. Organizations also face the pressure of granting benefits versus the challenge of containing costs associated with the granting of such provisions. Rosenbloom (2005, 3), for example, indicates that employee benefits "account for over 40 percent of an individual's total compensation." Even with such demands placed on organizational budgets, it still may seem difficult to believe that many organizations voluntarily provide benefits. Leave time, vacation pay, and medical and other health benefits are just a few examples of voluntary benefits granted by many employers that are not required to be provided by federal laws.

Most government and many private sector companies grant benefits to secure new talent or to retain current employees. Many experts believe that better benefits attract higher-quality job applicants. In addition, competitive benefits packages provide organizations the means to protect their valuable human capital investments. Employee separation, especially for key personnel, can be extremely costly to organizational productivity, creativity, service delivery quality, and performance. Thus, prudent employers, governmental employers included, must periodically assess the benefit package provided and adapt it in keeping with what other labor market competitors grant their workforces.

Effective benefit packages also allow employees greater opportunity to focus on work, knowing that they and covered family members have basic health and security needs provided through their benefit packages. Worker satisfaction also increases when organizations include significant program benefits.

Organizations also profit through the provision of employee benefits. One simple example can be seen (no pun intended) in granting vision and eye-care programs for the staff. Corrective eyeglasses or contact lenses for workers experiencing deteriorating vision often bring productivity gains and improve performance standards. Employee wellness initiatives also enhance performance outcomes. Numerous studies (Daly 2009) have demonstrated positive returns on investment for organizations providing these initiatives. Employee wellness programs in the long term often lead to reduced health costs and improved worker productivity as the employees' (and their family's) physical, mental, emotional, and financial needs are met.

TYPES OF BENEFITS: MANDATORY AND VOLUNTARY

Many, but not all, benefits provided to American workers are granted voluntarily. In this section we will focus first on those benefits that must be given to workers by law. We will then review some of the voluntary benefits that employers may choose to provide their workers.

Mandatory Benefits

Mandatory benefits consist of a group of provisions that employers provide because the law requires them to do so. What the individual employee receives varies based on the law's mandates, as well as the geographic area where the employee works. We will discuss only federally legislated benefit mandates. Nevertheless, state and local governments can pass laws affecting what benefits requirements are mandated in their jurisdiction, provided that these governments meet minimum higher-level government standards. Thus, as an example, Florida state government can mandate greater benefits for workers' compensation but not standards less than federal law mandates.

Among the most common security benefits mandated by law are unemployment compensation, Social Security—that is, Old Age Survivors and Disability Insurance (OASDI)—and workers' compensation. These mandated security laws originated in the economic disaster of the Great Depression of the 1930s. Today, these security benefits provide modest benefits to sustain a floor of protection against living in poverty by providing assistance when workers lose their job, retire from the workforce, or are temporarily or permanently disabled due to work-related injuries. These three primary security benefits are discussed briefly below.

Unemployment Compensation. Unemployment compensation (UC) was established in 1935 as a part of the Social Security Act. Its passage, then and now, provides subsistence provisions for individuals displaced from the workforce. Unemployment benefits are provided by state unemployment insurance programs utilizing guidelines established by federal law. State law determines eligibility, benefit coverage amounts, and coverage lengths (Doyle n.d.). UC benefits grant individuals modest compensation when they are unemployed, having lost their jobs for legitimate reasons (such as layoffs resulting from economic downturns or organizational failures that displace individuals from their jobs). Unemployed individuals seeking UC claims must demonstrate that they are actively seeking employment as justification for continued assistance. Traditionally, UC provisions cover individuals for a period up to twenty-six weeks. During times of sustained national economic downturns, like the near collapse of the U.S. economy in late 2008, Congress often has authorized coverage extensions beyond this twenty-six–week limitation.

The means for sustaining UC funding occurs through employer contributions as established through federal unemployment taxes (FUTA) and state unemployment taxes (SUTA). Presently, federal UC withholdings are obtained through a 6.2 percent fee paid by the employer from the employee's first $7,000 of earnings. It should also be noted that no direct payroll deductions come from employees' earnings to pay for UC premiums, although one might anticipate that this cost is factored in as part of the pay that employees ultimately receive. State unemployment taxes also apply the same current rate structure.

Old Age Survivors and Disability Insurance. In 2010 approximately 156 million workers paid into OASDI, commonly known as Social Security. This number accounts for approximately 93 percent of individuals in the workforce, either currently working for another employer or self-employed (Social Security Administration 2009b). Social Security came into being with the passage of the Old Age Survivors and Disability Insurance Act of 1935. Social Security started distributing benefits to qualified recipients on January 1, 1940. This program began as a social safety net for those who lost their life savings and/or pensions as a result of the banking and financial collapse during the Great Depression of the 1930s. Today, Social Security serves more than 52 million beneficiaries (i.e., people receiving monetary supplements) (Social Security Administration 2009b).

Social Security funding is provided through Federal Insurance Contributions Act (FICA) authorized payroll deductions, paid in equal portions (6.2 percent each) by the employer and employee. In 2010 the percentage of combined deduction is 12.4 percent of a worker's earnings, up to a wage base ceiling of $106,800 (Social Security 2009a). Payroll deductions end above this earning level.

Medicare also is a significant government administered social insurance program. Congress authorized it during President Lyndon B. Johnson's administration, as a part of the Social Security Act of 1965. It offers a medical and health care safety net through insurance reimbursements for individuals age sixty-five or older eligible to receive Social Security Insurance (SSDI) benefits. Individuals under sixty-five also may be eligible for Medicare if they are disabled and have received SSDI benefits for more than twenty-four months, or are diagnosed with an End-Stage Renal Disease, or are diagnosed with Amyotrophic Lateral Sclerosis (ALS), commonly known as Lou Gehrig's Disease (Medicare Interactive.org 2010). Like Social Security, Medicare requires the withholding of a percentage of earnings from the employee's paycheck that is matched by the employer. The 2010 tax rate is 1.45 percent for the employer and for the employee (resulting in a total deduction of 2.90 percent of earnings). However, unlike Social Security, Medicare has no ceiling limit, and contributions continue to be made with each additional dollar earned.

Social Security affords coverage for dependents under the age of eighteen when a qualified participant dies before reaching retirement eligibility. In addition, disability benefits are available for participants under the age of sixty-five when deemed totally disabled and unable to continue working.

Social Security was not designed to sustain a person's desired quality of life during retirement, but rather to supplement retirement income gained through other income sources (e.g., pension plan programs, personal savings, part-time employment). Unfortunately, many employees fail to grasp that Social Security benefits serve only as a safety net and do not provide full retirement coverage. This fact is worrisome, especially as society ages and enters into a period of increasing demands for Social

Security assistance due to the expected upswings caused by baby boomers' age-related retirements. Expected increases in recipient demands for services, coupled with Social Security's struggle to remain financially solvent, point to troubled waters ahead for American society. Difficult policy decisions will need to be considered over the next quarter century that certainly will displease recipients or further alienate individual wage earners and employers funding Social Security, if not both.

Workers' Compensation. Workers' compensation is the third major mandatory benefit requiring employer participation. The workers' compensation insurance program (commonly referred to as "workers' comp") is administered on a state-by-state basis. Thus, there tends to be greater variability in the benefits awarded as well as costs imposed. Generally, the rate paid by each employer depends on the record of claims sought by organizational members. Workers in accident-prone occupations with frequent injuries, like residential roofers, create demands for higher rate structures.

Workers' compensation programs provide insurance coverage for workers who suffer occupational-related injuries or illness. When warranted, workers' comp insurance provides coverage for medical, disability, and income assistance. In exchange for assistance, workers who suffer injuries resulting from their work give up their rights to sue employers.

Voluntary Benefits

Progressive benefits granted beyond those mandated by law (referred to here as voluntary benefits) provide organizations, public and private, with competitive human capital advantages in their local labor markets. Organizations, however, do have varying capacities to provide voluntary benefits, as there is no free lunch when finding resources to fund benefits programs. Sufficient resource capacity to offer competitive benefits packages, however, does not automatically mean that organizations will choose to do so. The organization's philosophy and belief about its moral responsibility to its employees' well being may impact positively or negatively its stance regarding provisions of voluntary benefits. An organization's history of granting competitive benefits may also influence positively its desire to continue offering such benefits. The goal of sustaining a desirable benefits package in comparison with competitors also may influence provision offerings. Some organizations believe that a strong benefits structure will fend off attempts at employee unionization, as the perception of limited benefits and protections might provide openings for union organizing efforts. Some organizations "educate" their employees that unionization might lead to the loss of benefits ("If you unionize, there is no guarantee that current benefits will continue") as a strategy for dissuading workers' support for union certification efforts. On the flip side, strong unions can pressure organizations to grant desirable benefits as a means of ensuring continued union workers' cooperation, productivity, and support.

Wide variation exists across benefit programs and payment-sharing plans for employees. Clearly, employees often prefer defined benefit plans (DBP) to defined contribution plans (DCP). DBP estimates retirement payouts on a formula basis, usually determined by the individual's pay history and length of employment. The higher one's salary and the longer one's employment service, the greater the pension payout will be when the employee retires. Historically, DBP have been funded through employer contributions without financial contributory participation by the employee. In recent years, organizations have been moving increasingly from DBP to DCP. DCPs differ from DBP, as the employer voluntarily contributes to an employee's controlled fund. Greater employee discretion over funding choices resides with the employee in DCP as compared with DBP, with some aggregate decision discretion allotted to the employee (e.g., whether or not to participate in a plan, which plans to select and offer, what the employer's level of contribution will be). In these instances, employers require some employee self-funding. Employers then contribute additional funds to the employee "owned" DCP. Furthermore, because employers now contribute to an employee's plan but do not in theory control it, employers may feel less obligated to continue support of such plans, especially during difficult economic times.

America's large organizations, those with more than 100 employees, customarily offer a variety of types of voluntary benefits. Some of the most common voluntarily provided benefits are discussed below.

Health Insurance Coverage. Group health and medical insurance demonstrates the most common form of voluntary benefits provided by employers. Estimates show that 85 to 90 percent of employers purchase insurance programs that are made available for their employees' participation. Within this category, benefits options might consist of prescription drugs, vision care, dental care, and mental health protections. Cost containment associated with continued health cost escalations remains among the biggest concerns for organizations when contemplating the benefits package that can be afforded for their employee pool. In addition, organizational workforce aging (as median age rises) and recent health services expenditures also influence health program costs and rising premiums. In an effort to stem rising health-care costs, some organizations utilize self-insured approaches. In these cases, the organization sets aside a pool of resources to cover "normal" medical care provisions provided to its employees. Often, such self-insured companies will also carry catastrophic medical coverage for unusually significant medical care costs associated with major illnesses. In these instances, once a covered member meets the threshold cost (e.g., once an employee's medical cost reaches $100,000 in any given policy coverage year), further yearly service reimbursements will be provided by an insurance company or underwriter as opposed to the employee's organization.

Health-care coverage may come from health maintenance organizations (HMOs), preferred provider organizations (PPOs), or other possible coverage arrangements that share and/or shift the burden from employer to employee (e.g., increased employee copayment responsibilities) (Reddick and Coggburn 2007).

Health Maintenance Organizations. HMOs have grown in popularity in recent years. Health policy experts view the HMO as the first real attempt to manage health care. It differs from traditional health-care approaches in its effort to reduce ultimate medical costs through preventive care as well as employee wellness (Mahoney 2005). As a means of reducing long-term health-care costs, HMOs more frequently utilize employee wellness, health-care screening, and immunization programs as compared to traditional health-care systems that act to "cure the patient" once declining health is identified. In addition, HMOs contain costs by deciding where the patient receives medical care, who should provide the care, and whether or not medical procedures are even needed. Utilization of family health-care physicians and general health-care practitioners (as opposed to field board-certified specialist physicians) provides a primary means for containing overall health-care outlays. One final distinction between the HMO and other forms of health care concerns fees provided in exchange for services granted. Organizations generally establish contract cost guidelines with the HMO, whereby one annual cost covers members' (and/or family members') health-care services. Thus, organizations know fairly well their annual outlays for health coverage and can factor these costs into their annual operating budgets. With more traditional pay-for-services health-care systems, the ability to contain costs becomes much more difficult; traditional coverage offers more discrete service provisions as opposed to blanket unit cost coverage for all health service provisions seen in an HMO.

Preferred Provider Organizations. PPOs comprise a group of medical providers (e.g., a hospital, medical group, insurance company) that offer varied medical care to one or more organizations (Mahoney 2005). The medical service provider is reimbursed on a fee-for-service basis as opposed to being paid a predetermined contractual amount for all services provided during the coverage period. PPOs typically provide individuals greater choice and discretion among health-care providers, as members can select associated medical providers for their medical services. In addition, since reimbursement depends on a fee-for-service basis, the level of pressure to limit health services (in order to remain profitable) lessens compared to HMO providers. Nevertheless, the determination of services granted is often determined by one's budget (for both organization and employee). HMOs are often less expensive for both employer and employee, but provide less discretion (and possibly say) about the services granted as compared with PPO systems.

Pension Plan Coverage. Workers highly value employee pension plans. These plans remain one of the most desired benefit provisions granted to workers. Clearly, with concerns over the future viability of Social Security, their importance will grow for younger workers.

Pension plans provide income for individuals during their retirement years. Thus, they serve to maintain one's preretirement lifestyle as well as offer income security to help offset likely increases in cost-of-living expenses that might otherwise be recouped if employed. The 401(k) plans and individual retirement accounts (IRAs) remain among the most commonly offered pension plan options. Generally employees prefer DBP, with their employer funding the pension costs and using a formula that provides retirement compensation levels based on their highest income earned and years of service. Defined contribution programs, however, are growing in application as employers seek to shift the burden toward employee self-funding, "ownership," and individual decision-making discretion over how pension resources are managed.

Paid Time Off, Paid Vacation, and Sick Leave. As previously noted, employers voluntarily offer time off as an incentive to attract, maintain, or reinvigorate individuals in their workforce. This section discusses three types of leave—paid time off (PTO), vacations, and sick leave. Traditionally in America, PTO has referred to work holidays provided to celebrate national or religious holidays. The most common national and religious holidays are New Year's Day, Christmas, Labor Day, Thanksgiving, Independence Day, Martin Luther King Day, Memorial Day, and Veterans Day. On average, employees receive ten days of holiday leave annually. Paid vacation leave also may vary significantly across organizations. In many instances, employees with one year of work will qualify for five days of vacation leave. As one's years of employment or service to the organization increase, so will the time granted for vacation leave time. For example, employees with five to ten years of continuous service might be granted two weeks (ten days) of paid vacation leave, those with eleven to twenty years of service three weeks (fifteen days) of paid vacation leave. It is less common for American workers to be granted more than four weeks of paid vacation leave, even with decades of employment service.

Sick leave is the final category discussed here. Taking sick leave remains among the most criticized form of leave granted by employers, as worker abuse (i.e., claiming time off due to illness when not sick) is common. Often the number of hours worked by the individual determines the granting of sick leave. For example, an employer might grant four hours of sick leave time for each eighty hours of work over a two-week pay period. Using this formula, individuals would accrue approximately 104 hours of sick leave per year (about thirteen sick leave days). Ideally, individuals use this leave for justified sick leave purposes, although cases of abused leave can be common in this area.

Work-Life Balance Benefits. Work and home life balance demands concern many employees. Balancing work demands against family responsibilities creates stress for individuals who want fulfilling career work but not at the expense of family life. Clearly, younger employees (digital generation members born after 1980 in particular) factor in employer work-life benefits and policies when choosing whom to work for and to remain with over time. Retention is critical, especially for knowledge workers (those individuals whose employment is critical to the continued creative success of their agencies), and can hinge on the quality of benefits provided in this category.

Examples of work-life benefits include child-care assistance, elder-care provisions, flexible work scheduling, employee assistance programs (EAPs), and employee wellness programs.

Childcare assistance serves as a mainstay of the American workforce benefits package in progressive organizations. Workers value childcare assistance, especially among younger families where, since about 1975, increasing numbers of women with children have entered and continued in the workforce. Recently, the U.S. Bureau of Labor Statistics indicated that 59 percent of women now work outside the home (or are actively seeking employment). For working mothers with children aged seventeen or younger, this statistic jumps to 66 percent (capturing both full- and part-time participation) (Parker 2009). U.S. lawmakers' awareness of demands for diverse benefits appears to be growing due to the changing workplace. The Patient Protection and

Affordable Care Act (PPAC) of 2010 best exemplifies this change. With this legislation's approval, nursing mothers in organizations with fifty or more employees must be provided reasonable work breaks any time up to one hour at a time. Break times may be unpaid, however, if occurring during work time. In addition, employers must provide a place (other than a restroom) shielded from view and free from intrusions where the nursing mother can express her milk (Barbieri 2010). Nursing mothers gain protection under this law during their first year of lactation, following childbirth.

Interest among workers for elder-care assistance (programs affording assistance to families with aging parents) has grown in America. The Social Security Administration estimates that the number of Social Security Old Age and Survivors Insurance beneficiaries per 100 workers will increase from 25 beneficiaries in 2000 to 26 in 2010, 32 in 2020, and 39 in 2030 (Smith and Toder 2005). Clearly, organizational benefit packages will adapt to meet the growing demands for elder-care provisions as society ages over the next two decades.

Flexible working schedules and telecommuting arrangements are strategies that employers offer to allow discretion among workers for balancing family responsibilities against the demands to maintain individual productive capacity. Flextime allows individuals to tailor their workdays to fit collective work and family responsibilities. Workers are expected to attend work during core periods (typically 10 A.M. through 3 P.M.), but they can adjust their work schedules to arrive earlier for work or remain later at work. For example, one employee might work from 6 A.M. to 3 P.M. while another may choose to work on-site from 10 A.M. to 7 P.M. Clearly, this arrangement has limits. The nature of working responsibilities, the need for face-to-face interaction between employees and customers, the organization's ability to accommodate flexible work schedules, and the number of facility shifts, such as one-shift (8 A.M. to 5 P.M.) versus three-shift (round-the-clock) operation, all must be considered.

Telecommuting allows workers to work from home—during all or part of their workweek. The benefits to the employee include decreased commuting time, flexibility, and personal convenience. Unfortunately, isolation from work and social interactions with supervisors and fellow workers might result. Often telecommuting employees spend part of their workweek on-site in order to sustain better knowledge and awareness of workforce influences that they might miss if totally separated from office dynamics. In addition, some concern exists that out-of-sight employees may not be granted similar opportunities for promotion as regular on-site employees. Thus, maintaining some face validity with the organization is important to individual growth and advancement. Organizations also benefit from telecommuting arrangements as often telecommuters prove to be more productive than on-site workers. In addition, reduced capital expenditures for dedicated office space and other operational cost savings may result.

The last work-life benefits categories discussed here are employee assistance programs (EAPs) and employee wellness programs (EWPs). EAPs began in the late 1930s as an outgrowth of efforts to address alcohol abuse and alcoholism in America's workforce (Daly 2009). Over time, EAPs grew to encompass drug abuse and other challenges facing employees (such as family and marital problems, nicotine addiction, personal finances). EWPs often cover those areas associated with EAPS, but also expand programs to sustain the health and well being of the workforce as opposed to dealing with problems once they arise. In this regard, EWPs might also provide health club facilities (or subsidies for joining such clubs), health screening programs, nutritional educational initiatives, stress reduction training, team athletic sports, and other related programs. These create opportunities for maintaining or increasing personal and health fitness within the workforce. EWPs cost-benefit research frequently finds a positive benefit return on the costs of such programs, thereby reducing financial outlays for health insurance as workers become healthier individuals.

KEY BENEFITS LEGISLATION

A myriad of legislation has been enacted in recent years to protect individuals' privacy as well as to ensure the integrity and fiscal soundness of benefits resources being set aside for employee retirement programs. Efforts to protect individuals against unethical misapplication of and illegal misappropriations of benefits monetary reserves, as in the case of Enron have resulted in increased mandated policies and protections. By 2001 when its fraudulent accounting practices were disclosed, Enron, a Texas energy corporation, had grown into America's seventh largest corporation employing 21,000 in more than 40 countries. Enron executives lied about corporation profits and concealed debt from its company's accounting reports (BBC 2002). Disclosure of its practices resulted in the largest U.S. corporate bankruptcy at that time, with losses of $50 billion for investors. In addition, Enron's bankruptcy left more than 20,000 of Enron's former employees and retirees participating in the company's pension and 401(k) retirement plans, with $1 billion in benefits losses (Iwata 2006). Actions of Enron, and more recently America's 2008 banking collapse have resulted in calls for increased mandated policies and protections. In addition, recent legislative initiatives provide regulatory guidelines for the application and practice of benefits administration. Five of the most important laws influencing benefits administration and practices are discussed briefly below. Clearly, this group serves only as a sampling of the legislative challenges facing benefits managers as they strive to administer programs and policies within their organizations.

Employee Retirement Income Security Act of 1974 (ERISA)

Approved in 1974, ERISA regulates private pension plans to ensure that funds placed in private pension plans are available when workers retire. In addition, ERISA mandates that employers who offer retirement plans provide their pension plan to all qualifying employees, not just selected individuals. Under ERISA standards, the Internal Revenue Service (IRS) can impose penalties for organizations failing to fund such pension offerings adequately. The goal of ERISA is to ensure the integrity of pension plans as well as to provide protections against misappropriations of pension plan resources. The act provides a modicum of protection for employees as they prepare for a financially secure life after work.

The Consolidated Omnibus Budget Reconciliation Act of 1985 (COBRA)

As it relates to benefits provisions, COBRA offers displaced employees and family members the opportunity to continue medical insurance following the loss of the employee's job. In these instances, the organization maintains former employees on its health insurance plan, although they are required to pay the health insurance premiums themselves. Generally, COBRA allows employees to maintain insurance coverage due to loss of employment for eighteen months. Under COBRA legislation, a spouse and dependent children who experience a second qualifying event may have their coverage extended for up to thirty-six months. Second qualifying events, as specified by the U.S. Department of Health and Human Services "may include the death of the covered employee, divorce or legal separation from the covered employee, the covered employee becoming entitled to Medicare benefits (under Part A, Part B or both), or a dependent child ceasing to be eligible for coverage as a dependent under the group health plan" (U.S. Department of Health and Human Services n.d., n.p.).

In 2009 Congress enacted the American Recovery and Reinvestment Act (ARRA), which mandated that 65 percent of federal COBRA group health continuation premium subsidies be paid by COBRA covered employers. Employers in return were granted increased tax deduction benefits. The ARRA subsidy mandate was designed with a sunset clause and expired on May 31, 2010. As of October 2010, ARRA has not been reenacted. Therefore, as was the case prior to ARRA, COBRA recipients pay all health coverage costs (in addition to a 2 percent administrative fee) for employer-sponsored health coverage to continue benefits. Thus, COBRA recipients again pay full coverage costs (102 percent of the true medical insurance cost) to receive health insurance, rather than a cap of 35 percent as was the case during ARRA's existence (Bell 2010).

The Family and Medical Leave Act of 1993 (FMLA)

Congressional approval of the Family and Medical Leave Act in 1993 reflected increased public opinion and union pressures to grant workers greater flexibility to care for personal family and medical needs. As the U.S. Department of Labor (n.d.) notes:

> FMLA applies to all public agencies, all public and private elementary and secondary schools, and companies with 50 or more employees. These employers must provide an eligible employee with up to 12 weeks of unpaid leave each year for any of the following reasons:
>
> - for the birth and care of the newborn child of an employee;
> - for placement with the employee of a child for adoption or foster care;
> - to care for an immediate family member (spouse, child, or parent) with a serious health condition; or
> - to take medical leave when the employee is unable to work because of a serious health condition.

During the last quarter of the twentieth century, the age and gender composition of the U.S. workforce changed. Increasingly, women entered and remained in the workforce. This created increased pressures on families in their efforts to balance work demands against family responsibilities. Improved longevity of elderly parents (and in some cases even grandparents) needing greater support from their children also influenced public policy relating to granting unpaid leave to care for family and/

or personal medical needs. Absent public policy mandating qualified leave, many businesses would not grant such time away from work (even unpaid absences). With FLMA, however, the law provides improved leave flexibility and affords greater protections against job loss for employees who need to care for documented family and medical needs.

Congress, realizing that FMLA would place hardships on small organizations, authorized that FLMA apply only to organizations with fifty or more full-time employees. In addition, employees seeking FMLA coverage do not qualify unless they have completed at least 1,250 hours of work during the past year. Furthermore, employees must request leave with thirty days prior notice (absent unforeseen emergencies). Two employees who are married to each other and work in the same organization qualify as one family unit and jointly share leave time (i.e., twelve weeks per year).

In 2008, Congress—through its passage of the National Defense Authorization Act—extended FMLA leave for up to twenty-six weeks per year to military personnel injured during military service or to family caregivers assisting them during their convalescence.

At the employer's discretion, employees may be required to use all existing vacation and sick leave time and simultaneously clock this leave as FMLA leave. Thus, an employee who has accrued six weeks of leave time may be required to take this time off and have it also counted as half of the twelve-week FMLA leave.

FLMA policies also allow organizations to identify 10 percent of their workforce as key employees, thereby excluding them from FMLA leave consideration. For example, a city manager with a seriously ill parent might be excluded by her city council from taking FMLA leave, provided this position has previously been identified as an FMLA key employee exception. Under these conditions, the city council may deny the FMLA leave request.

Uniformed Service Employment and Reemployment Rights Act (USERRA)

Enacted in 1994 by the Clinton administration, USERRA serves to protect civilians' employment rights and benefits for individuals serving in limited military service positions, such as military reservists and National Guard members. USERRA covers virtually all employers, including federal, state, and low governments. It requires employers to reemploy returning service personnel in the position and with the benefits that they would have had (including likely promotions and pay increases) had they not been called up for active duty. Employers must maintain employment protections for called-up service members for up to five years, with additional extensions and accommodations provided for special needs groups—such as disabled returning veterans.

The Health Insurance Portability and Accountability Act of 1996 (HIPAA)

As related to benefits administration, HIPAA created increased provisions to protect the security and privacy of health-related information. This law, administered by the U.S. Department of Health and Human Services, regulates who should have access to information associated with one's health and medical records and how that access would be protected. In an era of virtually universal accessibility of medical data, the privacy rights of the individual easily could be abridged. Under HIPAA's privacy rule, organizations with access to health information, such as health insurers, employers with health plans, medical service providers, and pharmacies, must follow stringent regulations designed to prevent the unlawful dissemination of individual medical records. HIPAA thus minimizes the potential for unwarranted use and abuse of such information.

Chapter Summary

As is evident from this chapter, compensation management and benefits administration are vitally important to both employer and employee. Keep in mind that we have only scratched the surface of the issues, as the policies and regulations in these two areas tend to be voluminous. That might explain why large organizations (local governments included) often hire experts specializing in compensation and benefits administration.

Local municipal leaders must carefully weigh multiple interests when making decisions affecting the application of local government compensation and benefits administration. On the one hand, city leaders must consider how much they can afford to provide for their employees. Leaders realize that inadequate compensation and benefits provisions will result in lessened interest on the part of better qualified applicants, shorter-term retention of existing employees, and high costs associated with increased turnover (especially in the areas of recruitment/selection and training/development replacement costs). On the reverse side of the equation, local governments must also consider how much burden can be placed on the taxpaying citizens who ultimately fund these programs through their tax dollars.

Key Concepts and Terms

American Recovery and Reinvestment Act (ARRA) of 2009

catastrophic medical coverage

childcare

child labor law policies and protections

closed and open pay systems

compensation management

compensation studies

Consolidated Omnibus Budget Reconciliation Act (COBRA) of 1985

defined benefits plans (DBPs)

defined contribution plans (DCPs)

elder care

elements of compensation: benefits, pay, pension, perks, work-life factors

employee assistance programs (EAPs)

employee Retirement Income Security Act (ERISA) of 1974

employee wellness programs (EWPs)

Equal Pay Act (EPA) of 1963

exempt employees

external compansation equity (ECE)

Fair Labor Standards Act (FLSA) of 1938

Family Medical and Leave Act (FMLA) of 1993

Health Insurance Portability and Accountability Act (HIPAA) of 1996

health maintenance organization (HMO)

holistic compensation

horizontal equity

internal compensation equity (ICE)

Lilly Ledbetter Fair Pay Act of 2009

mandatory benefits: Old Age Survivors and Disability Insurance (OASDI), unemployment compensation (UC), workers' compensation

meaning of compensation: growth indicator, instrumental value, psychological value

Medicare

minimum wage

non-exempt employees overtime

paid time off (PTO)

Patient Protection and Affordable Care Act (PPAC) of 2010

pay tunnel vision

preferred provider organizations (PPO)

security benefits

self-insured companies

sick leave

Social Security

telecommuting

traditional compensation

Uniformed Service Employment and Reemployment Rights Act (USERRA) of 1994

vacation pay

vertical equity

voluntary benefits

work-life balance benefits

PRACTICAL LEARNING ACTIVITIES

1. The instructor will separate class members into small groups of three to five students for this exercise. Team members will be identified as "pro-FLSA" and "anti-FLSA" proponents. Depending on your team's stance, discuss why the Fair Labor Standards Act regulations should or should not be maintained. Identify five to seven points that justify the retention or repeal of FLSA.
2. Review the results of Table 8.1 in this chapter. Wage comparisons point to evidence that compensation in the federal government often is better than that offered through private industry. What might explain this surprising finding?
3. Early in the chapter the concept of "pay tunnel vision" is discussed, indicating that many young professionals choose employment positions based only, or almost only, on the pay. What other forms of compensation, in addition to salary, should job prospects consider when deciding which job offer to accept?
4. If given the opportunity to choose between a DBP and a DCP, which type of pension would you select? Why?
5. Select a large organization in your local labor market that you believe offers progressive benefits to its employees. Review this organization's benefits plan and assess the extent to which it offers work-life benefits versus more traditional benefits. What, if anything, in this company's benefits plan appears to be an innovative benefit that might attract job prospects?

REFERENCES

Anonymous. 2008. The Quote Garden. www.quotegarden.com/money.html.
Barbieri, C. 2010. Federal heath care law provides for breaks for nursing mothers. FLMA Blog, March 31. http://fmla.foxrothschild.com/tags/patient-protection-and-afford.
BBC News. 2002. Enron scandal-at-a-glance. http://news.bbc.co.uk/2/hi/business/1780075.stm.
Bell, A. 2010. Expired COBRA subsidy gets mixed reviews. *National Underwriter Life & Health*, August 11. www.lifeandhealthinsurancenews.com/News/2010/8/Pages/Expired-COBRA-Subsidy-Gets-Mixed-Reviews.aspx.
Bowman, J. 2010. The success of failure: The paradox of performance pay. *Review of Public Personnel Administration* 30, 1 (March), 70–88.

Cauchon, D. 2010. Federal pay ahead of private industry. *USA Today*, March 8. www.usatoday.com/news/nation/2010-03-04-federal-pay_N.htm.

Daly, J. 2009. Government and the utilization of employee assistance programs. In *Employee Assistance Programs: Wellness/Enhancement Programming* (4th ed.), ed. M.A. Richard, W.G. Emener, and W.S. Hutchison Jr. Springfield, IL: Charles C. Thomas.

Doyle, A. n.d. Unemployment—unemployment compensation: Unemployment offices, benefits and rates. About.com. http://jobsearch.about.com/od/unemployment/a/unemployment.htm.

Florida Department of Business and Professional Regulations. 2011. Child Labor Laws. www.myfloridalicense.com/dbpr/reg/childlabor/documents/childlaborposter0709.pdf.

Greenhouse, S. 2008. Wal-Mart to pay $54 million to settle suit over wages. *New York Times*, December 10. www.nytimes.com/2008/12/10/business/10walmart.html.

Iwata, E. 2006. The Enron trials. *USA Today*.www.usatoday.com/money/industries/energy/2006-01-29-enron-legacy-usat_x.htm.

Mahoney, D. 2005. Evolving health plan designs. In *The Handbook of Employee Benefits* (6th ed.), ed. J. Rosenbloom. New York: McGraw-Hill.

Medicare Interactive.org. 2010. Am I eligible for Medicare if I am under 65? www.medicareinteractive.org/page2.php?topic=counselor&page=script&slide_id=15.

Quick, B. 2009. No change seen in city wage floor. *New Mexican*, December 21. www.santafenewmexican.com/localnews/No-change-seen-in-city-wage-floor.

Parker, K. 2009. The harried life of the working mother. Pew Research Center, October 1. http://pewresearch.org/pubs/1360/working-women-conflicted-but-few-favor-return-to-traditional-roles.

Reddick, C., and J. Coggburn. 2007. State employee health benefits in the United States: Choices and effectiveness. *Review of Public Personnel Management* 27, 1, 5–20.

Rosenbloom, J. 2005. The environment of employee benefit plans. In *The Handbook of Employee Benefits* (6th ed.), ed. J. Rosenbloom. New York: McGraw-Hill.

Smith, K., and E. Toder. 2005. Changing demographics of the retired population. *Older Americans' Economic Security: The Retirement Project* 5 (November). Urban Institute. www.urban.org/publications/900895.html.

Social Security Administration. 2009a. General W-2 filing information. Social Security Online. www.socialsecurity.gov/employer/gen.htm.

Social Security Administration. 2009b. Social Security program fact sheet. Social Security Online. www.socialsecurity.gov/OACT/FACTS/.

U.S. Department of Health and Human Services. n.d. COBRA Extended Periods of Coverage. www.cms.gov/COBRAContinuationofCov/06ExtendedPeriodsofCoverage.asp.

U.S. Department of Labor. 2009. Wages and hours worked: Minimum wage and overtime pay. Fair Labor Standards Act of 1938 (FLSA), as amended (29 USC §201 et seq.; 29 CFR Parts 510 to 794). www.dol.gov/compliance/guide/minwage.htm.

U.S. Department of Labor. 2010. Minimum wage laws in the states, July 1. www.dol.gov/esa/minwage/america.htm.

U.S. Department of Labor. n.d. Leave benefits: Family and medical leave. www.dol.gov/dol/topic/benefits-leave/fmla.htm.

9 Employment and Labor Relations Management

Have the courage to act instead of react.

—Earlene Larson Jenks

After reading this chapter, you will

- comprehend the significant roles that employee relations specialists play in creating positive and productive work cultures;
- understand work conduct guidelines affecting employees and organizations;
- appreciate the challenges of resolving conflicts using dispute resolution techniques;
- gain insights about employee discipline approaches, including the application of progressive disciplinary programs, to rectify poor employee performance and to correct unsanctioned work behaviors; and
- gain increased familiarity with collective bargaining as used in public sector settings.

The public sector faces immense challenges not experienced at this level since the Great Depression of the 1930s. Revenue declines point to an increased likelihood for employee layoffs and reductions in force. Fiscal declines result in growing employee concerns over benefits losses, especially in the areas of pension provisions and medical and health benefits. Thus, employees' support for local government leadership and for sustaining service delivery may be replaced with increasing levels of distrust, growing conflict within, and lessening commitment and loyalty to public service (Society for Human Resource Management 2010b). Effective employee and labor relations management becomes increasingly significant during these times of economic disparity.

This final chapter explores employee relations and collective bargaining activities in the public sector. Together, these areas encompass an organization's employee relations management process. Employee relations entail the development, implementation, and oversight of programs, policies, and practices affecting the employer-employee relationship for workers who are not represented through collective bargaining agreements. In most instances, but not all, the same or similar work expectations and workforce policies apply to unionized employees. In the case of union-represented employees, however, issues affecting the work relationship, such as wages, benefits, working conditions, and work rules, frequently must be specified in a collectively bargained contract agreed to by management and ratified by union members' votes.

Both employee relations and labor relations exert substantial influences over the organization's culture, at times positively and on other occasions negatively. The first half of this chapter focuses on employee relations, including the roles that employee relations specialists play and the programs and activities that they oversee in their organizations. In the second half of the chapter, the discussion turns to the collective bargaining process as applied in public organizations.

EMPLOYEE RELATIONS

As individuals, we expect fair and equitable treatment when dealing with others. These same expectations hold true when the individual joins an organization. Organizational leaders expect their employees to follow basic rules of behavior, especially with reference to proper workplace conduct and employee productivity and performance. Violations of standards can result in sanctions, including termination of employment. The organization's personnel policies handbook generally documents proper employee conduct, as well as the organization's rules and policies stipulating the consequences for employees when violations occur. The Society for Human Resources Management (2010a) summarizes workplace conduct rules within the following four categories:

- On-the-job conduct: attendance, tardiness, alcohol and substance abuse, fighting, use of profanity
- Disciplinary issues: insubordination, rules violations, theft of organizational property
- Dress and appearance: dress code, facial hair, jewelry, body piercing, tattoos, and headwear
- Harassment: sexual, racial, ethnic, and religious harassment, bullying.

A myriad of employee relations issues—such as excessive absenteeism and abuse of sick leave, illicit substance use and chemical dependency, and harassing treatment of fellow employees—requires the attention of experienced employee relations facilitators. All these undesirable behaviors rob employees of their ability to achieve desired performance outcomes. Moreover, if left unattended, actions like these destroy the potential for positive organizational cultures in the long term.

EMPLOYEE RELATIONS SPECIALIST ROLES

Employee relations specialists play essential roles in facilitating the creation and development of positive and sustainable work cultures in their organizations. Often, they serve in a critical liaison role, providing assistance through the fielding of questions from operational supervisors. The specialist offers advice about the best approaches for implementing organizational employee relations policies. In addition, when disputes occur, the specialist accepts employee complaints, investigates their validity, and provides resolution strategies. These activities significantly affect the organization's ability to develop a strong and positive working environment that fosters synergistic performance outcomes.

Creating successful service-oriented organizations requires careful planning and commitments of organizational resources. Talented employee relations specialists must possess a clear vision of the goals the organization seeks to achieve and, as Earlene Jenks notes above, the courage to act, rather than to react, when conditions warrant action. Employee relations specialists must inspire others as true believers in the power and benefits of progressive employee relations systems. As often seems the case, employees pay little attention to organizational policies when those policies do not directly affect their job responsibilities, job performance, or rewards structure. Thus, serving as champions for the development of positive working environments, employee relations specialists must communicate passionately the values of adhering to the organization's policies. These specialists achieve this outcome by understanding the appropriate communication channels to employ that will capture and keep the employees' attention. Lastly, employee disputes arise frequently in work settings. These disputes can be cancerous to the organization. Employee relations specialists, in such cases, must act quickly as counselors, mediators, or dispute resolution facilitators to resolve nagging dispute issues.

The following sections identify the following five primary roles performed by employee relations specialists:

- Compliance officer
- Policy-maker
- "Culture of excellence" champion
- Employee attitudinal monitor
- Dispute mediator

COMPLIANCE OFFICER

As noted in discussions of employment opportunity management in Chapter 3, federal and state laws mandate that employers dedicate extensive efforts to protect employees and job applicants from victimization resulting from illegal discrimination practices. Employee relations units and their equal employment opportunity compliance officers handle complaints of discriminatory treatment as defined by federal and state legislation and regulation. Areas where discriminatory complaints commonly arise within organizations include talent acquisition, performance evaluation, compensation awards, and employee discipline. Often, claims of unfair or discriminatory treatment involve the complainant's race, gender, age, ethnicity or national origin, religion, or disability. Compliance oversight also occurs in a number of other areas, including health and safety, privacy and protections of privileged information (e.g., employees' medical records), and compensation administration.

Compliance officers also serve in a training capacity, seeking to inform managers and employees about recent updates in recent legislation, regulations, and judicial outcomes affecting compliance standards. Educating the workforce about such changes creates an ethically and legally sound organization. Court judgments, for example, often take into consideration the organization's efforts in establishing and updating policies as well as educating employees about new standards and practices. Thus, the organization that has developed new written policies, trained its employees in these policies, communicated through multiple channels its stance on an issue, and acted appropriately and quickly on employees' complaints may suffer reduced culpability compared to another organization that took little to no proactive steps to protect its workforce. Utilizing an affirmative defense strategy, the employer with robust policies and protections in place may mitigate the award damages granted to a successful plaintiff.

POLICY-MAKER

Employee relations specialists keenly understand that human resource (HR) management constantly changes in dynamic ways, especially as a result of the environmental forces discussed in Chapter 2. Among the most significant external forces influencing employee relations management are federal and state legislation and judicial decisions. Policy changes occur frequently as new HR laws gain approval and as existing policies change due to policy updating and modifications.

Employee relations specialists become their system's experts as HR policy evolves. New laws and the updates of existing regulations cannot take into consideration the unique characteristics and needs of each system. Thus, the employee relations specialist, with an in-depth understanding of the organization's unique culture and operational needs, crafts and reshapes system standards and practices to remain in statutory compliance while minimizing systems disruptions. For example, increasing acts of terrorism and terrorist threats forced many local governments to add security personnel in previously unprotected areas. In many cases, federal and state governments mandated new security standards but failed to offer commensurate federal and/or state funds to pay for increased security protection. In these instances, local governments had no choice but to reallocate resources from other service areas. Frequently, employee relations personnel participate in crafting new strategies for meeting emerging standards while ensuring that the damage in other service areas remains minimal. More importantly, fiscal aid provided by federal or state resources comes with restrictions that allow expenditures only for their intended purpose. In the attempt to resolve one issue, in this case providing increased law enforcement securities and protection, the organization must ensure that it has not reallocated resources illegally from other areas. Significant policy influence and insights may be required from the employee relations expert before policy decisions can be implemented.

"CULTURE OF EXCELLENCE" CHAMPION

High-quality organizations possess distinctive characteristics that demonstrate their commitment to the achievement of their organizational mission. Clearly, the ultimate purpose of local governments is to provide high-quality, affordable services in the public's interest. Peters and Waterman (1982), in their book *In Search of Excellence*, offer the following eight characteristics that they found common in excellent organizations:

- a bias for action,
- remaining in close contact with customers (and citizens),
- possessing an entrepreneurial spirit,
- valuing employees,
- understanding that the organization's mission drives actions,
- sticking to what the organization does well,
- maintaining simple structures with lean staffs,
- allowing for decentralized decision-making, provided that the organization's core values remain intact

Characteristics similar to these drive highly successful employee relations management systems. Not only do employee relations specialists need these qualities to promote strong and positive employee relations cultures, but most units of government and their employees need these qualities as well. Bryson (1995) refers to individuals creating opportunities for excellence as "process champions." These champions commit to providing quality services and exceed their own expectations about continuous improvements in their (and others') operating units. Champions like these individuals seek to promote positive cultures by advancing employee and community engagement. They are unrelenting in their belief that an improved system is possible, and they work collectively with others to achieve such improvements. The City of Coral Springs, Florida (n.d.) serves as an example of such an organization. In 2008 it became the first state or local government in America to receive the prestigious Malcolm Baldrige National Quality Award for organizational excellence.

EMPLOYEE ATTITUDINAL MONITOR

Increasingly, pressures affecting organizational sustainability and survival require an effort to change and improve. Changing organizational structures and processes often creates resistance in the organization's workforce. Many employees have long-term memories of past reform and change efforts that failed. These employees feel burned and remember the scars of failure. Thus, failed change efforts create lukewarm support for reform, if not outright resistance and open hostility. Clearly, workforce attitudes and climate should be measured before launching any new change initiatives. Organizations often enlist employee relations specialists to evaluate workforce climate and employee satisfaction prior to initiating change. Studies of this kind can determine existing employees' attitudes and beliefs, as well as identify factors of resistance and levels of distrust that could sabotage the success of change efforts (Bryson 1995).

Organizations often utilize climate surveys and employee satisfaction surveys to gauge the workforce's general mood and to assess the potential backlash once discussions about change initiatives surface. Connelly (2002) illustrates the difference between climate and employee satisfaction surveys:

> Climate surveys: These surveys are intended to gauge the general work environment. Do hostile feelings abound or are workers sharing weekend barbecues? Are departments acting mutually exclusively or cooperatively? Is management admired or despised? Climate surveys are designed to address these types of broad reaching issues. If your organization is facing large-scale change, a climate survey may help with strategy.
>
> Employee satisfaction surveys: These surveys are built to dig a little deeper. Employees are questioned on specific topics relevant to their business. Satisfaction surveys may unearth some of the same insights as climate surveys, but typically at a more local level. If you are consulting with individual departments, an employee satisfaction survey may be more useful to you.

Employee relations officers and organizational leaders need insights about the mood of the workforce if they hope to frame a change initiative properly. Knowing the points creating resistance to change as well as the loci for resistance provides valuable information and insights about the next best steps of action. Significant dissatisfaction among the workforce or a high degree of distrust for the organization's leadership may point to the ill advisability of launching high-risk change initiatives. In such cases, systems might do best to maintain the status quo while working to repair attitudinal deficiencies in the workforce.

DISPUTE MEDIATOR

Unrelenting increases in the cost of employee disputes factor into the growing application of internal dispute resolution (IDR) techniques to resolve workplace disagreements. Attorneys' fees in the District of Columbia in 2008–2009, for example, ranged from $225 to $465 per hour, depending on the attorney's years of prior experience (U.S. Attorney Office 2008). Cost containment associated with disputes is expensive, so organizations actively value IDR alternatives.

The use of dispute resolution techniques is not a new phenomenon, as exemplified by President George Washington's last will and testament, which included a provisional clause for resolving disputes over his estate (Society for Human Resource Management 2009). IDR provides opportunities for resolving disputes in-house, leading to cost savings and increased efficiency in dispute resolution as compared to court-imposed outcomes. Like union grievance processes, IDR attempts to resolve disputes at the lowest possible level within the organization. Employee relations specialists trained in dispute resolution techniques often serve to mediate employee disagreements, whether the disputes are with the organization or with fellow employees. Often a complaint procedure is established through HR's employee relations representative with a process for appealing lower-level disputes to a higher level. In some instances, individuals may have voluntarily waived their right to litigation (i.e., waived their right to sue in court) in exchange for accepting a job offer. In these situations, the disputant might have no legal recourse other than to utilize the IDR process designed to arbitrate the case. Often, arbitration through neutral third parties may apply as the means of finalizing and settling the dispute.

EMPLOYEE CONDUCT

Appropriate on-the-job conduct is a necessity to organizations as a means of minimizing substantial disruptions. Individuals need to understand what behaviors and practices gain acceptance as normal work expectations versus those lacking approval. Typically, organizations communicate these work expectations to employees through distribution of the employee handbook at orientation training and through departmental communiqués to supervisors. In recent years, the introduction of Intranet systems in large organizations has created greater opportunities to disseminate conduct policy changes and other information updates directly to employees.

Employee conduct policies incorporate standards to maintain a sense of workplace civility and professional demeanor. These conduct standards demonstrate adherence to honest, open, and professional government, as well as an abiding commitment to public service in the citizens' best interest. Codes of ethics generally contain a broader scope of reference than do conduct codes, but elements of ethics codes often appear in municipal employee handbooks.

The International City/County Management Association's Code of Ethics (2004) offers accepted principles of behavior for city managers, senior level staff, and other municipal employees. These guidelines, relating to a variety of conduct issues, include:

- demonstrated integrity and honesty in action,
- commitment to serving for a minimum of two years,
- open disclosure of information to elected officials,
- avoiding role conflicts and conflicts of interest,
- adhering to equal employment opportunity for all,
- neither soliciting nor accepting gifts affecting judgment in action, and
- disclosing any investments, personal relationships, or private employment that might interfere with the individual's duties or lead to the appearance of a conflict of interest.

Common categories for determining appropriate on-the-job conduct are attendance and tardiness; alcohol and substance abuse; workplace violence, including fighting and use of profanity; disciplinary issues, including insubordination, rules violations, and theft and malfeasance of community property; dress and appearance code; and any form of unacceptable harassing behavior. The breadth of each topic could fill pages, and often does, in employee handbooks. A brief discussion of some of these topics is included here. Clearly, the extent of discipline and punishment for errant behavior on the job varies based on the severity of the conduct violation. Persistent patterns of repeated behavior even when reprimands have been issued, and the legal consequences to the organization for allowing the violation to continue unabated, play some part in disciplinary actions taken. As an example, an individual worker arriving a few minutes late for work two to three times during an evaluation cycle might receive a verbal warning but probably will not be terminated for this indiscretion. On the other hand, the police chief arrested for driving under the influence (DUI), during working hours or not, will face severe consequences for such conduct.

Alcohol or drug abuse among employees is a serious form of misconduct, especially when such conduct creates an immediate threat to the welfare and safety of the workforce and/or general public. Thus, a municipal transit system bus driver testing DUI while on the job may not only lose his job but will face stiff criminal penalties resulting from the loss of the public's trust for his conduct. Local governments, recipients of federal government contracts, also must abide by provisions of the Drug-Free Workplace Act of 1988. This law requires federal contractors to take actions to eliminate employee drug use in the workplace. Organizations that fail to take appropriate steps to control substance abuse among workers jeopardize contract continuation and loss of its funding.

Most conduct policies also prohibit harassing another worker, including bullying. The most recognized form of harassment today is sexual harassment, which is considered a form of gender discrimination and a violation of Title VI of the Civil Rights Act of 1964. According to the U.S. Equal Employment Opportunity Commission (EEOC) (2002), sexual harassment exists "when submission to or rejection of this conduct explicitly or implicitly affects an individual's employment, unreasonably interferes with an individual's work performance or creates an intimidating, hostile or offensive work environment."

The EEOC distinguishes two types of sexual harassment, quid pro quo and hostile work environment. Organizations are held accountable for the actions of their employees under both forms of sexual harassment. The first type is referred to as quid pro quo (literally meaning "this for that"). Quid pro quo sexual harassment occurs when an employer's agent requires the satisfaction of sexual demands as a condition for a job benefits or continued employment or that influences employment decisions (positively or negatively) affecting an employee. Clearly greater litigation awards tend to be granted for quid pro quo violations when the perpetrator of the harassing behavior holds a position of power or authority over the victimized individual. Generally, immediate supervisors and higher-level managers fall into the category of possessing such power and authority. One violation of quid pro quo sexual harassment constitutes violation of the law. By comparison, the second type of sexual harassment, creating a hostile work environment, results from intimidating or offensive behavior of a sexual nature that affects the ability of another to perform work duties or creates a psychologically threatening environment for the victim. Normally, one offensive incident does not constitute this form of sexual harassment, but repeated incidents, especially when the perpetrator is informed that the behavior is distasteful and offensive, create a pattern. As a rule of thumb, organizations must take sexual harassment (and all other forms of harassing behavior) seriously. Active policies prohibiting all forms of harassment should be clearly and frequently communicated to all employees. When necessary, dedicated training to prevent harassing behavior and practices should be offered. In addition, employees should receive warnings against any form of retaliation applied against the complainant. A zero-tolerance standard should be applied, and its violation should warrant severe disciplinary actions, including potential job loss.

PROGRESSIVE DISCIPLINARY PROGRAMS

Workers frequently perceive employee discipline as an early warning sign of impending termination. Unfortunately, this communicates a parent-child relationship between supervisor and employee, one that potentially creates future conflict and tension in the operating unit. Disciplinary programs do signal troubling issues, most often in the areas of poor performance, unsanctioned behavior, or rules violations. Counseling employees about errant behavior or poor work performance serves to advise individuals that problems exist and need corrections.

As indicated in the discussion about performance management in Chapter 6, organizations have an ethical and, in some instances, contractual obligation to alert their workers about less than satisfactory levels of performance or on-the-job conduct. In cases where employees' due process rights apply, courts review the actions of the organization prior to imposing adverse disciplinary actions to determine if reasonable notification occurred. For these reasons, organizations must be careful to document effectively prior counseling to individuals not serving on an "at-will" status. In municipal governments, an employee's right to proper notification prior to adverse disciplinary actions exists in most civil service systems and/or for those individuals represented through union collective bargaining contracts. Good disciplinary systems alert the individual that concerns exist, identify remediation strategies to bring the employees' performance or behavior back to satisfactory status, and, when necessary, discharge employees unable to achieve the level of performance or behavioral standards to maintain and protect the integrity of the organizations.

Most organizational disciplinary programs utilize an approach (or modified variation) commonly referred to progressive discipline. Progressive discipline provides increasing steps of discipline for failure to comply with organizational expectations of performance or conduct. The number of steps in this disciplinary model may vary, especially in collectively bargained union contracts, but all progressive disciplinary models contain the following four steps:

- *Verbal warning (documented):* A supervisor indicates concern about the offense and requesting corrective action from the employee.
- *Written reprimand (documented with remediation training):* The supervisor reiterates in writing that the inappropriate behavior or performance has continued. In this case, remediation in the form of retraining occurs.
- *Employee suspension (documented):* The employee is subject to paid or unpaid suspension. This step varies across organizations and may be influenced by the nature of the issue.
- *Employee termination (documented):* This step is applied to individuals who are unable to return to organizational standards or where immediate termination is warranted.

Progressive discipline, especially during the written reprimand step, provides remedial training to the employee experiencing performance deficiencies. In cases of conduct such as alcohol abuse, the individual may also be required to meet with employee assistance counselors and complete sponsored alcohol intervention programs as a condition of retaining employment. Employee discipline and the use of the progressive disciplinary model seek to alert employees to work-related problems and allow them to correct their behavior.

Often supervisors hesitate to impose sanctions against their employees for a variety of reasons. These include friendship with the employee, concerns for reduced productivity and staffing levels during remediation, fear of legal entanglements caused by the disciplinary actions, and a sense of remorse that they may be partially at fault. Employee relations specialists should work not only with the individual receiving disciplinary counseling, but also with the department to support the need for remediation and disciplinary action. In such cases, they reassure the reporting supervisor that her actions were not only appropriate (when they were) but also in the best interest of the employee and the organization. In addition, support in terms of additional resources may be warranted, especially by adding temporary replacement workers during the disciplined worker's remediation period to maintain performance expectations within the unit.

PUBLIC SECTOR UNIONIZATION TODAY

The second half of this chapter focuses on aspects of labor relations in public sector settings. As is likely evident at this point in the chapter, the organization-employee relationships change when a collective bargaining unit considers workers a part of it. When a worker is employed within a bargaining unit, whether a dues-paying union member or not, the union must afford representation and the rules of that bargaining unit still apply. Clearly, many more employees in American public sector organizations gain protection and representation from unions than just union members.

Union membership in the United States declined significantly over the past fifty years. At its peak in 1954, 35 percent of all U.S. workers held union membership (Ahrens 2010). By 2009 the number of dues-paying union members dropped to 12.3 percent of the total workforce (Greenhouse 2010). In addition, for the first time in U.S. history, more union members are employed in the public sector than in the private sector. Estimates from the Bureau of Labor Statistics in 2009 indicate that 15.3 million U.S. workers hold union membership. Currently, 7.9 million hold public sector employment with the remaining 7.4 million union members working in private sector jobs (Greenhouse 2010). Without the support of public sector unions, the overall percentage of the unionized workforce population would easily fall below 10 percent. A focus on collective bargaining in the public sector remains significant, because management-union relationships affect so many employees in public service. High percentages of law enforcement and fire service employees in local governments hold union membership. Thus, the quality of service received by the citizenry might be directly influenced by the quality of relationship existing between the union and city hall.

Kearney (2001, 86) defines collective bargaining as "the continuous process in which representatives of the employer (government) and employees (union) meet jointly to establish the terms and conditions of employment for workers in a bargaining unit." Public sector collective bargaining allows rank-and-file employees (most often below the supervisory level) to gain a voice in work policies and working conditions affecting their lives. This occurs through participation in a union once a union establishes legal recognition by the employer to negotiate in the employee group's interest. In most instances, exclusive recognition of an agent to represent employees does not occur without a union certification election. Public sector employers can voluntarily agree to recognize the legitimacy of the union to represent an employee group, but in most cases they first request input from their state's public employee relations board (PERB), which identifies which groups of employees will be included in the certification vote. PERBs, discussed below, also administer certification elections to ensure the integrity of the process, count the votes, and determine if an exclusive agent (union) official represent the unit's interests. Certification elections, if won by the union, affirm that employees seek representation by an identified union to negotiate with management over aspects of their work, such as wage and compensation factors, benefits, working conditions, and work rules.

Statutory approval of collective bargaining through the selection of exclusive bargaining agents representing state and local government workers is relatively new in many state and local governments. Limits to the use of collective bargaining and allowance of union activities prior to the 1950s resulted from governmental adherence to the sovereignty doctrine. Kearney (2001, 15) provides a succinct summary of this principle:

> the sovereignty argument contends that in a representative democracy the people are sovereign, and their will is served by their elected representatives. If government, through these representatives' appointees or civil servants, bargains over terms and conditions of employment with a union, then sovereignty is violated through the illegal delegation of the people's sovereign power.

Public sector unions increasingly challenged this doctrine's application, arguing that it abridged their individual First Amendment rights to freedom of speech and freedom of association. Court decisions and, in some states, legislation allowing public sector collective bargaining won over the sovereignty doctrine. Princeton University's Henry Farber's research on public sector unionization demonstrates this point. He determined that in 1955 only one state government allowed public sector collective bargaining. By 1965 the number had grown to ten states (Edwards 2010). Currently, twenty-six states allow collective bargaining for virtually all public sector employees (below the supervisory level), with twelve additional states granting collective bargaining privileges for a portion of their state or local public sector employees, provided they collectively approve a representative through certification elections (Edwards 2010). Twelve states, most in the South, still have no statutory authorized public sector collective bargaining in their jurisdictions, although many still allow workers to "meet and confer" with management about their needs.

PUBLIC SECTOR UNION OVERSIGHT

A national unified code such as that established for private sector labor relations issues, including determining unit composition, certification of elections, and adjudication of disputes and impasses, does not exist in the public sector. The National Labor Relations Board (NLRB), which gained its authority with passage of the National Labor Relations Act of 1935 (commonly referred to as the Wagner Act), functions to ensure consistency in application of labor relations rules and standards. Congress, however, did not authorize the NLRB oversight authority for public sector labor relations within this approved legislation.

In the federal government, the Federal Labor Relations Authority (n.d.), an independent administrative federal agency that was created by Title VII of the Civil Service Reform Act of 1978, provides administrative oversight to most nonpostal federal labor relation occupations. Postal employees' unions occur under the authorization granted through the Postal Reorganization Act of 1970.

Many states that grant statutory authority for collective bargaining to state or local government employees have established PERBs. In similar fashion to the NLRB and FLRA, PERBs oversee the establishment of certification processes and adjudicate labor relations disputes. PERBs also mediate impasses when glitches occur in ratifying collective bargaining agreements or when disputes occur over the interpretation or intent of existing contracts during the contract administration phase.

PUBLIC SECTOR CERTIFICATION PROCESS AND UNIT DETERMINATION

UNION CERTIFICATION PROCESS

Union representation approval requires exceptional dedication and determination, as the process for formation of a union can be extensive. Employees interested in forming a union must demonstrate that sufficient interest exists among fellow employees. Generally, at least 30 percent of bargaining unit employees sign "authorization cards" designating a union to represent them (Kearney 2001). Once the state PERB determines that a sufficient show of interest exists and identifies the logical unit composition of membership, it establishes procedures for conducting an election to determine if a union should serve as the exclusive representative for the unit. Normally, if more than 50 percent of the eligible employees approve the union, the union will be approved to negotiate exclusively with management over that unit's composition interests.

UNIT DETERMINATION

Unit determination refers to the composition of membership included in the collective bargaining agreement. Typically, PERBs consider what makes logical sense in terms of employee groups' inclusion in bargaining units. City leaders, in most instances, would prefer to limit the number of units that they must bargain with when new contracts negotiation and administration occur. They balance this desire against the unique needs of employees represented. For example, does it make sense to combine occupations in one bargaining unit? Should police and fire unions be integrated into one collective bargaining unit, or do their individual occupation interests, needs, and working condition mandate the formation of separate units? According to Kearney's research on the factors influencing bargaining unit formation (2001), unit formation can be specified by a state administrative agency (PERB), when mandated by state statute; determined on a case-by-case basis; or agreed to by management based on evidence of majority support from members of a primary bargaining unit.

In instances where unit formation occurs on a case-by-case basis, the public sector employee relations board considers a number of factors about the best structural arrangement. This includes judging the logic of combining multiple occupational groups within one unit and determining the effect on operations of combining occupational groups together into the unit. Past historical bargaining practices, commonality of interests across occupational categories, and the advantages of efficiency in management-labor operations versus the impact of administering all aspects of the contract effectively also are considered. Generally, law enforcement and fire service units maintain separate collective bargaining status. In the administrative staff, maintenance, and business operations units, occupational categories are often combined. The number of potential members also may influence combinations of occupation in order to allow for the funding and sustainability of the union and its activities.

Support for union coordination frequently comes from national labor relation organizations such as the American Federation of Labor and Congress of Industrial Organizations (AFL-CIO). Readers may be surprised to learn that the AFL-CIO is not a union. Rather, it is a confederation of unions existing together under one unified structure. A selected list of public sector unions supported by the AFL-CIO (2010) and working in the interests of public sector employees includes the following:

- American Federation of Government Employees (AFGE)
- American Federation of State, County and Municipal Employees (AFSCME)
- American Federation of Teachers (AFT)
- American Postal Workers Union (APWU)
- Communication Workers of America (CWA)
- International Association of Fire Fighters (IAFF)
- International Union of Police Associations (IUPA)

The Service Employees International Union (SEIU) also represents a number of public sector employees, especially in the fields of health care, public educational services, building services and maintenance, and nursing home care. It stands as America's second largest public service union, with more than 1 million members (SEIU 2010).

COLLECTIVE BARGAINING PROCESS

Envision a haggard union representative coming to a microphone after an all-night bargaining session with management and announcing that the union has finally struck an acceptable deal with the city. This might represent for many a common view of the collective bargaining process. In reality, collective bargaining requires thorough planning long before the announcement of a satisfactory negotiated agreement. Both management and union must assemble their teams, assess revenues and expenditure projections in the coming budget year, and determine future operating costs, especially in the area of benefits administration. In addition, they also compare current compensation levels against other organizations in their relevant labor market, prepare their presentations and their final best offers, and anticipate the moves of their opponent once negotiations begin. In reality, the party that plans haphazardly for collective bargaining suffers at the negotiating table by negotiating from a position of weakness rather than strength. This diminishes the stakeholders' interests and outcomes.

All labor laws concerning labor negotiation mandate that both sides (management and the union) bargain fairly and honestly. Bargaining in good faith refers to the willingness of each party to meet and discuss mutual interest for consideration as a part of a new collective bargaining contract. Bargaining in good faith, as required during the administration of existing contracts, however, does not mean that a party must agree to the terms or conditions proposed by the other side. On the other hand, both sides must demonstrate that they make a good faith effort to consider alternative solutions to their mutual concerns.

Two aspects of collective bargaining must remain in the mind's eye of both management and union representatives when bargaining. First, both parties must come to the negotiating table with a willingness to bargain in good faith. In addition, members must make certain that their actions do not intentionally inhibit efforts to gain consensus and a new employment contract. If they do, they may be guilty of an unfair labor practice. The following behaviors during collective bargaining exemplify unfair labor practices (Fecteau n.d.):

- seeking to discourage members' support for the union negotiators through the use of threats, punishments, promises, or discrimination;
- refusing to supply information required for the union to bargain intelligently;
- attempting to bargain directly with employees instead of through their official union negotiating team;
- refusing to abide by the ground rules for negotiating previously agreed to by both parties;
- refusing or failing to meet at reasonable times;
- management's dictating who it will or will not negotiate with or unilaterally dictating what will be the terms of the final agreement; and
- engaging in surface bargaining by going through the motions of bargaining, but taking positions that indicate no willingness to give and take on bargaining issues.

Collectively bargained agreements play a significant role in a local government's budget process. In some state statutes, a mechanism for automatically declaring impasse occurs if disagreement continues past a specified deadline, such as sixty days before the commencement of a city's next annual budget.

An impasse takes place when management and the union are unable to come to an agreement over all aspects of a new (or existing) contract. Once a declaration of impasse occurs, outside services like the Federal Mediation and Conciliation Service, the American Arbitration Association, and the state's PERB can be called in to help move negotiations forward. Mediation remains the most popularly used approach. Here an outside mediator meets with both sides, collectively and individually, and attempts to facilitate voluntary resolution of pending issues impeding agreement (Van Asselt 1972). Arbitration, also available to some governments, involves the identification of an outside neutral arbitrator. The arbitrator listens to each side's positions, reviews documents and practices, then requests each party's best alternative recommendation package for resolving the impasse. Ultimately, the arbitrator decides the final outcome. The use of arbitration varies across states based on individual state labor statutes. In Florida, for example, arbitration is allowed for grievances relating to existing collective bargaining contracts, but not for impasses associated with the negotiation of new contracts. Ultimately, most parties come to an agreement over the terms of a new contract. Collective bargaining negotiations hold significant interest for both organizational concerns and local government employees as the outcomes affect all of them. In reality, however, the true challenge is continued labor-management cooperation during the administration of the collective bargaining contract.

ADMINISTRATION OF CONTRACTS AND GRIEVANCE RESOLUTION PROCEDURES

The true test of the quality of a collective bargaining agreement occurs during the contract administration phase. Following the ratification of an agreement, HR systems must act quickly to train operational personnel (especially unit supervisors) about the new aspects and changes in the contract. Educating the workforce is a necessary step in the successful launching of a new contract. Nevertheless, during the administration of a contract, unanticipated glitches and disputes will arise that require continued negotiation and conversations across the bargaining table. The next two sections offer a brief discussion of two common methods used to minimize problems and resolve issues during the administration phase of the contract: labor-management committees and impasse resolution.

LABOR-MANAGEMENT COMMITTEES

Cooperation between labor and management remains vital, and continuous consultation should occur during the agreement's execution. Yet disputes, disagreements, and grievances arise even in the best contracts. The threat and use of a strike, considered the ultimate weapon available in the private sector, remain illegal in most public sector union contracts. State statutes prohibit union strikes, as well as related activities such as work slowdowns and intermittent walkouts, because of the critical need to provide public services, such as law enforcement, fire protection, and waste and health management, without interruption. Public services, often provided by municipalities on a sole source basis (although this has changed for a number of services in recent years, garbage collection as one example), therefore necessitate "no-strike clauses." Strike prohibition results from the immediate concern for the threat and harm to the public's health and safety that a strike would cause, as well as the inability to locate immediate alternative service providers to stem such threats.

Massachusetts and Indiana were the first states to employ labor-management committees (LMCs), beginning in 1978 (Midwest Center for Public Sector Labor

Relations 1980). Often local government will create LMCs to address and resolve disputes or emerging issues. The committees focus on sustaining ongoing and open communications about existing or potential concerns, so that potential solutions can be identified before small problems turn into major issues. It is not uncommon in large municipal governments for one member of management to dedicate a significant portion of time to maintaining and ensuring cooperative relations with the city's unions. With reference to the benefits of labor-management cooperation, Rubin and Rubin (2006, 284) note that "organization management theorists have documented that collaborative management improves labor-management relations in the public sector. When designed and implemented effectively, collaborative strategies satisfy both organizational and individual needs and building lasting relationships between managers and employees."

LMCs work best in environments with strong positive respect for unions and union employees. In situations where unions lack respect, the potential for successful labor-management collaboration and cooperation diminishes. In addition, the success and effectiveness of LMCs benefit most when economic conditions are strong and the prospect for reductions in force are low.

GRIEVANCE IMPASSE RESOLUTION: MEDIATION, FACT-FINDING, ARBITRATION

Disputes and conflicts that arise often require the assistance of outside, neutral third-party professionals. Disputes frequently occur as a result of poorly developed collective bargaining agreements. A flawed contract that creates increased potential for disputes may be poorly worded, using legalese and/or ambiguous wording that creates confusion; may be subject to misinterpretation of its meaning or intent; or may simply make no mention or reference to the issue at hand.

Van Asselt's (1972, 114) seminal research offers four successive stages for resolving impasses:

- *direct negotiations:* a process used by management and the union to resolve differences over contract terms;
- *mediation:* the intervention of a neutral third-party mediator who attempts to persuade the parties to reach a settlement voluntarily;
- *fact-finding:* the appointment of a neutral party (or panel) to study the key facts in a dispute and to recommend nonbinding terms for settlement; and
- *arbitration:* referral of the dispute to an impartial third party who determines the final outcome.

Van Asselt's model follows the path for resolution most often taken when disputes arise. The parties first attempt to settle disputes internally without outside intervention. Costs and the time required for dispute resolution involving outside experts can be extensive, especially with fact-finding and arbitration, where reports documenting the findings and the rationale for the decision are often required. Thus, both management and the union have an incentive to resolve the dispute internally and quickly, if at all possible. Finally, arbitrated outcomes signal failure on the part of both management and union, as they lose decision-making control and authority to an outside third-party actor. Political fallout from such decisions is often excessive, suggesting that every effort to resolve disputes internally should occur first.

CHAPTER SUMMARY

This chapter addresses the significance of cultivating strong employee relationships within an organization's workforce. Work-life balance factors continue to grow in importance for both organizations and employees. Employee relations specialists play an active role in seeking to identify and develop programs and processes that create and sustain high-quality organizational cultures. Positive cultures improve employee performance and strengthen workers' job satisfaction. Employee relations specialists also serve significant roles ensuring that organizational policies comply with HR laws while serving their organization's needs. In times of conflict, the employee relations specialists oversee disputes and provide mediation assistance designed to resolve disputes in the workforce.

The character of employee relations shifts and becomes more formal when workers opt for union representation. Decisions affecting working conditions may require prior discussion with union representatives. Dispute resolution requires union representation involvement and discussion and, if impasse occurs, possibly the assistance of third-party mediators, fact-finders, or arbitrators.

Under both circumstances, whether or not the individual received union representation, employee relations systems and their specialists must focus on developing strong, cooperative working environments. These are achieved through the investment in people, addressing not only the organization's needs for efficiency and the citizens' demands for improved services, but also the needs of the employees, who remain the organization's most valuable asset.

KEY CONCEPTS AND TERMS

authorization cards

bargaining units

climate surveys

Drug-Free Workplace Act of 1988

employee conduct

employee disciplining

employee relations management

employee relations specialist roles: compliance officer, "culture of excellence" champion, dispute mediator, employee attitudinal monitor, policy-maker

employee satisfaction surveys

Federal Labor Relations Authority

First Amendment freedoms and unionization

impasse resolution

internal dispute resolution (IDR)

International City/County Management Association (ICMA) Code of Ethics

labor-management committees

National Labor Relations Act of 1935 (Wagner Act)

National Labor Relations Board

progressive discipline

sexual harassment: quid pro quo and hostile work environment

sovereignty doctrine

unfair labor practices

Van Asselt's methods for resolving impasses

PRACTICAL LEARNING ACTIVITIES

1. Review Peters and Waterman's characteristics of organizational excellence on page 166. Assess an organization that you work for or your own university. How many of these points of excellence can you identify in your chosen organization? What examples can you provide demonstrating evidence of excellence in your organization? What changes would you recommend to help your organization achieve higher potentials for excellence?
2. Does your university mandate a dress code policy for its faculty and for its students? If yes, how well is it received by organizational members? Is the policy enforced? If not, should one be required? Why or why not? What factors influence the need for an organizational dress code?
3. Public statutes, in most instances, do not allow public sector labor unions to strike, even when impasses exist. Under what conditions, if any, would you allow public employees the authorization to strike for better working conditions? What factors about public service influence your stance about strikes in public settings?

REFERENCES

Ahrens, F. 2010. Are unions still the answer to sustaining the middle class? *Washington Post*, January 25. http://voices.washingtonpost.com/economy-watch/2010/01/are_unions_still_the_answer_to.html.

American Federation of Labor–Congress of Industrial Organizations (AFL-CIO). 2010. Unions of the AFL-CIO. www.aflcio.org/aboutus/unions.

Bryson, J. 1995. *Strategic Planning for Public and Nonprofit Organizations: A Guide to Strengthening and Sustaining Organizational Achievement*. San Francisco: Jossey-Bass.

City of Coral Springs, Florida. n.d. Coral Springs is recipient of the Malcolm Baldrige National Quality Award. www.coralsprings.org/baldrige/index.cfm.

Connelly, B. 2002. Developing/delivering climate surveys/employee surveys via corporate Intranet. www.shrm.org/Research/Articles/Articles/Pages/CMS_000087.aspx.

Edwards, C. 2010. Public-sector unions. *Tax & Budget Bulletin* 61 (March). Cato Institute. www.cato.org/pubs/tbb/tbb_61.pdf.

Fecteau, M. n.d. Legal boundaries of collective bargaining. Labor Studies Center, Wayne State University. www.clas.wayne.edu/multimedia/usercontent/File/Labor%20Studies%20Center/collectivebargaing.pdf.

Federal Labor Relations Authority. n.d. Introduction to the FLRA. www.flra.gov/introduction-flra.

Greenhouse, S. 2010. Most U.S. union members are working for the government, new data shows. *New York Times*, January 23. www.nytimes.com/2010/01/23/business/23labor.html?_r=1.

International City/County Management Association. 2004. ICMA Code of Ethics with Guidelines. http://icma.org/en/Page/72/The_ICMA_Code_of_Ethics_with_Guidelines.

Jenks, E. n.d. Famous Quotes & Authors. www.famousquotesandauthors.com/topics/courage_and_bravery_quotes.html.

Kearney, R., with D. Carnevale. 2001. *Labor Relations in the Public Sector* (3rd ed.). New York: Marcel Dekker.

Midwest Center for Public Sector Labor Relations. 1980. *Impasse Resolution in the Public Sector: New Directions*. Bloomington: Indiana University School of Public and Environmental Affairs.

Peters, T.J., and R.H. Waterman Jr. 1982. *In Search of Excellence: Lessons from America's Best-Run Companies*. New York: HarperCollins.

Rubin, B., and R. Rubin. 2006. Labor-management relations: Conditions for collaboration. *Public Personnel Management* 35, 4 (Winter), 283–298.

Service Employees International Union (SEIU). 2010. Our union. www.seiu.org/our-union/index.php?via=navbar.

Society for Human Resource Management. 2009. Resolving workplace disputes internally. www.shrm.org/Research/Articles/Pages/ResolvingDisputesInternally.asp.

Society for Human Resource Management. 2010a. Introduction to the human resources discipline of employee relations. www.shrm.org/hrdisciplines/employeerelations/Pages/EmpRelIntro.aspx.

Society for Human Resource Management. 2010b. Succession planning. *Workplace Visions* 6. www.shrm.org/Research/FutureWorkplaceTrends/Documents/100722%20Workplace%20Visions%206.pdf.

U.S. Attorney Office for the District of Columbia. 2008. Laffey matrix 2003–2009. www.justice.gov/usao/dc/Divisions/Civil_Division/Laffey_Matrix_7.html.

U.S. Equal Employment Opportunity Commission (EEOC). 2002. Facts about sexual harassment. June 27. www.eeoc.gov/facts/fs-sex.html.

Van Asselt, K. 1972. Impasse resolution. *Public Administration Review* 32, 2 (March–April), 114–119.

Index

About the Author

John L. Daly is an associate professor and director of public administration in the Department of Government and International Affairs at the University of South Florida in Tampa. He received his doctorate in public policy from Indiana University's School of Public and Environmental Affairs in Bloomington. John has extensive local and international experience working with government and public administrators. In 1998–1999 and again in 2005–2006, he served as the Fulbright Senior Scholar to the Kingdom of Swaziland. In 2005, M.E. Sharpe published his book *Training in Developing Nations: A Handbook for Expatriates*. John also serves as president of Creative Insights Corporation, a management consulting company focusing on issues affecting local governments. John and his wife, Debra, reside in Lutz, Florida. John welcomes your feedback; his e-mail address for correspondence is jdaly@usf.edu.